2007

Praise for
Leading at a Higher Level

"At Southwest Airlines, we have always strived to lead at a higher level. We truly believe that profit is the applause you get for taking care of your internal and external customers. We have always insisted upon a happy, carefree, team-spirited—yes, even fun—working environment, which we think results in motivated employees who will do the right thing for their internal and external customers. Reading this book will make a positive difference in your organization."

Colleen C. Barrett, *President, Southwest Airlines*

"If you want to have a great company, you don't have a choice but to lead at a higher level. When you do that, you excite your people, they take care of your customers, and your cash register goes ca-ching."

Horst Schulze, *President and CEO, The West Paces Hotel Group, LLC;*
Founding and former President & COO,
The Ritz-Carlton Hotel Company, LLC

"Leading at a higher level is a must today if leaders are to rebuild trust and credibility, as we are doing at Tyco. This book will teach you how."

Eric Pillmore, *Senior Vice President of Corporate Governance,*
Tyco International

"*Leading at a Higher Level* translates decades of research and 25 years of global experience into simple, practical, and powerful strategies to equip leaders at every level to build organizations that produce bottom-line results. At Nissan, we have made these principles a core part of our leadership philosophy, better equipping our managers to bring out the great energies and talents of our employees."

Jim Irvine, *Vice President of Human Resources,*
Nissan North America

The concepts in *Leading at a Higher Level* have been used by high performing organizations around the world, including:

Abbott Laboratories

AMF Bowling Worldwide, Inc.

Anthem Blue Cross and Blue Shield

Applebee's International, Inc.

Bayer AG

Big Lots Stores, Inc.

Biogen Idec Inc.

Bose® Corporation

Bowater® Incorporated

Burger King®

Callaway Golf Company

Caterpillar Inc.

Cellular One

Chick-fil-A®, Inc.

Children's Hospital

The Coffee Bean and Tea Leaf®

Comerica Incorporated

Compaq

CompUSA®

ConocoPhillips

Domino's Pizza

Dow Corning Corporation

Energy Northwest

Exxon Mobil Corporation

Fairmont Hotels & Resorts

FedEx Kinko's Office and Print Services

Fireman's Fund Insurance Company®

Foster Farms

Genentech, Inc.

Georgetown University

Hilton Hotels Corporation

Home Depot

Host Hotels & Resorts, (formerly known as Host Marriott)

Hyatt Corporation

Jack in the Box Inc.

Kennedy Space Center

Krispy Kreme Doughnut Corporation

L'Oréal

Mattel, Inc.

Marriott International

MCI, Inc.

Merck & Co., Inc.

The Michelin Group

Microsoft Corporation

Nabisco

Nissan Motor Co.

Northrop Grumman Corporation

Novartis AG

Pepperdine University

Polaris Industries

The Ritz-Carlton Hotel Company

Royal Caribbean Cruises Ltd.®

Safeco Corporation

San Diego Padres

S.C. Johnson & Son, Inc.

Six Continents Retail

Sony Corporation of America

Staples, Inc.

Toshiba Corporation

Toyota Motor Corporation

TRW Automotive Inc.

Tyson Foods, Inc.

UCLA

United States Postal Service®

UPS™

Verizon

Victoria's Secret

Wal-Mart Stores, Inc.

Washington State Criminal Justice Training Commission

WD-40 Company

Wells Fargo & Company

Wendy's International, Inc.

Yellow Pages (GTE)

LEADING
AT A
HIGHER
LEVEL

CONTRIBUTING AUTHORS

Ken Blanchard

Marjorie Blanchard

Scott Blanchard

Don Carew

Eunice Parisi-Carew

Fred Finch

Susan Fowler

Laurence Hawkins

Judd Hoekstra

Fay Kandarian

Alan Randolph

Jesse Stoner

Drea Zigarmi

Pat Zigarmi

LEADING AT A HIGHER LEVEL

Blanchard on Leadership and Creating High Performing Organizations

The Founding Associates and Consulting Partners
of The Ken Blanchard Companies

*with an Introduction
by Ken Blanchard*

PEARSON
Prentice
Hall

Vice President and Editor-in-Chief: Tim Moore
Editorial Assistant: Susie Abraham
Development Editor: Russ Hall
Associate Editor-in-Chief and Director of Marketing: Amy Neidlinger
Cover Designer: Bill Chiaravalle
Managing Editor: Gina Kanouse
Senior Project Editor: Lori Lyons
Copy Editors: Gayle Johnson and Karen Gill
Senior Indexer: Cheryl Lenser
Interior Designer and Composition: Gloria Schurick
Production Assistance: Jennifer Cramer, Terra Dalton, Tammy Graham, and Karen Opal
Manufacturing Buyer: Dan Uhrig

© 2007 by Blanchard Management Corporation
Publishing as Prentice Hall
Upper Saddle River, New Jersey 07458

Prentice Hall offers excellent discounts on this book when ordered in quantity for bulk purchases or special sales. For more information, please contact U.S. Corporate and Government Sales, 1-800-382-3419, corpsales@pearsontechgroup.com. For sales outside the U.S., please contact International Sales, 1-317-581-3793, international@pearsontechgroup.com.

Company and product names mentioned herein are the trademarks or registered trademarks of their respective owners.

Situational Leadership® is a registered trademark of The Center for Leadership Studies. Ken Blanchard and Paul Hersey first developed the theory of Situational Leadership in the late 1960s. In 1985, Blanchard and the Founding Associates of The Ken Blanchard Companies—Marjorie Blanchard, Don Carew, Eunice Parisi-Carew, Fred Finch, Laurence Hawkins, Drea Zigarmi, and Pat Zigarmi—created a new generation of the theory called Situational Leadership® II.

Raving Fans® is a registered trademark of Blanchard Family Partnership and Ode to Joy Limited.

HPO SCORES™ is a trademark of The Ken Blanchard Companies.

The SERVE model presented in Chapter 12 is owned by CFA Properties, Inc. and is included herein by permission.

The information presented in Chapter 2 is adapted from "From Vision to Reality," © 1993 by Jesse Stoner and Drea Zigarmi and *Full Steam Ahead!* (Berrett-Koehler) © 2003 by Jesse Stoner and Blanchard Family Partnership, and is included with the permission of the authors.

Printed in the United States of America

First Printing November 2006

ISBN 0-13-234772-5

Pearson Education LTD.
Pearson Education Australia PTY, Limited.
Pearson Education Singapore, Pte. Ltd.
Pearson Education North Asia, Ltd.
Pearson Education Canada, Ltd.
Pearson Educatión de Mexico, S.A. de C.V.
Pearson Education—Japan
Pearson Education Malaysia, Pte. Ltd.

CIP data is available upon request.

Dedicated to all leaders in the world
who are trying every day to lead at a higher level.
May you keep your energy high and know
that what you are doing makes a difference.

CONTENTS

Contents

Contents

Contents

LIST OF ILLUSTRATIONS

Introduction

LEADING AT A HIGHER LEVEL

Ken Blanchard

This past year, my wife, Margie, and I went on a safari in South Africa with some family and friends. Margie and I have been on a number of safaris over the past 20 years. This time I saw some things I'd seen before but never quite as vividly. What I observed is how vicious, competitive, and territorial the jungle is. If you've ever heard a lion roar, it brings chills up your back. When our long-time guide, Gary Clarke from Topeka, Kansas, imitates the roar, he shouts, "It's mine, mine, mine, mine!" That's because when the lion roars, what he's really saying is, "This is my territory. Don't mess with me." In fact, lions will kill their sons if they challenge their control over the father's territory.

The reason I saw this more vividly than ever before is that I had decided on this trip that I was going to find out as much as I possibly could about Nelson Mandela. We had been at a dinner party where people around the table were asked to share what person—of anyone in the world—they would love to have dinner with. It was a quick decision for me. I said, "Nelson Mandela. I would love to have dinner with a man who was in prison for 28 years and treated cruelly, yet came out of that experience full of love, compassion, and reconciliation." On the trip, I began to read Mandela's book *Long Walk to Freedom*.

When I compared what I saw in the jungle with how Mandela had reacted to his treatment, I realized that in many ways we as human beings are just intelligent animals. And being intelligent animals, we can choose between being self-serving and serving. The animals in the jungle can't make that choice. A rhino can't get up in the morning and say, "I'm going to make friends with the lion today." It's just not in their temperament. And yet, just as Mandela did, we can make choices to live and lead at a higher level. But when you look at the leaders around the world— whether they're running countries, businesses, churches, educational institutions, or what have you—too many people are choosing to be self-serving rather than serving. Why is that? Because they don't have a different leadership role model.

When I contemplated this dilemma, my thinking took me back to my days in graduate school, when I studied Paulo Freire, a revolutionary from Brazil. He wrote a fascinating book called *The Pedagogy of the Oppressed*. Freire argued that the problem with oppression is that once the oppressed throw off the oppressor, the only leadership role models they have are the very people who oppressed them. Thus, the oppressed become the new oppressors. The ramifications of this are disheartening—not only for countries, but for every enterprise imaginable. This phenomenon creates a new breed of self-serving leaders overseeing a system where all the money, power, and recognition move up the hierarchy and away from the people the organization was established to serve.

I think the only answer to this recurring cycle is a different leadership role model. That's what this book is all about—helping individuals and organizations lead at a higher level.

Leading at a Higher Level

What is leadership? For years we defined leadership as an *influence process.* We believed that anytime you tried to influence the thoughts and actions of others toward goal accomplishment in either your personal or professional life, you were engaging in leadership. In recent years, we have changed our definition of leadership to *the capacity to influence others by unleashing their power and potential to impact the greater good.* We made this change for an important reason.

When the definition of leadership focuses on goal accomplishment, you can think that leadership is only about results. Yet when we talk about leading at a higher level, just focusing on goal accomplishment is not enough. The key phrase in our new definition is "the greater good"—what is best for all involved. We think leadership is a high calling. Leadership should not be done purely for personal gain or goal accomplishment; it should have a much higher purpose than that.

What is a higher purpose? It is not something as internally focused and self-centered as making money. As Matt Hayes and Jeff Stevens contend in *The Heart of Business,* when it becomes obvious that profit, which is a legitimate goal, is the driving reason for being in business, everyone—stockholders, top managers, employees, customers, suppliers, and the community—quickly becomes self-serving, with a focus on their own agenda and personal enrichment. Employee loyalty and passion often go out the window as the point of work becomes simply to get as much as you can for as little effort as possible.[1]

What is the answer to this dilemma? A higher purpose—a key element of what we will refer to throughout this book as a *compelling vision.* In Hayes and Stevens' terms, it is outwardly focused, must require sacrifice—in other words, it takes precedence over any short-term goal such as profit—and is intrinsically honorable.

Leaders can be successful in the short run if they emphasize only goal accomplishment. What tends to fall by the wayside is the condition of the human organization. Leaders don't always take morale and job satisfaction into consideration—only results count. They forget what the point is. They don't have a higher purpose. In business, with that kind of leadership, it is a short leap to thinking that the only reason to be in business is to make money. There is an either/or added to people and results. Leaders falsely believe that they can't focus on both at the same time.

When you are leading at a higher level, you have a both/and philosophy. The development of people—both customers and employees—is of equal importance to performance. As a result, the focus in leading at a higher level is on long-term results and human satisfaction. Leading at a higher level, therefore, is a process. We define it as *the process of achieving worthwhile results while acting with respect, care, and fairness for the well-being of all involved.* When that occurs, self-serving leadership is not possible. Why?

Self-serving leaders think that leadership is all about them and not about the best interests of those they serve. They forget about acting with respect, care, and fairness for all involved. Everything is about their own self-interest. It's only when you realize that it's not about you that you begin to lead at a higher level.

Why Are We Writing This Book?

We are writing this book for several reasons. First, our dream is that someday everyone will know someone who is leading at a higher level. Self-serving leaders will be a thing of the past, and leadership throughout the world will be composed of people who, as Robert Greenleaf said, "Serve first and lead second."[2] We are writing this book to help make our dream a reality.

Second, the vision of The Ken Blanchard Companies is focused on leading at a higher level. This kind of leadership begins with a vision. Jesse Stoner and I wrote a book called *Full Steam Ahead!* about the power of visioning. To us, a compelling vision tells you *who you are* (your purpose), *where you're going* (your preferred picture of the future), and *what will drive your journey* (your values).

The purpose of The Ken Blanchard Companies is to help individuals and organizations lead at a higher level. Our mission statement reflects our new definition of leadership:

Unleash the power and potential of people and organizations for the greater good.

Our picture of the future is

- Everyone is trained to lead at a higher level.
- Every organization is led by people leading at a higher level.
- People are motivated to lead at a higher level by observing people who lead at a higher level.

Our operating *values* are

- **Ethical**—Doing the right thing
- **Relationships**—Developing mutual trust and respect
- **Success**—Operating a profitable and well-run organization
- **Learning**—Always growing, inquiring, and developing

These values are ordered by rank. In other words, we won't do anything to improve the profitability of the company that is unethical or that doesn't honor the relationships we have with our customers, our people, our suppliers, and our community. We realize that making money is not the higher purpose of our business.

You might say that this all sounds like Pollyanna—overly optimistic. That may be, but these are the standards we have set for ourselves. And these are the same high standards we want to help you and the people in your organization reach through this book. Helping individuals and organizations lead at a higher level is our passion, for both your organization and our own.

Finally, in many ways this book spells out our leadership point of view. Extensive research shows that effective leaders have a clear leadership point of view and are willing to share with others these beliefs about leading and motivating people. We hope reading this book will impact your leadership point of view.

How This Book Is Organized

Over the years, I have found that in organizations where leading at a higher level is the rule rather than the exception, people do four things well:

- They set their sights on the right target and vision.
- They treat their customers right.
- They treat their people right.
- They have the right kind of leadership.

This book is organized into four sections. Section I focuses on *the right target and vision* and integrates our work on the triple bottom line, the characteristics of a high performing organization, and creating a compelling vision.

Section II highlights *treating the customer right* and integrates our work on legendary service, raving fans, and customer mania. Today, everybody should realize that their customers are the reason their organization exists.

Section III focuses on *treating your people right*. This is where the rubber meets the road. If you don't empower your people and treat them right, they won't take care of your customers, and in the long run, you won't get your desired results. This is the longest section of the book, because your treatment of people is leadership in action. This is what The Ken Blanchard Companies has been focusing on for more than 25 years. In this section, we start with empowerment and then examine four leadership domains: self leadership, one-on-one leadership, team leadership, and organizational leadership.

Effective leadership of people starts with looking at yourself—who you are, what you stand for, and how you take initiative when you don't have position power. Without this kind of perspective, it's hard to be effective at one-on-one leadership, where building a partnership based on trust is key. Once you know how to work with individuals, you can begin to build a team and a sense of community. Leading a team is much more complicated than one-on-one leadership and is a precursor to engaging in organizational leadership, which is the most complex leadership domain.

Section IV zeros in on *the right kind of leadership*. Here we're not talking about leadership style; we're talking about character and intentionality. My travels over the years through organizations of all shapes and sizes have convinced me of two things: Effective leadership starts on the inside, and the right kind of leadership is servant leadership. This is a leadership not based on false pride or fear, but one that's grounded in humility and focused on the greater good. With the right kind of leadership, leading at a higher level can become a reality.

This section also includes our thoughts on determining your leadership point of view. This turns the focus to you. Here we assist you in pulling together many of the concepts you have learned and help you integrate and apply that knowledge to your own leadership situation.

Writing this book has been a labor of love. It pulls together our best thinking from more than 25 years of working together. It truly is *Blanchard on Leadership*. It includes not only Margie's and my thinking, but also all the wonderful contributions of our founding associates—Don Carew, Eunice Parisi-Carew, Fred Finch, Laurie Hawkins, Drea Zigarmi, and Pat Zigarmi—and other fabulous consulting partners who have really made Blanchard "the home of the authors," including Alan Randolph, Jesse Stoner, Fay Kandarian, Susan Fowler, Judd Hoekstra, and our son, Scott Blanchard.

We think everyone can lead at a higher level, whether at work, at home, or in the community. We hope that, regardless of your position, the size or type of your organization, or the kind of customers or people you serve, you will learn some important information in this book that will help you lead at a higher level and create a high performing organization that not only accomplishes your desired results but is a welcome harbor for the people you touch. May good come out of your reading of this book.

Ken Blanchard
San Diego, California
Fall 2006

SET YOUR SIGHTS
ON THE
RIGHT TARGET AND VISION

Chapter 1

IS YOUR ORGANIZATION HIGH PERFORMING?

Don Carew, Fay Kandarian,
Eunice Parisi-Carew, Jesse Stoner,
and Ken Blanchard

Marksmen will tell you that if you're going to aim for a target, you should go for the bull's-eye. The reason for that is if you miss the bull's-eye, you're still on the target. But if all you do is aim for the target and you miss, you're nowhere. Don Shula, who coauthored *Everyone's a Coach* with Ken Blanchard, always told his Miami Dolphins football team that the target they were aiming at was to win every game. Was that possible? Obviously not, but if you don't shoot for excellence, you never have a chance of getting there. That's probably why Don Shula's teams won more football games than those of any coach in the history of the NFL and why his 1972 Dolphins is still the only team in history to go undefeated for an entire season. So the target you aim for has a lot to do with your performance.

Wall Street and the pressures of business today make many people think that the only target that counts is financial success. Yet few, if any, businesspeople would want their epitaph to include their company's bottom line—their stock price or profit margin. They might, however, want people to remember their contribution to the creation of a high performing organization.

Those who want to lead at a higher level need to understand what a high performing organization looks like and what is necessary to create one. They need to aim for the right target.

The Right Target: The Triple Bottom Line

In high performing organizations, everyone's energy is focused on not just one bottom line, but three bottom lines—being the **provider of choice**, the **employer of choice**, and the **investment of choice**. This triple bottom line is the right target and can make the difference between mediocrity and greatness.[1] The leaders in high performing organizations know that their bottom line depends on their customers, their people, and their investors. These leaders realize the following:

Profit is the applause you get for taking care of your customers and creating a motivating environment for your people.

Provider of Choice

Being the provider of choice is becoming increasingly more challenging. Competition is fierce as new competitors emerge unexpectedly. Customers are more demanding with many more options at their fingertips. They expect to get what they want when they want it, and they want to have it customized to suit their needs. The world has changed in such a way that today the buyer, not the seller, is sitting in the driver's seat. These days, nobody has to convince anybody that the customer reigns. People are realizing that their organizations will go nowhere without the loyalty and commitment of their customers. Companies are motivated to change when they discover the new rule:

4

---

*If you don't take care of your customers,
somebody else will.*

In *Raving Fans®: Satisfied Customers Are Not Enough*, Sheldon Bowles and Ken Blanchard argue that to keep your customers today, you can't be content just to satisfy them; you have to create raving fans. They describe raving fans as customers who are so excited about how you treat them that they want to tell everyone about you; they become part of your sales force. Let's look at a simple yet powerful example.

What's the most common wake-up call that you get in a hotel in America today? The phone rings at the allotted hour, but when you pick it up, no one is there. At least they got the machine to call your room at the designated hour. The second most common wake-up call greets you with a recording. But again, no one's there. Today if you pick up the phone on a wake-up call and there's a human being on the other end of the phone—someone you can actually talk to—you hardly know what to say. A while back, one of our colleagues was staying at the Marriott Convention Hotel in Orlando. He asked for a 7:00 wake-up call. When the phone rang and he picked it up, a woman said, "Good morning; this is Teresa. It's 7:00. It's going to be 75 and beautiful in Orlando today, but your ticket says you're leaving. Where are you going?"

Taken aback, our colleague stammered, "I'm going to New York City."

Teresa said, "Let me look at the *USA Today* weather map. Oh, no! It's going to be 40 degrees and rainy in New York today. Can't you stay another day?"

Now where do you think our colleague wants to go when he gets to Orlando? He wants to go to the Marriott so that he can talk to Teresa in the morning! Raving fans are created by companies whose service far exceeds that of the competition and even exceeds customer expectations. These companies routinely do the unexpected and then enjoy the growth generated by customers who have spontaneously joined their sales force.

Employer of Choice

Being the employer of choice is equally challenging. With highly mobile, competent workers in demand, employers must find ways to attract and keep their best people. Good pay is no longer the only answer. It is true that some competent workers will go elsewhere for a higher wage; however, today's workers generally want more. They seek opportunities where they feel like their contributions are valued and rewarded—where they are involved and empowered, can develop skills, can see advancement opportunities, and can believe they are making a difference.

You will get little argument today if you tell managers that people are their most important resource. Some even argue that the customer should come second, because without committed and empowered employees, a company can never provide good service. You can't treat your people poorly and expect them to treat your customers well.

Several years ago, a friend of ours had an experience in a department store that illustrates this point well. He normally shops at Nordstrom but found himself in a competitor's store. Realizing that he needed to talk to his wife, he asked a salesperson in the men's department if he could use their telephone. "No!" the salesperson said.

He said, "You have to be kidding me. You can always use the phone at Nordstrom."

The salesperson said, "Look, buddy! They don't let *me* use the phone here. Why should I let you?"

People who are treated poorly tend to pass that attitude on to their customers.

Another reason that your people are so important today is because these days your organization is evaluated on how quickly it can respond to customer needs and problems. "I'll have to talk to my boss" doesn't cut it anymore. Nobody cares who the boss is. The only people customers care about are the ones who answer the phone, greet them, write up their order, make their delivery, or respond to their complaints. They want top service, and they want it fast. That means you need to create a motivating environment for your people and an organizational structure that is flexible enough to permit them to be the best that they can be.

Investment of Choice

Growing or expanding requires investment, regardless of whether the company is publicly owned, privately held, government, or nonprofit. All organizations require funding sources, through stock purchases, loans, grants, or contracts. To be willing to invest, people must believe in the organization's viability and performance over time. They need to have faith in the leadership, the quality of the people, the product and services, the management practices, and the resilience of the organization.

If the financial success of an organization is a function of revenue minus expenses, you can become more sound financially by either reducing costs or increasing revenues. Let's look at costs first, because in today's competitive environment, the prize goes to those who can do more with less. More organizations today are deciding that the only way for them to be financially effective is to downsize. There's no doubt that some personnel reduction is necessary in large bureaucracies where everyone just has to have an assistant, and the assistant has to have an assistant. Yet downsizing is an energy drain, and it's by no means the only way to manage costs.

There's a growing realization that another effective way to manage cost is to make all your people your business partners. For instance, in some companies, new people can't get a raise until they can read their company's balance sheet and understand where and how their individual efforts impact the company's profit-and-loss statement. When people understand the business realities of how their organization makes and spends money, they are much more apt to roll up their sleeves and help out.

Traditionally, managers have been reluctant to share financial information. Yet these days, many organizations are responding with open book management. That's because they realize the financial benefits that come from sharing previously sensitive data. For example, in working with a restaurant company, one of our consulting partners was having a hard time convincing the president of the merits of sharing important financial data with employees. To unfreeze the president's thinking, the consulting partner went to the firm's largest restaurant one night at closing time. Dividing all the employees—cooks, dishwashers, waiters, waitresses, bus people, hostesses—into groups of five or six, he asked them to come to an agreement about the answer to a question: "Of every sales dollar that comes into this restaurant, how many cents do you think fall to the bottom line—money that can be returned to investors as profit or reinvested in the business?"

The least amount any group guessed was 40 cents. Several groups guessed 70 cents. In a restaurant, the reality is that if you can keep 5 cents on the dollar, you get excited—10 cents, and you're ecstatic! Can you imagine the attitude among employees toward such things as food costs, labor costs, and breakage when they thought their company was a money machine? After sharing the actual figures, the president was impressed when a chef asked, "You mean, if I burn a steak that costs us 6 dollars and we sell it for 20, at a 5 percent profit margin, we have to sell six steaks for essentially no profit to make up for my mistake?" He already had things figured out.

8

---

*If you keep your people well informed
and let them use their brains,
you'll be amazed at how they can
help manage costs.*

What about revenues? If you develop committed and empowered people who create raving fan customers, you can't help but increase your revenues. Why? Because raving fan customers want to brag about you. They become part of your sales force or PR department, which increases your sales and/or visibility and makes your organization more attractive as an investment. Now you are a leader of a high performing organization.

A High Performing Organization Scores Every Time

Provider of choice, employer of choice, and investment of choice—the three elements of the triple bottom line—form the right target. If you aim for only one of the three elements, you won't hit the target, and your organization won't be able to sustain high performance. Once leaders understand the importance of the target, questions naturally arise, such as "What is a high performing organization?" and "What does a high performing organization that hits the target look like?"

To answer these questions, Don Carew, Fay Kandarian, Eunice Parisi-Carew, and Jesse Stoner conducted an extensive research project to define and identify the characteristics of a high performing organization.[2] Their first step was to define "high performing organization." While many organizations rise quickly and then plateau or topple, some continue to thrive, somehow reinventing themselves as needed. The researchers focused on these kinds of organizations, creating the following definition:

---

*High performing organizations are enterprises
that over time continue to produce
outstanding results with the highest level of
human satisfaction and commitment to success.*

Because of their flexibility, nimbleness, and responsive systems, high performing organizations (HPOs) remain not only successful and respected today but also poised to succeed in the future. HPOs demonstrate results consistently over time.

The HPO SCORES™ Model

As a result of their research, Drs. Carew, Kandarian, Parisi-Carew, and Stoner created the HPO Scores model. "Scores" is an acronym that represents the six elements evident in every high performing organization. A high performing organization scores—hits the target consistently—because it demonstrates strength in each of these six elements. The following pages describe these elements in greater detail.

S = Shared Information and Open Communication

In high performing organizations, information needed to make informed decisions is readily available to people and is openly communicated. Sharing information and facilitating open communication builds trust and encourages people to act like owners of the organization. Information is power. The more readily available information is, the more empowered and able people are to make solid decisions aligned with the organization's goals and values. Open communication is the lifeblood of the organization. Encouraging dialogue lessens the danger of territoriality and keeps the organization healthy, agile, flexible, and fluid.

C = Compelling Vision

A compelling vision is the hallmark of a high performing organization. It answers the question "What's the point?" When everyone supports such an organizational vision—including purpose, picture of the future, and values—it creates a deliberate, highly focused culture that drives the desired business results toward a greater good. In these organizations, people are energized by, excited about, and dedicated to such a vision. They can describe the vision, are deeply committed to it, and clearly see their role in supporting it. They have a noble sense of purpose that creates and focuses energy. As a result, their personal values are aligned with the values of the organization. They can describe a clear picture of what they intend to create. Everyone is aligned and going in the same direction.

O = Ongoing Learning

High performing organizations constantly focus on improving their capabilities through learning systems, building knowledge capital, and transferring learning throughout the organization. Organizational learning is different from individual learning. High performing organizations engage in both. Everyone is always striving to get better, both individually and as an organization.

R = Relentless Focus on Customer Results

No matter what industry they are in, high performing organizations understand who their customer is and measure their results accordingly. They produce outstanding results, in part because of an almost obsessive focus on results. However, what is unique is the way in which they focus on those results: from the viewpoint of the customer.

The HPO SCORES™ Model

Shared Power and High Involvement
Power and decision making are shared and
distributed throughout the organization and
not guarded at the top of a hierarchy.
Participation, collaboration, and
teamwork are the way of life.

**Shared Information and Open
Communication**
High performing organizations employ a broad
definition of what is relevant and necessary
information. Information needed to make
informed decisions is readily available
to employees.

HPO
SCORES™

SHARED POWER
and HIGH
INVOLVEMENT

SHARED
INFORMATION
and OPEN
COMMUNICATION

Employer of Choice • Provider of Choice
*Unleashing
Potential
and Power*
• Investment of Choice

ENERGIZING
SYSTEMS
and
STRUCTURES

COMPELLING
VISION:
PURPOSE and
VALUES

RELENTLESS
FOCUS on
CUSTOMER RESULTS

ONGOING
LEARNING

Organization
Knowledge
and Capabilities

Individual
Learning

**Energizing
Systems and
Structures**
Systems, structures,
processes, and practices
are aligned to support the
organization's purpose, values,
strategic direction, and goals—which
makes it easier for people to get their
jobs done.

Compelling Vision
Organizational vision,
including purpose and
values, are clearly
understood and passionately
supported by all—which creates
a deliberate, highly focused culture
that drives the desired business results.

Relentless Focus on Results
High performing organizations produce
outstanding results, in part because of an almost
obsessive focus on results. However, what is unique
is the way in which they focus on those results—
from the perspective of their customer.

Ongoing Learning
High performing organizations are constantly focused
on improving their capabilities through learning
systems, building knowledge capital, and transferring
learning throughout the organization.

The six essential elements of the HPO SCORES™ Model operate interdependently to produce
sustainable high performance and human satisfaction. Refer to the "High Performing
Organizations: SCORES" article for more information on each of the elements and the research
behind them.

E = Energizing Systems and Structures

The systems, structures, processes, and practices in high performing organizations are aligned to support the organization's vision, strategic direction, and goals. This makes it easier for people to get their jobs done. Energizing systems and structures provide the platform for rapid response to obstacles and opportunities. The bottom-line test of whether the systems and structures are energizing is to look at whether they help people accomplish their jobs more easily or make them more difficult.

S = Shared Power and High Involvement

In high performing organizations, power and decision making are shared and distributed throughout the organization, not guarded at the top of the hierarchy. Participation, collaboration, and teamwork are a way of life. When people feel valued and respected for their contributions, are allowed to make decisions that impact their lives, and have access to information to make good decisions, they *can* and *will* function as valuable contributors to the purpose and vision of the organization. In high performing organizations, a sense of personal and collective power exists.

High performing organizations use the best of what people have to offer for the common end. Centralized power and authority are balanced with participation and do not become obstacles to agility and responsiveness. When people are clear about goals and standards and have clear boundaries of autonomy, they act with commitment toward accomplishing results.

Leadership Is the Engine

If becoming a high performing organization is the destination, leadership is the engine. While the HPO SCORES model describes the characteristics of a high performing organization, leadership is what moves the organization in that direction.

In high performing organizations, the role of formal leadership is radically different from traditional organizations. High performing organizations do not rely on cultivating a great, charismatic leader but on building a visionary organization that endures beyond the leader. The role of leadership shifts from privileged status and power for its own sake toward a more complex, participative, long-term process. As this book will continually emphasize, once leaders establish the vision, they assume the attitude and behavior of a servant leader. Because they are so important, the attitudes and actions of servant leadership are discussed in detail in Chapter 12, "Servant Leadership."

In high performing organizations, leadership practices support collaboration and involvement. Leadership is assumed at every level of the organization. Top leaders live the organization's values. They embody and encourage a spirit of inquiry and discovery. They help others think systematically. They act as teachers *and* lifelong learners. They are visible in their leadership and have the strength to stand firm on strategic business decisions and values. They keep everyone's energy focused on the bull's-eye of excellence.

In high performing organizations, leadership is not the province of formal leaders alone; leadership emerges everywhere. Individuals with expertise come forward as needed throughout the organization. High performing organizations do not depend on a few peak performers to guide and direct; rather, they have broadly developed leadership capabilities. This allows for self-management, ownership, and the power to act quickly as the situation requires.

The HPO SCORES Quiz:
How Does Your Organization Score?

To begin to see how your organization scores, take a few moments to complete the following quiz. It is based on a few of the questions from the HPO SCORES Profile, an organizational assessment that was developed as part of the research project.[3] We've also included some supplemental questions on leadership.

HPO SCORES Quiz

On a scale of 1 to 7 , to what extent do you disagree or agree with the following statements?

1 = Strongly Disagree

2 = Disagree

3 = Slightly Disagree

4 = Neutral

5 = Slightly Agree

6 = Agree

7 = Strongly Agree

Shared Information and Open Communication

___ 1. People have easy access to the information they need to do their job effectively.

___ 2. Plans and decisions are communicated so that they are clearly understood.

Compelling Vision: Purpose and Values

___ 1. Leadership in your organization is aligned around a shared vision and values.

2. The people in your organization have passion around a shared purpose and values.

Ongoing Learning

___ 1. People in your organization are actively supported in the development of new skills and competencies.

___ 2. Your organization continually incorporates new learning into standard ways of doing business.

Relentless Focus on Customer Results

__ 1. Everyone in your organization maintains the highest standards of quality and service.
__ 2. All work processes are designed to make it easier for your customers to do business with you.

Energizing Systems and Structures

__ 1. Systems, structures, and formal and informal practices are integrated and aligned.
__ 2. Systems, structures, and formal and informal practices make it easy for people in your organization to get their job done.

Shared Power and High Involvement

__ 1. People have an opportunity to influence decisions that affect them.
__ 2. Teams are used as a vehicle for accomplishing work and influencing decisions.

Leadership[4]

__ 1. Leaders think that leading is about serving, not being served.
__ 2. Leaders remove barriers to help people focus on their work and their customers.

How Does Your Organization Score?

It is possible to receive a total of 14 points for each of the elements and for the supplemental questions on leadership.

Add the scores for each element to determine how strong your organization is in that element.

Score 12–14 = High performing
Score 9–11 = Average
Score 8 or below = Opportunity for improvement

How Should I Use My Quiz Results?

Although this quiz may help you begin to determine if your organization is high performing, it should not be used as an organizational analysis. The main purpose of the quiz is to guide your reading. While the sections and chapters of this book are sequenced for good reason, they may not be laid out in the order that most matters to you and your organization today.

While it makes perfect sense to us to focus first on setting your sights on the right target and vision, it may make more sense for you to start with having the right kind of leadership. For example, some of our clients have a long history of having the right target and vision, but in recent years, some self-serving leaders have risen to the top and have been causing a gap between the espoused vision and values and the vision and values in action. Other clients have a real sense of the right target and vision, but a culture has emerged that is not treating their customers right. If that sounds familiar to you, you might want to start with Section II, "Treat Your Customers Right." However, if you are just beginning your journey to becoming a high performing organization, we recommend that you start with Section I, "Set Your Sights on the Right Target and Vision." Then move through the planned sequence of sections from how you treat your customers and your people to a hard look at whether you have the right kind of leadership.

We recommend that you first skim the entire book in sequence. Then go back and read the book more closely, beginning with the corresponding section(s) and chapters that address any element on the HPO SCORES quiz on which you scored 8 or less.

The sections and chapters that address specific HPO SCORES elements follow.

Shared Information and Open Communication

Section III, "Treat Your People Right"

Chapter 4: "Empowerment Is the Key"

Chapter 9: "Situational Team Leadership"

Chapter 10: "Organizational Leadership"

Chapter 11: "Strategies for Managing a Change"

Compelling Vision: Purpose and Values

Section I, "Set Your Sights on the Right Target and Vision"

Chapter 2: "The Power of Vision"

Ongoing Learning

Section III, "Treat Your People Right"

Chapter 4: "Empowerment Is the Key"

Chapter 5: "Situational Leadership® II: The Integrating Concept"

Chapter 6: "Self Leadership: The Power Behind Empowerment"

Chapter 7: "Partnering for Performance"

Chapter 8: "Essential Skills for Partnering for Performance: The One Minute Manager®"

Chapter 9: "Situational Team Leadership"

Chapter 10: "Organizational Leadership"

Chapter 11: "Strategies for Managing a Change"

Relentless Focus on Customer Results

Section II, "Treat Your Customers Right"

Chapter 3: "Serving Customers at a Higher Level"

Energizing Systems and Structures

Shared Power and High Involvement

Leadership

Chapter 2

THE POWER OF VISION

Jesse Stoner, Ken Blanchard,
and Drea Zigarmi

When leaders who are leading at a higher level understand the role of the triple bottom line as the right target—to be the provider of choice, employer of choice, and investment of choice—they are ready to focus everyone's energy on a compelling vision.

The Importance of Vision

Why is it so important for leaders to have clear vision? Because...

...leadership is about going somewhere.
If you and your people don't know
where you are going,
your leadership doesn't matter.

Alice learned this lesson in *Alice in Wonderland* when she was searching for a way out of Wonderland and came to a fork in the road. "Would you tell me, please, which way I ought to go from here?" she asked the Cheshire Cat. "That depends a good deal on where you want to go," the cat responded. Alice replied that she really did not much care. The smiling cat told her in no uncertain terms: "Then it doesn't matter which way you go."

Jesse Stoner conducted an extensive study that demonstrated the powerful impact of vision and leadership on organizational performance.[1] She collected information from the team members of more than 500 leaders. The results were striking. Leaders who demonstrated strong visionary leadership had the highest performing teams. Leaders with good management skills but without vision had average team performance. Leaders who were identified as weak in vision and management skills had poor-performing teams.

The biggest impediment blocking most managers from being great leaders is the lack of a clear vision for them to serve. In fewer than 10 percent of the organizations we have visited were members clear about the vision. This lack of shared vision causes people to become inundated with multiple priorities, duplication of efforts, false starts, and wasted energy—none of which supports the triple bottom line.

A vision builds trust, collaboration, interdependence, motivation, and mutual responsibility for success. Vision helps people make smart choices, because their decisions are being made with the end result in mind. As goals are accomplished, the answer to "What next?" becomes clear. Vision allows us to act from a proactive stance, moving toward what we want rather than reactively away from what we don't want. Vision empowers and excites us to reach for what we truly desire. As the late management guru Peter Drucker said, "The best way to predict your future is to create it."

A Compelling Vision Creates a Culture of Greatness

A compelling vision creates a strong culture in which the energy of everyone in the organization is aligned. This results in trust, customer satisfaction, an energized and committed workforce, and profitability. Conversely, when an organization does not live up to its stated values, employee and customer trust and commitment erode, negatively impacting all aspects of the bottom line. For example, Ford lost credibility and market share when its stated value—"Quality Is Job One"—was tested by its hesitation to take responsibility in the recall of the defective Firestone tires on its Explorer sport utility vehicle in 2000.[2]

High performing organizations (HPOs) have a strong and distinct culture. There is no denying that the illusive phenomenon called culture is a powerful definer of organizational excellence. Culture may be described as the context within which all practices exist. It is the organization's personality—it's "how things are done around here." Culture consists of the values, attitudes, beliefs, behaviors, and practices of the organizational members. Culture not only underlies all that an organization does but also determines its readiness for change. When organizations seek greatness, they often find aspects of their organizational culture that need change. A strong, focused organizational culture starts with a compelling vision and is supported by each of the key elements.

Vision Is the Place to Start

Research clearly demonstrates the extraordinary impact of a shared vision, or core ideology, on long-term financial performance. The cumulative stock returns of the HPOs researched by Collins and Porras were six times greater than the "successful" companies they examined and 15 times greater than the general market over a 50-year period![3] For this reason, vision is the place to start if you want to improve your organization's HPO SCORES and hit the target.

Research has demonstrated time and again that an essential characteristic of great leaders is their ability to mobilize people around a shared vision.[4]

If it's not in service of a shared vision, leadership can become self-serving. Leaders begin to think their people are there to serve them, instead of the customer. Organizations can become self-serving bureaucracies where leaders focus their energies on recognition, power, and status, rather than the organization's larger purpose and goals. The results of this type of behavior have been all too evident recently at Enron, WorldCom, and others.

Once the leader has clarified and shared the vision, he can focus on serving and being responsive to the needs of the people, understanding that the role of leadership is to remove barriers and help people achieve the vision. The greatest leaders mobilize others by coalescing people around a shared vision. Sometimes leaders don't get it at first, but the great ones eventually do.

Louis Gerstner, Jr. is a perfect example. When Gerstner took the helm of IBM in 1993—amidst turmoil and instability as the company's annual net losses reached a record $8 billion—he was quoted as saying, "The last thing IBM needs is a vision." A lot of people asked us what we thought about that statement. Our reply was, "It depends on how he defines vision. If he means a 'pie-in-the-sky' dream, he's absolutely right. The ship is sinking. But if all he's doing is plugging the holes, the ship isn't going anywhere." We were amused to read an article in the *New York Times*[5] two years later. In that article, Gerstner conceded that IBM had lost the war for the desktop operating system, acknowledging that the acquisition of Lotus signified that the company had failed to plan properly for its future. He admitted that he and his management team now "spent a lot of time thinking ahead." Once Gerstner understood the importance of vision, an incredible turnaround occurred. He became clear that the company's source of strength would be in integrated solutions, and he resisted pressures to split the company. In 1995, delivering the keynote address at the computer industry trade show, Gerstner articulated IBM's new vision—

that network computing would drive the next phase of industry growth and would be the company's overarching strategy. That year, IBM began a series of acquisitions that positioned services to become the fastest-growing segment of the company, with growth at more than 20 percent per year. This extraordinary turnaround demonstrated that the *most important* thing IBM needed was a vision—a shared vision.

If an organization's vision is compelling, the triple bottom line is served. Success goes way beyond mere financial rewards. Vision generates tremendous energy, excitement, and passion, because people feel they are making a difference. They know what they are doing and why. There is a strong sense of trust and respect. Managers don't try to control but rather let others assume responsibility, because people know they are part of an aligned whole. People assume responsibility for their own actions. They take charge of their future, rather than passively waiting for it to happen. There is room for creativity and risk taking. People can make their contributions in their own way, and those differences are respected because people know they are in the same boat together—all part of a larger whole going "full steam ahead!"

Vision Can Exist Anywhere in an Organization

You don't have to wait for an organizational vision to begin. Vision is the responsibility of every leader at every level of the organization. It's possible for leaders of departments or teams to create shared visions for their departments even when the rest of the organization doesn't have one. Consider our work helping a tax department in a Fortune 500 company. The leader of the department stated:

> "We began to understand our own and each others' hopes and dreams and discovered how close they were. As a result, we found ways to work together more effectively and began to enjoy work a lot more. We discovered what business we were really in: 'Providing

financial information to help leaders make good business decisions.' As a result, we began to partner more effectively with business leaders. Our department gained more credibility in the company, and other departments began asking us what we had done to make such a turnaround. They became interested in creating a vision for their own department. It was contagious."

Too often, leaders complain that they can't have a vision because the larger organization doesn't have one. Again, it's not necessary to wait. The power of vision will work for you and your team, regardless of your level in the organization.

Effective Versus Ineffective Vision Statements

A lot of organizations already have vision statements, but most of them seem irrelevant when you look at the organization and where it's going. Are these vision statements misguided, and if so, how can we improve them? The purpose of a vision statement is to create an aligned organization where everyone is working together toward the same desired ends.

The vision provides guidance for daily decisions so that people are aiming at the right target, not working at cross-purposes with each other.

How do you know if your vision statement works? Here's the test: Is it hidden in a forgotten file or framed on a wall solely for decoration? If so, it's not working. Is it actively used to guide everyday decision making? If the answer is yes, your vision statement is working.

Creating a Vision That Really Works

Why don't more leaders have a vision? We believe it's a lack of knowledge. Many leaders—such as former president George H. W. Bush—say they just don't get the "vision thing." They acknowledge that vision is desirable, but they're unsure how to create it. To these leaders, vision seems elusive—something that is magically bestowed only on the fortunate few. Intrigued by the possibility of making vision accessible to all leaders, Jesse Stoner teamed up with Drea Zigarmi to identify the key elements of a compelling vision—one that would inspire people and provide direction. In "From Vision to Reality," Jesse and Drea identified three key elements of a compelling vision:[6]

- **Significant purpose**—What business are you in?
- **A picture of the future**—What will the future look like if you are successful?
- **Clear values**—What guides your behavior and decisions on a daily basis?

A vision must include all three elements to be inspiring and enduring. Let's explore these elements with some real-world examples.

Significant Purpose

The first element of a compelling vision is a significant purpose. This higher purpose is your organization's reason for existence. It answers the question "Why?" rather than just explaining what you do. It clarifies, from your customer's viewpoint, what business you are *really* in.

CNN is in the "hard spot news-breaking business." Their customers are busy people who need breaking news on demand. Their business is to provide hard news as it unfolds—not to provide entertainment. According to CNN, the typical family today is too busy to sit in front of the television at 7 P.M. Dad has a second job, Mom is working late, and the kids are involved in activities. Therefore, CNN's purpose is to provide news 24 hours a day. This helps CNN employees answer the questions "What are my priorities?" and "Where should I focus my energy?"

Walt Disney started his theme parks with a clear purpose. He said, "We're in the happiness business." That is very different from being in the theme park business. Clear purpose drives everything the cast members (employees) do with their guests (customers). Being in the happiness business helps cast members understand their primary role in the company.

A wonderful organization in Orlando, Florida, called Give Kids the World, is an implementation operation for the Make-A-Wish Foundation. Dying children who always wanted to go to Disney World, SeaWorld, or other attractions in Orlando can get a chance through Give Kids the World. Over the years, the organization has brought more than 50,000 families to Orlando for a week at no cost to them. The organization thinks having a sick child is a family issue; therefore, the whole family goes to Orlando. When you ask the employees what business they are in, they tell you they're in the memory business—they want to create memories for these kids and their families.

On a visit to Give Kids the World, one of our colleagues passed a man who was cutting the grass. Curious about how widely understood the organization's mission was, our colleague asked the man, "What business are you in here at Give Kids the World?"

The man smiled and said, "We make memories."

"How do *you* make memories?" our associate asked. "You just cut the grass."

The man said, "I certainly don't make memories by continuing to cut the grass if a family comes by. You can always tell who the sick kid is, so I ask that youngster whether he or she or a brother or sister wants to help me with my chores."

Isn't that a wonderful attitude? It keeps him focused on servicing the folks who come to Give Kids the World.

Great organizations have a deep and noble sense of purpose—a significant purpose—that inspires excitement and commitment.

When work is meaningful and connected to what we truly desire, we can unleash a productive and creative power we never imagined. But purpose alone is not enough, because it does not tell you where you're going.

Picture of the Future

The second element of a compelling vision is a picture of the future. This picture of the end result should not be abstract. It should be a mental image you can actually see. The power of imagery has been described by many sports psychologists, including Charles Garfield in *Peak Performance: Mental Training Techniques of the World's Greatest Athletes*. Numerous studies have demonstrated that not only does mental imagery enhance performance, but it enhances intrinsic motivation as well.[7]

CNN's picture of the future is not something vague like being the premier network news station or being "number one." It's a picture you can actually create a mental image of: "To be viewed in every nation on the planet in English and in the language of that region."

Walt Disney's picture of the future was expressed in the charge he gave every cast member: "Keep the same smile on people's faces when they leave the park as when they entered." Disney didn't care whether guests were in the park two hours or ten hours. He just wanted to keep them smiling. After all, they were in the happiness business. Your picture should focus on the end result, not the process for getting there.

At Give Kids the World, their picture of the future is that in the last week of the lives of youngsters who have been there, they will still be laughing and talking to their families about their time in Orlando.

Some people mistakenly use the Apollo Moon Project as an example of a vision. It is a wonderful example of the power of creating a picture of the future, but it's not an example of a vision. In 1961, when President John F. Kennedy articulated a picture of the future—to place a man on the moon by the end of the 1960s and bring him home safely—the United States had not even invented the technology to accomplish it. To achieve that goal, NASA overcame seemingly insurmountable obstacles, demonstrating the power of articulating a picture of the future. However, once the goal was achieved, NASA never re-created its spectacular achievement because it was not linked to a significant purpose. There was nothing to answer the question "Why?" Was the purpose to "beat the Russians" or to "begin the Space Defense Initiative" or—in the spirit of *Star Trek*—"to boldly go where no one has gone before"? Because there was no clear purpose, there was no way to guide decision making going forward and answer the question "What next?" The second element—a picture of the future—is powerful, but it alone does not create an enduring vision.

Clear Values

The third element of a compelling vision is having clear values. High performing organizations have clear values. Values define leadership and the way employees act on a day-to-day basis while doing their work.

Values provide guidelines on how you should proceed as you pursue your purpose and picture of the future. They answer the questions "What do I want to live by?" and "How?" They need to be clearly described so that you know exactly what behaviors demonstrate that the value is being lived. Values need to be consistently acted on, or they are only good intentions. They need to resonate with the personal values of the members of the organization so that people truly choose to live by them.

The values need to support the organization's purpose. Because CNN is in the journalism business, not the entertainment business, its values are "to provide accurate, responsible journalism and to be responsive to the news needs of people around the world." These values help reporters and producers make on-the-spot decisions about news coverage and would be quite different if CNN were in the entertainment business.

Robert Johnson founded Johnson & Johnson for the purpose of alleviating pain and disease. The company's purpose and values, reflected in its credo, continue to guide the company. Using its values to guide its decision making, Johnson & Johnson quickly recalled all Tylenol capsules throughout the United States during a 1982 tampering incident that was localized in the Chicago area. The immediate cost was substantial, but not knowing the extent of the tampering, the company didn't want to risk anyone's safety. In the end, Johnson & Johnson's triple bottom line was served, demonstrated by the company's long-term gains in reputation and profitability.

Most organizations that do have values either have too many values or have not rank-ordered them.[8] Research done by Ken Blanchard and Michael O'Connor shows that people can't focus on more than three or four values that really impact behavior. They also found that values must be rank-ordered to be effective. Why? Because life is about value conflicts. When these conflicts arise, people need to know which value they should focus on.

The Disney theme parks have four rank-ordered values: safety, courtesy, the show, and efficiency. Why is safety the highest-ranked value? Walt Disney knew that if guests were carried out of one of his parks on a stretcher, they would not have the same smiles on their faces leaving the park as they had when they entered.

The second-ranked value, courtesy, is all about the friendly attitude you expect at a Disney park. Why is it important to know that it's the number-two value? Suppose one of the Disney cast members is answering a guest question in a friendly, courteous manner, and he hears a scream that's not coming from a roller coaster. If that cast member wants to act according to the park's rank-ordered values, he will excuse himself as quickly and politely as possible and race toward the scream. Why? Because the number-one value just called. If the values were not rank-ordered and the cast member was enjoying the interaction with the guest, he might say, "They're always yelling in the park," and not move in the direction of the scream. Later somebody could come to that cast member and say, "You were the closest to the scream. Why didn't you do something?" The response could be, "I was dealing with our courtesy value." Life is a series of value conflicts. There will be times when you can't act on two values at the same time.

One of our colleagues recently experienced firsthand what happens when a company has not articulated values. Driving home one evening, she arrived to find two people working in her yard. A local teenager was mowing her lawn in the back. A man from her tree service company was spraying insecticide on a fruit tree in her front yard. The wind was blowing the spray into the backyard and directly onto the teenager mowing her lawn.

Shocked, our colleague jumped out of her car, ran up to the man who was spraying her trees, and cried, "Stop! Can't you see that the spray is blowing on that boy in the backyard?"

The man replied evenly, "That's okay. I asked him, and he said he didn't mind."

This is what happens in organizations that do not articulate their values. Decisions are left up to the judgment of individuals to determine how best to fulfill their job and the purpose of the organization. How much better would it have been if the tree company had articulated values such as "safety" and "in an environmentally friendly manner"? Then the man spraying our colleague's trees might have known to come back later. If he saw an open window in a house, he might know to knock on the door and ask the homeowner to shut the window. Or if he saw children's toys in the yard, he might move them before spraying. In this particular case, the tree company lost a valued customer.

For a vision to endure, you need all three elements—a significant purpose, a picture of the future, and clear values—to guide behavior on a day-to-day basis. Martin Luther King, Jr. outlined his vision in his "I Have a Dream" speech. By describing a world where his children "will not be judged by the color of their skin but by the content of their character," he created powerful and specific images arising from the values of brotherhood, respect, and freedom for all—values that resonate with the founding values of the United States. King's vision continues to mobilize and guide people beyond his lifetime because it illuminates a significant purpose, provides a picture of the future, and describes values that resonate with people's hopes and dreams.

Make Your Vision a Reality

In their book *Full Steam Ahead!: Unleash the Power of Vision*, Ken Blanchard and Jesse Stoner define vision as "knowing who you are, where you're going, and what will guide your journey."[9] *Knowing who you are* means having a significant purpose. *Where you're going* means having a picture of the future. *What will guide your journey* are clear values. However, vision alone is not enough. For a leader to ensure that the vision becomes a reality— a shared vision that mobilizes people—Ken and Jesse identify three important guidelines that people must follow: how the vision is created, how it's communicated, and how it's lived.

How It's Created

The process of creating the vision is as important as what the vision says. Instead of simply taking the top management to a retreat to put the vision together and then announcing it to others, encourage dialogue about the vision. While the initial responsibility for drafting an organizational vision rests with the top management, the organization needs to put in place mechanisms to allow others to have an opportunity to help shape the vision—to put their thumbprint on it.

For a departmental or team vision, it's possible to craft the vision as a team. Although the leader must have a sense of where he's going, it's important that he trusts and utilizes the knowledge and skills of the people on the team to get the best vision.

Regardless of how you initially draft the vision, it's important that you get input from those it affects before you finalize it. Ask people these questions: "Would you like to work for an organization that has this vision? Can you see where you fit in the vision? Does it help you set priorities? Does it provide guidelines for making decisions? Is it exciting and motivating? Have we left anything out? Should we delete anything?" Involving people will deepen their understanding and commitment and create a better vision.

How It's Communicated

Creating a vision—for your organization or department, for your work, and for your life—is a journey, not a one-time activity.

In some organizations, a vision statement may be found framed on the wall, but it provides no guidance or, worse, has nothing to do with the reality of how things actually are. This turns people off. Visioning is an ongoing process; you need to keep it alive. It's important to keep talking about the vision and referring to it as much as possible. Max DuPree, the legendary former chairman of Herman Miller and author of *Leadership Is an Art*, said that in his visionary role, he had to be like a third-grade teacher. He had to keep saying it over and over and over until people got it right, right, right! The more you focus on your vision, the clearer it will become, and the more deeply you will understand it. In fact, aspects of what you thought was the vision may change over time, but its essence will remain.

How It's Lived

The moment you identify your vision, you need to behave as if it were happening right now. Your actions need to be congruent with your vision. As others see you living the vision, they will believe you are serious, and this will help deepen their under-standing and commitment. Two strategies will support your efforts to live your vision:

- **Always focus on your vision**—Your vision should be the foundation for your organization. If an obstacle or unforeseen event throws you off-course, you may have to change your short-term goals, but your vision should be long-lasting. Change is bound to happen. Unforeseen events are bound to occur. Find a way to reframe what is happening as a challenge or opportunity on the road to living your vision.

- **Show the courage of commitment**—True commitment begins when you take action. There will be fears; feel them and move ahead. It takes courage to create a vision, and it takes courage to act on it. In the words of Goethe, "Whatever you can do, or dream you can, begin it. Boldness has genius, power, and magic in it."

Vision and Leadership

Vision always comes back to leadership. People look to their formal leaders for vision and direction. While leaders should involve people in shaping direction, the ultimate responsibility for ensuring and maintaining a vision remains with the leaders and cannot be delegated to others. Creating a vision is not an activity that can be checked off a list. It's one of the most critical ongoing roles of a successful leader. It means the difference between high and average performance, whether it's an entire organization, a department, or a team.

Once a vision is agreed upon, the leader's role is to ensure that people throughout the organization are responsive to this vision. The leader's job is to support people in accomplishing the vision by removing barriers; by ensuring that policies, practices, and systems make it easier for them to act on the vision; and by holding themselves, their peers, and their people accountable for acting consistently with the vision. Then people naturally serve the vision, not the leader.

Vision calls an organization to be truly great, not merely to beat the competition and get big numbers. A magnificent vision articulates people's hopes and dreams, touches their hearts and spirits, and helps them see how they can contribute. It starts everything in the right direction.

Visit **www.LeadingAtAHigherLevel.com** to access the free virtual conference titled *Set Your Sights on the Right Target and Vision.* Use the password "Target" for your FREE access.

TREAT
YOUR CUSTOMERS
RIGHT

Chapter 3

SERVING CUSTOMERS AT A HIGHER LEVEL

Ken Blanchard, Jesse Stoner,
and Scott Blanchard

The second step in leading at a higher level is to treat your customers right. While everybody seems to know that, few organizations are creating raving fans—devoted customers who want to brag about them. Organizations with legendary service are rare.

Scoring with Your Customers

In Chapter 1, "Is Your Organization High Performing?," we discussed HPO SCORES; one of the key elements was *relentless focus on customer results*. In high performing organizations, everyone passionately holds and maintains the highest standards for quality and service from their customers' perspective. These organizations use the customer experience to evaluate how well they are doing in every aspect of the organization. Processes are designed with the customer in mind. Those who are in contact with the customer can make decisions. Accountability is to the customer.

In high performing organizations, everything starts and ends with the customer. This is a radical shift from organizations whose business design puts the customer as the end receiver of the chain. For example, at the renowned Golden Door Spa, all systems are set up to wow the customer. Employees know that their job is to exceed expectations and to back up the key frontline person at that moment. Customer needs and trends drive innovation, new products, and services. High performing organizations design work processes from the customer backward to ensure a flow that makes sense from a customer's perspective. Internal cross-functional relationships and structures are organized around customer needs. High performing organizations ensure that they are able to respond quickly to customer needs and adapt to changes in the marketplace. They anticipate trends and get in front of them. Innovations in processes are developed to make it easier for customers to do business. This creates constant innovation in operating practices, market strategies, products, and services.

In high performing organizations, management has regular face-to-face contact with customers—not only with devoted customers, but also with those who are frustrated, angry, or not using the organization's products and services. Leaders are passionate about developing sophisticated knowledge of customers and sharing the information broadly throughout the organization. Working with the people they serve and listening intently allows high performing organizations to respond rapidly and flexibly to changing conditions.

Connecticut's Trader Joe's Grocery exceeds expectations by making sure the customer gets the best of what he wants. One of the HPO SCORES researchers, Fay Kandarian, had a recent experience with this when she brought red tulips to the checkout line. The associate checked the tulips before ringing them up and suggested looking for a fresher bunch. Together they went to look at other tulips, and after checking for red ones, the associate picked out the freshest-looking tulips, which were pink and white. After ringing up the new tulips, the associate said, "Since I need to throw away these red tulips, I'm going to give them to you to enjoy for the few days they will last." This is another example of how high performing organizations encourage those who touch the customer to create the best possible customer experience and act on their ideas.

Nordstrom's core ideology, "service to the customer above all else," has been a way of life for the company long before customer service programs became stylish.[1] Planning starts with the customer, and execution focuses on the customer. For example, planning the sale environment exceeds the effort put into planning sale advertising. To ensure customer comfort, sale planning may involve valet parking, extra fitting rooms, and additional sales staff. A key aspect of the orientation of new associates is teaching them how to say "no problem" and mean it. To ensure that their frontline people put all their initiative into serving customers, Nordstrom's rule of thumb and main guideline for employees is that they should always use their best judgment. In fact, that is the only rule that is really enforced. Combining the service ethic with best judgment has resulted in legendary tales of clothes being pressed, Macy's packages being wrapped, outfits being personally delivered, and two different-sized shoes being sold as a pair to fit a customer's different-sized feet. The result? Customers are dedicated to Nordstrom with almost as much passion as Nordstrom's long-term associates, who also enjoy profit sharing year after year.

Serving Customers at a Higher Level

In *Raving Fans*, Sheldon Bowles and Ken Blanchard contend that there are three secrets to treating your customers right and turning them into raving fans: Decide, Discover, and Deliver Plus One Percent.[2] All these concepts came alive when Ken Blanchard, Fred Finch, and Jim Ballard studied Yum! Brands, the world's largest quick-service restaurant corporation. Their book, *Customer Mania: It's Never Too Late to Build a Customer-Focused Company*, documents Yum! Brands' journey to satisfy customers in more than 30,000 restaurants located in 100 countries.[3]

Decide What You Want Your Customer Experience to Be

If you want to create raving fans, you don't just announce it. You have to plan for it. You have to decide what you want to do. What kind of experience do you want your customers to have as they interact with every aspect of your organization? Some people would argue that you should ask your customers first. While you do want input from your customers, they often are limited to certain things they like and don't like. They don't know what the possibilities are beyond their own experience. They don't see the big picture. It's important that *you* determine from the beginning what you want your customer's experience to be. That doesn't mean that customers' opinions aren't important. In *Full Steam Ahead*, Ken Blanchard and Jesse Stoner describe how the needs of your customers should determine the Law of the Situation— what business you are really in. Understanding what your customers really want when they come to you helps you determine what you should offer them.

A good example of how this works is Domo Gas, a full-service gasoline chain in Western Canada cofounded by Sheldon Bowles. Back in the 1970s, when everybody was going to self-service gasoline stations, Sheldon knew that if people had a choice, they would never go to a gas station. But people have to get gas, and they want to get in and out as quickly as possible. The customer-service vision that Sheldon and his cofounders imagined was an Indianapolis 500 pit stop. They dressed all their attendants in red jumpsuits. When a customer drove into one of Sheldon's stations, two or three people ran out of the hut and raced toward the car. As quickly as possible, they looked under the hood, cleaned the windshield, and pumped the gas. A California station that got excited about the concept gave customers a cup of coffee and a newspaper and asked them to step out of their cars while the interior was vacuumed. As customers pulled away, they were given flyers that said, "P.S. We also sell gas."

In deciding what experience you want your customers to have, you are creating a picture of what things would look like if everything were running as planned. World-class athletes often picture themselves breaking a world record, pitching a perfect game, or making a 99-yard punt return. They know that power comes from having a clear mental image of their best potential performance. Developing a clear picture of how you want to serve your customers is almost like producing a movie in your mind.

We had a chance to work with the top management and the heads of dealerships for Freightliner, a leading manufacturer of large trucks. Jim Hibe, the president at the time, spearheaded the creation of a new picture of service for their dealerships—one that permitted them to go way beyond their competition. In preparation for their key annual conference, Freightliner produced a 30-minute video that illustrated two hypothetical dealerships. The first, called Great Scott Trucking, typified the present mode of operating for many of the dealerships: limited hours (8 to 5 Monday through Friday and 9 to 12 on Saturday); uncommitted employees; few, if any, extras (like donuts and coffee for truckers waiting for their vehicles); and so on. When you entered the dealership, everything seemed to be organized to serve the policies, rules, and regulations and not the customers. For example, suppose the manager comes in about 11:45 on Saturday. Seeing a long line in the parts department, he says, "Make sure you shut her down at 12. The line will make for a good Monday."

The other hypothetical dealership, called Daley Freightliner, was a customer-centered operation with 24-hour service. Seven days a week, committed and trained employees were willing to go the extra mile and provide all kinds of services for the truckers. They had a lounge with recliners and a huge TV showing first-run movies. There was a quiet, dark room with bunk beds in case the truckers wanted to sleep. Employees drove repaired trucks to the front rather than making the drivers retrieve them from the back lot.

Many of the dealerships were closer to Great Scott Trucking than they were to Daley Freightliner. So when the conference opened with the video, it made some people squirm. But it beautifully depicted the new service vision for all to see and experience. Throughout the conference, dealers who were closest to the positive image shared their success stories. That program was an excellent way to convey a customer service vision.

The Moments of Truth concept that Jan Carlzon used to create a customer-focused culture when he was president of the Scandinavian Airlines System (SAS) is most helpful in deciding what you want your customer experience to be. A Moment of Truth is as follows:

> Any time a customer comes in contact with anyone in our organization in a way that they can get an impression. How do we answer the phone? How do we check people in? How do we greet them on our planes? How do we interact with them during flights? How do we handle baggage claim? What happens when a problem occurs?

For Carlzon and other great service providers, Moments of Truth could cover every detail, including coffee stains. When he was chairman of People Express Airlines, Donald Burr contended that if the flip-down trays were dirty, customers would assume that the plane's engines were not well maintained either.[4] When looking for a place to stay after a long day's drive, how many people would choose a motel with a sign that is missing some lights?

While most of our examples have focused on external customers, it is important to recognize that everyone has a customer. An external customer is someone outside your organization who you serve or provide with a service. A person who takes orders at a quick-service restaurant is a good example of someone who serves external customers. An internal customer is someone within your organization who may or may not serve external customers. For example, people who work in the human resources field have mainly internal customers. And some people, like those in the accounting department, have both external and internal customers. They send bills and invoices to external customers, and they provide reports and information to internal customers. The point is, everyone has a customer.

Great customer service organizations analyze every key interaction they have with customers, whether they are external or internal, and they determine how they would like that scenario to play out. One of the ways to think about that is to suppose that the word has gotten out about how fabulously you are serving customers. Ecstatic customers are running all over the place, bragging about you. A well-known television station gets word of this and decides it wants to send a crew in to film what is going on in your organization. Who would you want them to talk to? What would your people tell them? What would these folks see?

Creating raving fans starts with a picture—an image of what kind of experience you want your customers to have. Analyzing your Moments of Truth for each department and deciding how you want them played out is a good start. This will serve as your guide as you target new customers and adjust to changing conditions.

Discover What Your Customers Want

After you decide what you want to have happen, it's important to discover any suggestions your customers may have that will improve their experience with your organization. What would make their experience with you better? Ask them! But ask them in a way that stimulates an answer. For example, how many times have you been eating at a restaurant when the manager comes over and says, "How is everything tonight?" Isn't your usual response "Fine"? That gives the manager no information. A better conversation would be, "Excuse me. I'm the restaurant manager. I wonder if I could ask you a question. Is there anything we could have done differently tonight that would have made your experience with us better?" That question invites an answer. If the customer says "No," you can follow it up with a sincere "Are you sure?"

High performing organizations regularly
solicit customer and market feedback.

Organizations that provide raving fan service are masters of discovering what the customer is thinking. They use real-time information on production activities, quickly adapting to changing environments and demands.

Sometimes you have to be creative in discovering what customers want. Tom Cullen, a teaching colleague of Ken's at the hotel school at Cornell University, shared a wonderful story about listening to customer feedback. Tom was having dinner with a family that included a 13-year-old son and two younger kids at a fine gourmet hotel restaurant in New York City. When their waiter gave each of the three children a children's menu, the older boy was upset. The attentive waiter, reading the boy's nonverbal cues, quickly brought him an adult menu.

The two younger kids ordered macaroni and cheese from the children's menu. When dinner came, they played with the macaroni but didn't eat much. When Tom tasted it, he thought it was something to die for—it was the best macaroni and cheese he'd ever tasted. When the waiter asked the kids if something was wrong with their meal, they said, "It's yucky! It's not Kraft!" The waiter responded, "If you come here tomorrow night, I guarantee you I'll have Kraft."

Where do you think the kids wanted to eat the next night? Obviously, that restaurant. When the family appeared at the hostess's desk, the waiter from the previous night spotted them and came right over to the kids. "I was hoping you would come back. I got Kraft for you." With that, he went to the kitchen and returned with a box of Kraft macaroni and cheese.

Listening to customers and then taking action often makes raving fans out of them. The waiter was certainly a good listener. Can you imagine what a special relationship he must have had with the chef for that kind of adaptability to take place? Is it any wonder that that restaurant is flourishing? Listening and adapting are key.

When a customer tells you something, you have to *listen without being defensive*. One reason people get uptight when they listen to customers is because they think they always have to do what the customer wants. They don't understand that listening has two parts. The first is, as Steve Covey says, "Seek first to understand." In other words, listen for understanding. Try saying, "That's interesting. Tell me more. Can you be more specific?"

The second aspect of listening is deciding if you want to do anything about what you heard. You have to separate that from the understanding aspect of listening. And it is important to realize that you don't have to decide right after you understand what the person is suggesting. You can do it later, when you have some time to think about it or talk it over with others. Realizing that you have time to think something over will make you less defensive and a better listener. First listen to understand, and then decide what you want to do about what you've heard.

In the mall recently, one of our colleagues saw an example of defensive listening. He was walking behind a woman who had an eight- or nine-year-old son. As they walked past the sporting goods store, the kid looked over and saw a beautiful red bicycle outside the store. He stopped in his tracks and said to his mother, "Boy, would I like a bike like that." His mother nearly went crazy and started screaming: "I can't believe it! I just got you a new bike for Christmas! Here it is March, and you already want another one! I'm not going to get you another $%&*^! thing!" Our colleague thought the mother was going to nail this kid's head to the cement. Sadly, she didn't distinguish the need to separate listening for understanding from deciding. If she had said to the kid, "Honey, what do you like about that bike?" he might have said, "See those streamers coming out of the handlebars? I really like them." And those streamers could have been a cheap birthday present. After listening to what he liked about the bike, the mother could have said, "Honey, why do you think I can't get you that new bike?" The kid was no fool. He probably would have said, "I just got a new one for Christmas."

Listening without being defensive is also helpful if you make a mistake with a customer. Defending what you've done will only irritate the customer. When customers are upset, all they want is to be heard. In fact, we have found that if people listen to a complaining customer in a nondefensive, attentive way and then ask, "Is there any way we could win back your loyalty?," more often than not the customer will say, "You've already done it. You listened to me."

If a customer makes a good suggestion or is upset about something that makes sense to change, you can add that suggestion to your customer-service picture. For example, recently we got a letter from a man who owns three quick-service restaurants in the Midwest. Some of the restaurant's elderly customers suggested that during certain parts of the day, the restaurant should have tablecloths on the tables, have people take their order at the table, and deliver the food to where they were sitting. After thinking about it, the owner realized it was a pretty good idea. Now, between 4 and 5:30 in the afternoon, the tables have tablecloths and candles, and the people behind the counter come out and wait on the customers. The elderly are pouring in to his restaurants during those hours.

When you put together what you want your customers to experience with what they want to have happen, you will have a fairly complete picture of your desired customer service experience.

Listening to customers, fitting their needs into your framework, and then consistently improving your level of service will turn your customers into raving fans.

Deliver Your Ideal Customer Service Experience

Now that you have a clear picture of the experience you want your customers to have that will satisfy and delight them and put smiles on their faces, you have to figure out how to get your people excited about delivering this experience, plus a little bit more.

As we emphasized in Chapter 2, "The Power of Vision," the responsibility for establishing a shared vision rests with the senior leadership. And that responsibility includes strong images of what excellent customer service looks like. Once your desired customer experience is set and people are committed to it, the implementation aspect of leadership begins. It is during implementation that most organizations get into trouble. The traditional pyramid is kept alive and well, leaving customers uncared for at the bottom of the hierarchy. All the energy in the organization moves up the hierarchy as people try to please and be responsive to their bosses, instead of focusing their energy on meeting the needs of their customers. Now the bureaucracy rules, and policies and procedures carry the day. This leaves unprepared and uncommitted customer-contact people to quack like ducks.

Wayne Dyer, the great personal-growth teacher, said years ago that there are two kinds of people: ducks and eagles. Ducks act like victims and go "Quack! Quack! Quack!" Eagles, on the other hand, take initiative and soar above the crowd. As a customer, you can always identify a bureaucracy if you have a problem and are confronted by ducks who quack: "It's our policy. I didn't make the rules—I just work here. Do you want to talk to my supervisor? Quack! Quack! Quack!"

Implementation is all about equipping people throughout the organization to act and feel like owners of the vision. It's about allowing people to take a proactive role in carrying out the organization's vision and direction so that they can soar like eagles and deliver great customer service rather than quack like ducks.

Our colleague's experience trying to rent a car in New York is a perfect example of this phenomenon. He is a trustee emeritus at Cornell University. A while back, he was heading to a meeting in Ithaca, New York, the small upstate town where Cornell is located. He wanted to rent a car that he could drop off at Syracuse, which is about an hour and a half away. Those who travel enough know that if you drop off a car at a different place than where you rented it, the company charges a big drop-off fee. You

49

can avoid that drop-off fee if you rent a car that came from where you are going. Knowing this, our colleague asked the woman behind the counter, "Do you have a Syracuse car?"

She said, "You're lucky. I happen to." Then she went to the computer and prepared his contract.

Our colleague is not a particularly detail-oriented person, but as he was signing his contract, he noticed a $75 drop-off fee. He said, "What's that $75 drop-off fee?"

She said, "I didn't do it. Quack! Quack!"

He said, "Who did?"

She said, "The computer. Quack! Quack!"

He said, "How do we tell the computer it was wrong?"

"I don't know. Quack! Quack!"

He said, "Why don't you just cross it out?"

She said, "I can't. My boss will kill me. Quack! Quack!"

"You mean I have to pay a $75 fee because you have a mean boss?" he asked.

"I remember one time—quack! quack!—my boss let me cross it out."

"When was that?"

"When the customer worked for Cornell. Quack! Quack!"

He said, "That's great. I'm on the Cornell board of trustees!"

She asked, "What does the board do? Quack! Quack!"

"We can fire the president."

"What's your employee number? Quack! Quack!"

"I don't have one."

"What should I do? Quack! Quack!"

It took our colleague 20 minutes of psychological counseling to get out of this drop-off fee. He used to get angry at these front-line people but doesn't anymore because he realizes that it's not really their fault.

Who do you think this woman worked for, a duck or an eagle? Obviously, a duck. If she worked for an eagle, the eagle would eat the duck. We call the supervisory duck the head mallard, because he just quacks higher up the bureaucracy. He tells you all the rules and regulations and laws that apply to your situation. Who do you think the supervisory duck works for? Another duck, who works for whom? Another duck, who works for whom? Another duck. And who sits at the top of the organization? A great big duck. Have you ever been hit by an eagle turd? Obviously not, because eagles soar above the crowd. It's the ducks that make all the mess.

How do you create an organization where ducks are busted and eagles can soar?

> The traditional pyramid hierarchy
> must be turned upside down so
> that the frontline people who are closest
> to the customers are at the top.

Here the frontline people can be **responsible**—able to respond to their customers. In this scenario, leaders **serve** and are **responsive** to people's needs, training and developing them to soar like eagles so that they can accomplish established goals and live according to the vision you have of the customer experience.

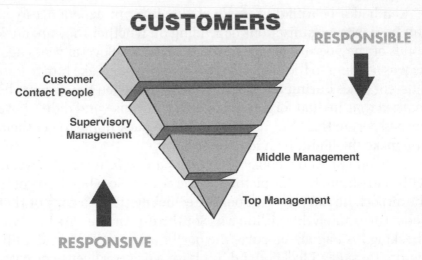

Figure 3.1   The Implementation Role of Leadership

If the leaders in an organization do not respond to the needs and desires of their people, these folks will not take good care of their customers. But when the frontline customer-contact people are treated as responsible owners of the vision, they can soar like eagles and create raving fans rather than quack like ducks.

Permitting People to Soar

One of our consulting partners experienced an eagle incident when he went to Nordstrom one day to get some perfume for his wife. The woman behind the counter said, "I'm sorry; we don't sell that perfume here. But I know where I can get it in the mall. How long will you be in our store?"

"About 30 minutes," he said.

"Fine. I'll go get it, bring it back, gift wrap it, and have it ready for you when you leave." This woman left Nordstrom, went to another store, got the perfume our colleague wanted, came back to Nordstrom, and gift wrapped it. You know what she charged him? The same price she paid at the other store. So Nordstrom didn't make any money on the deal, but what *did* they make? A raving fan.

Ken had a beautiful example of the different experiences you can have with organizations depending on whether they are duck ponds or they permit people to soar like eagles. Several years ago, he was heading to the airport for a trip that would take him to four different cities during the week. As he approached the airport, he realized that he had forgotten his driver's license and didn't have his passport, either. Not having time to go back home to get them and make the flight, he had to be creative.

Only one of Ken's books, *Everyone's a Coach*, which he wrote with Don Shula, has his picture on the cover.[5] So when Ken got to the airport, he ran into the bookstore; luckily, it had a copy of that book. Fortunately, his airline was Southwest Airlines. As Ken was checking his bag at the curb, the porter asked to see his identification. He said, "I feel bad. I don't have a driver's license or passport. But will this do?" And he showed him the cover of the book.

The man shouted, "The man knows Shula! Put him in first class!" (Of course, Southwest doesn't have first class.) Everybody out by the curb check-in started to high-five Ken. He was like a hero. Then one of the baggage handlers said, "Why don't I go in the terminal with you? I know the folks in security. I think I can get you through there, too."

Why did that happen? Herb Kelleher, who cofounded Southwest, not only wanted to give his customers the lowest possible price, but he also wanted to give them the best possible service. He set up the whole organization to empower everyone—right down to the frontline baggage check folks—to make decisions, use their brains, and be customer maniacs so that they could create raving fans. Kelleher (who has now retired and turned over the presidency to Colleen Barrett) felt that policies should be followed but that people could use their brains in interpreting them. Why do they ask for identification at the airport? To make sure that the person getting on the plane is the same person as the name on the ticket. That was an easy decision for the Southwest Airlines frontline person.

Wallowing in a Duck Pond

The next airline Ken had to fly on before his office could overnight his driver's license was an airline in financial trouble. The baggage handler at the curbside check-in looked at Ken's picture on the book and said, "You've got to be kidding me. You'd better go to the ticket counter."

When Ken showed the book to the woman at the ticket counter, she said, "You'd better talk to my supervisor." Ken was moving up the hierarchy fast. He thought maybe pretty soon he would get to the mayor and then finally to the governor. Quack! Quack! Quack! In the troubled airline, the hierarchy was alive and well. All the energy was moving away from pleasing the customers and toward serving the hierarchy—following the policies, procedures, rules, and regulations to the letter.

Giving Your People Wings

Horst Schultze, one of the founders of the Ritz-Carlton Hotels, retired a few years ago as president and CEO. During his reign, after orientation and extensive training, every employee was given a $2,000 discretionary fund that they could use to solve a customer problem without checking with anyone. They didn't even have to tell their boss. Horst loved to collect stories about people using this empowerment to make a difference. One of our favorites is about a businessman who was staying at one of the Ritz-Carlton properties in Atlanta. That day he had to fly from Atlanta to Los Angeles and then from Los Angeles to Hawaii, because the next day at 1:00, he was making a major speech to his international company. He was a little disorganized as he was leaving. On his way to the airport, he discovered that he'd left behind his laptop computer, which contained all the PowerPoint slides he needed for his presentation. He tried to change his flights, but he couldn't. So he called the Ritz-Carlton and said, "This is the room I was in, and this is where my computer was. Have Housekeeping get it and overnight it to me. They have to guarantee delivery by 10:00 tomorrow morning, because I need it for my 1:00 speech."

The next day Schultze was wandering around the hotel, as he often did. When he got to Housekeeping he said, "Where's Mary?" Her coworkers said, "She's in Hawaii." He said, "Hawaii? What's she doing in Hawaii?"

He was told, "A guest left a computer in his room, and he needs it for a speech today at 1:00—and Mary doesn't trust overnight carrier services anymore." Now you might think that Mary went for a vacation, but she came back on the next plane. And what do you think was waiting for her? A letter of commendation from Horst and high fives around the hotel. That's really empowering people and giving them wings.

You might wonder if this story is really true. The answer is yes. If you create an environment where the customers rule and your people can use their brains to take care of customer needs, stories like this become commonplace, even legendary. People who spread these stories—including your customers—sometimes love to embellish them. For example, a legendary story developed about Nordstrom's "no questions asked" return policy. It was rumored that somebody returned snow tires to Nordstrom and, even though they didn't sell them, the store took them back. When cofounder Bruce Nordstrom was asked about this, he laughed, because Nordstrom actually does sell snow tires—in its Alaska store.

Going Above and Beyond Customer Service

Creating raving fans means going above and beyond customer service and delivering wherever possible. This creates unforgettable experiences—like that of Milt Garrett, a resource trainer from Albuquerque, New Mexico, who has worked with us over the years. Milt's story is an excellent demonstration of the above-and-beyond principle. At the end of a week of training, Milt and his wife, Jane, took a walk on Friday night. Jane said to him, "Milt, you missed my anniversary this week."

Surprised, Milt said, "What anniversary?"

"Five years cancer-free," said Jane. Five years ago, Jane had had a mastectomy. She and Milt celebrated every year that she was cancer-free.

Milt felt awful. He couldn't believe he had forgotten. The week before, when he and Jane had been talking one night, they'd decided that she needed a new car. Since their son was still in college in Australia, they'd decided to wait a year until he graduated. That night, Milt said to himself, "Why am I waiting? I am so lucky that Jane is still in my life."

The next morning, he called the Saturn dealership in Albuquerque and talked to one of their salespeople, whose name was Billy Graham. (No, we're not kidding.) Milt explained the situation to Billy, saying that his kids had told him Jane really wanted a white car. "Could you get me a white Saturn by next Saturday when I get back home from training?" Milt asked.

Billy told Milt that white Saturns were hard to get. "But if you'll come in next Saturday, I'll have one ready," he said.

The next Saturday morning Milt told Jane that he was running a bunch of errands, but he invited her to come with him so that they could go out to lunch. During their drive, they passed the Saturn dealership. Milt told Jane he had to stop in for some materials, because he was giving a speech about Saturn to the Chamber of Commerce. When they entered the dealership, they saw only one car: a white Saturn in the center of the showroom.

"Milt, that's the kind of car I'd love to have!" Jane said. She ran over to the Saturn and, with a big grin on her face, got in. When she got out of the car and walked around to the front of it, she let out a scream and began to cry. Milt had no idea what had happened. When he got to the front of the car, he saw a beautiful sign on the hood of the car that read:

> Yes, Jane, this is your car!
> Congratulations on five years cancer-free.
>
> Love,
> Milt, Billy, and the whole Saturn staff

When Billy saw them coming, he got everyone out of the showroom and into the parking lot so that Milt and Jane could be alone. As they were crying in each other's arms, all of a sudden they heard applause. They looked up to see everyone giving them a hand.

The people at the Saturn dealership in Albuquerque took giving great service seriously and lived it on an ongoing basis. Saturn became a company known for these kinds of stories. For example, a pregnant woman bought a Saturn from a dealership in San Diego. She loved the car, but three months later, she learned she was going to have twins. The car wasn't big enough, so she called the dealership and told them about her situation. They told her that they would give her money back and help her find another car that better met her needs.

Exceeding customer expectations is not just a theory; it's a practice. Raving fan service inspires customers to tell stories about your company. When customers tell positive stories about you and your level of service, you cannot ask for better publicity.

Recovering quickly from your mistakes will also make your customers want to brag about your service. If you make a mistake with a customer, do whatever you need to fix the problem and create or win back a devoted customer. Legendary service is not about arguing over who is right or finding someone else to blame—it's about fixing the problem for the customer.

For example, a hotel in Southern California had a history of poor guest ratings. When foreign owners took over the hotel, they felt the poor ratings were mainly the result of the dilapidated condition of the aging property. They decided to put millions of dollars into refurbishing the hotel. During the renovation—which would take nine months to a year—the management decided not to tell their customers. They felt that if the customers knew the extent of the renovations, they would move their meetings to other locations. Given that strategy, the general manager brought together all the hotel workers and told them this:

"It will be tough sledding around here for the next twelve months or so. The noise and inconvenience may not be popular with our guests. Do whatever it takes to recover from any inconvenience caused by our remodeling. If you want to send someone a bottle of champagne, do so. If you want to hire a babysitter for them, do it. Do whatever it takes to recover from this trying situation."

With that recovery strategy, the hotel entered its remodeling phase. To the amazement of management, during the renovations, their guest ratings were the highest they had ever received. Even though things were bad for the guests, their memories of their experience with the hotel were formed by the customer-oriented staff who recovered quickly when things went wrong for guests. Management had empowered their frontline people to be all-out recovery experts. The results showed in highly satisfied customers.

If you empower people to do what's necessary to serve the customers' best interests to begin with, you are more likely to exceed customer expectations and minimize the need to recover. Most businesses believe that only a small percentage of people are out to take advantage of them, while the vast majority are basically honest and loyal. That's why Nordstrom decided to train its customer contact people to use the phrase "no problem" as their first response to customer concerns. Yet because many businesses set policies, procedures, and practices to try to catch the small percentage of unethical customers, they miss servicing the honest majority. Have you ever attempted to try on clothes that have so many safety gadgets that it's almost impossible? There are risks to providing raving fan service, but the gains can far outweigh the drawbacks, particularly when your customers start acting like part of your sales force. That's when you know you're treating your customers right.

Making It All Happen

Now that we've talked about raving fan service and all the elements that need to go into implementing it, how do you set it up in your own organization? So often, talking about leading at a higher level seems so far off and distant to people.

---

*How do you help all people serve
at a higher level and
realize that they can—
and do—make a difference?*

Two things have to be in place. First, you have to focus everybody's energy on making customers their first priority. Second, you have to make sure that you have energizing systems and structures.

Making Customers the First Priority

At The Ken Blanchard Companies, we wanted to make sure that we were constantly practicing what we were preaching to our customers. To do that, we needed to focus everyone's energy on the customer. We were inspired by Fergal Quinn, who owns one of the highest medals in Ireland for his tremendous work in customer service. Fergal thinks everyone should provide Boomerang Service. Some of us got introduced to his thinking on a golf trip to his homeland. Our group went to a restaurant where everybody was wearing boomerangs on their outfits. When we asked the waitress what the boomerangs were for, she said:

"What happens when you throw a boomerang?"

And we all said, "It comes back."

She said, "Exactly. That's what we want you to do—come back."

To help us on our customer service journey, we decided to have all the people in our organization remember a time when they received outstanding customer service and a time when they received poor customer service. Then we asked each person to write a story about those experiences.

Here are two examples.

A Story About Great Customer Service

I had a low front tire for several days. Not knowing where to go to evaluate whether I needed a new tire, I called a friend for advice. She immediately said, "Discount Tire, off Grand Avenue." I drove straight to Discount Tire, entered a clean and neat storefront with an attached garage, and was immediately greeted by the man working behind the counter, even though he was helping another customer.

When he finished with the customer ahead of me, I told him my problem. He came around the counter and said, "Show me your car." He approached the car, felt the tire (something that didn't occur to me), and said, "Here is your problem. Look at this huge nail." At that point, I saw the writing on the wall—$200 for a new tire. He said, "Let me have your keys. We'll do this right away." He then said, "How would you like to pay?" I asked how much it would be and how long it would take. When his response was, "$15 and about 15 minutes," I was truly amazed and delighted. He showed me back to the storefront, where there was a waiting area with several magazines and newspapers, coffee, and water.

In a short time, an attendant pulled my car up to the front door, opened the door for me, gave me my receipt, and said, "Keep this receipt, because if you buy a tire from us within the next year, you can deduct this $15."

A Story About Poor Customer Service

I arranged for a construction company to install new lighting in my kitchen and outside porch. I made several appointments for the installer to meet with me to discuss options and plans. He canceled at the last minute on three of these appointments, apologizing profusely. Each time, I was charmed by his "This won't happen again" speech. On the fourth appointment, he didn't show up or even call. When he finally got in touch a few days later, I was angry. I not only informed him that his services were no longer needed, but I also told him that it was the worst customer experience of my life and that I didn't appreciate being so blatantly disrespected and ignored.

After people wrote their stories, we asked them a few questions: What did they think and feel about that experience? What conclusions did they draw from that experience? What would they remember about the organization as a result of that experience? What would they tell others about that experience?

Answering these questions helped them determine what values would guide their own behavior when serving customers. Once people reflected on how they wanted to serve customers, we asked them to fill in the blanks in the following statement:

> When working with or responding to my internal or external clients or customers—those I serve—I want them to think that I am _____ and _____. I want them to feel _____ and I want them to believe _____.

After people reflected on how they wanted customers to think and feel about them and the organization, they were ready to write their own personal customer service philosophy. We asked them to write it so that they would be proud to have it on their business card. Here is one example.

My Personal Customer Service Philosophy

I always strive to treat internal and external customers with love, caring, respect, honesty, integrity, and empathy. I want people to go away from encounters with me feeling respected and cared for and knowing that our organization is a very special place.

The process of having people personalize a customer service philosophy excited them about keeping customers coming back.

Creating Energizing Systems

In high performing organizations, having energizing systems and structures is one of the important elements in scoring with customers. In many typical organizations, the systems and structures derail people. The organization may be aligned at one point, but policies and procedures make getting the job done harder instead of easier. People's purpose may start off aligned with the purpose of the organization, but the organization's systems or structure steer them in the wrong direction. In high performing organizations, on the other hand, systems and structures are aligned with the vision. For example, if your organization has a vision that involves creating raving fan customers, it must also develop systems that reward people for going the extra mile for customers.

In their theme parks, Disney masters aligned systems and structures. From recruitment to training to terminology, their systems and structures spell out *a great guest entertainment experience*. All "cast members" are aware of their role in creating this experience. One of the HPO SCORES researchers, Jesse Stoner, saw this in action during a Disney visit. After waiting longer than usual for the bus to Disney World's entrance, she herded her family aboard the tardy bus. To her surprise, the bus driver was visibly upset, despite the fact that the delay had been beyond his control. As the driver shared with her, "I know I'm the first person our guests have contact with during their day at Disney. I'm the one responsible for starting a great day. When the bus is late and they are frustrated, I can't do my job."

Once you have the energizing systems and structures in place, the next step is to unleash the power of people to create outstanding results.

Creating *Raving Fan* Customers Requires *Gung Ho* People

When Ken Blanchard and Sheldon Bowles published *Raving Fans*, a lot of excitement was generated around the importance of customer service. The most frequent question leaders asked, though, was "How can you create raving fan service when you have uncommitted, unmotivated people?" Answering that question led Ken and Sheldon to write *Gung Ho*.[6] They found there are three requirements for turning on the people in any organization.

First, people need to have *worthwhile work*. To make the world a better place, people need a higher purpose and shared values that guide all plans, decisions, and actions. Worthwhile work gets people up in the morning with a spring in their step.

Second, people need to *be in control of achieving the goal*. When people know why they are working and where they're going, they want to bring their brains to work. Being responsible demands people's best and allows them to learn and act like owners.

Third, to continue to generate energy, people need to *cheer each other on*. Of all the things we've taught over the years, we can't overemphasize the power of catching each other doing things right and accentuating the positive.

In many ways, Chapter 2, "The Power of Vision," was all about *worthwhile work. Being in control of achieving the goals* and *cheering each other on* turn our focus to Section III, "Treat Your People Right," the third practice that is characteristic of organizations where leading at a higher level is alive and well. The next chapter, "Empowerment Is the Key," zeros in on *being in charge of achieving the goal.*

COMPANION
ONLINE
RESOURCE

Visit **www.LeadingAtAHigherLevel.com** to access the free virtual conference titled *Treat Your Customers Right.* Use the password "Customers" for your FREE access.

section III

TREAT YOUR PEOPLE RIGHT

Chapter 4

EMPOWERMENT IS THE KEY

Alan Randolph
and Ken Blanchard

H ow do the best-run companies in the world beat the competition day in and day out? As we pointed out in the previous chapter, they treat their customers right. They do that by having a workforce that is excited about their vision and motivated to serve customers at a higher level. So how do you create this motivated workforce? The key is ***empowerment***.

Empowerment means letting people bring their brains to work and allowing them to use their knowledge, experience, and motivation to create a healthy triple bottom line. Leaders of the best-run companies know that empowering people creates positive results that are just not possible when all the authority moves up the hierarchy and managers shoulder all the responsibility for success.

---

*People already have power through their
knowledge and motivation.
The key to empowerment is
letting this power out.*

Ideally, people's power will be focused not only on organizational outcomes—such as outstanding customer service and financial goals—but also on the greater good.

We believe organizations work best when they can depend on individual contributors who take the initiative to go beyond problem spotting to problem solving. Yet because most of us have experienced only hierarchical organizations, people at all levels have much to learn about moving to a culture of empowerment.

What Is Empowerment?

Empowerment is the process of unleashing the power in people—their knowledge, experience, and motivation—and focusing that power to achieve positive outcomes for the organization. Creating a culture of empowerment consists of only a few key steps, yet because they challenge most people's assumptions, these steps are often difficult for managers and direct reports alike.

Empowerment requires a major shift in attitude.
The most crucial place that this shift must occur
is in the heart of every leader.

For empowerment to succeed, leaders must make a leap of faith and fight the battle against habit and tradition. For example, most managers continue to define empowerment as "giving people the power to make decisions." Perhaps this misguided definition explains why so many companies have difficulty engaging the minds and hearts of their people. Defining empowerment as "the manager giving power to the people" still regards the manager as controller and misses the essential point: namely, that *people already possess a great deal of power*—power that resides in their knowledge, experience, and internal motivation. We prefer the following definition:

Empowerment is the creation of an organizational climate that releases the knowledge, experience, and motivation that reside in people.

Unfortunately, this is easier said than done. Other players can block this release of power, and a strong force of past history often inhibits the shift to empowerment.

Direct reports, too, misunderstand empowerment. Many of them feel that if they are empowered, they will be given free rein to do as they please and make all the key decisions about their jobs. Direct reports often fail to grasp that the price of freedom is a sharing of risks and responsibilities. This is particularly true in a post-Sarbanes-Oxley environment of accounting oversight and corporate responsibility.[1] Indeed, an empowerment culture requires much greater accountability from direct reports than a hierarchical culture does. Yet, it is precisely this frightening increase in responsibility that engages people and gives them a sense of fulfillment. The opportunities and risks of empowerment invigorate direct reports and managers alike.

The Power of Empowerment

Does empowerment work in the real world? You bet it does! Several researchers have found that when people are empowered, their organizations benefit overall. For example, Edward Lawler found that when people are given more control and responsibility, their companies achieve a greater return on sales (10.3 percent) than companies that do not involve their people (6.3 percent).[2] Trader Joe's is a niche retailer in the food industry well known for pushing decision making to the store level. It found over an eight-year period that its annual sales growth increased from 15 percent to 26 percent, sales per store increased 10 percent per year, and the number of stores increased by almost 100 percent. In addition, overall sales volume increased in excess of

500 percent. While other factors contributed to these increased sales, empowered employees were deemed a major element of Trader Joe's success.[3]

Not only is there clear evidence of a positive relationship between empowerment and performance, but scholars such as Thomas Malone believe that empowerment is essential for companies that hope to succeed in the new knowledge-based economy.[4]

How Past History Blocks Change to Empowerment

Most people have a history of exposure to command-and-control thinking, rather than a culture of empowerment. The majority of us are quite accustomed to working under external guidance and control. The following questions are all too familiar to us:

At school: "What does my teacher want me to do to get good grades?"

At work: "What does my boss want me to do?"

Having spent our lives in a framework of hierarchical thinking, we are far less accustomed to dealing with questions like these:

At school: "What do I want to learn from this class?"

"How will I know I have learned something I can use?"

At work: "What do I need to do to help my company succeed?"

These are the kinds of questions that arise—and require answers—when an organizational culture begins to support empowerment. President Kennedy made a call for these kinds of questions when he challenged Americans: "Ask not what your country can do for you; ask what you can do for your country."[5]

Many of us possess hard-earned parenting, teaching, and managing skills that fulfill role expectations for leaders based on an assumption of hierarchical responsibility. Indeed, we feel it is our responsibility as parents, teachers, or managers to tell people what to do, how to do it, and why it needs to be done. We feel it would be avoiding our responsibility to ask children, students, or direct reports questions such as these:

"What do you think needs to be done, and why is it important?"

"What do you think your goals should be?"

"How do you think you should go about achieving your goals?"

Because managers know they will still be held accountable for outcomes, many are reluctant to relinquish control to direct reports. This reluctance points to one of the main sources of resistance to empowerment: managers who feel their control is threatened by empowerment. Ironically, it is through the development of self-directed individuals and teams as a replacement for the hierarchy that managers can most easily assume their new and more empowering roles as coaches, mentors, and team leaders.

Tapping the Power and Potential of People: A Real-World Example

While there is a learning curve from a hierarchical to an empowerment culture, the benefits can be well worth the effort, as the following case study shows.

In 1983, a management team of a large organization was struggling with a severe traffic problem on the road leading to its location. The road crossed four miles of protected wetlands, so it could not be widened without significantly impacting the environment. Each morning, the traffic leading to the site was backing up the entire four-mile length of the road, adding an hour to commuting time. The resulting delay and aggravation caused a significant drop in productivity.

Three years earlier, the management team had hired traffic consultants to solve the problem. Their work focused on a future widening of the road and looked promising, but their attempts to devise short-term solutions failed miserably. As a last resort, management decided to assemble a team of engineers, clerical personnel, line workers, and union representatives to address short-term solutions. This team met twice a week for a month. At the end of that time, the team provided a series of practical recommendations that ultimately improved the traffic flow both into and out of the site.

The simplicity of the team's recommendations surprised management. For example, the team suggested that trucks be prohibited from making deliveries to the site between the hours of 6 and 9 a.m. Since there were many deliveries to the site at this time, this recommendation immediately removed some of the slowest, most cumbersome traffic clogging the road. Other recommendations also contributed to easing the problem. The result was almost-instantaneous improvement in the traffic flow.

At the outset, management had doubted that this team could solve the problem. After all, experts had been studying the dilemma for three years. Yet in turning to their own people, they tapped into a hidden reservoir of knowledge, experience, and motivation—and found a solution.

Learning the Language of Empowerment

Moving to an empowerment culture requires learning a new language. To understand the differences between the command-and-control structure and the culture of empowerment, consider the following phrases:

Hierarchical Culture	Empowerment Culture
Planning	Visioning
Command-and-control	Partnering for performance
Monitoring	Self-monitoring
Individual responsiveness	Team responsibility
Pyramid structures	Cross-functional structures
Workflow processes	Projects

Managers	Coaches/team leaders
Employees	Team members
Participative management	Self-directed teams
Do as you are told	Own your job
Compliance	Good judgment

As you compare the words in the two lists, the differences in attitude, expectations, and associated behaviors become clear. For example, *planning* suggests a step-by-step, controlled process, while *visioning* suggests a more holistic and inclusive approach. *Command-and-control* suggests that the manager tells you what to think and do, while *partnering for performance* suggests that how you achieve the vision is left open for discussion and input by everyone involved. *Monitoring* suggests that someone—usually the manager—should check on each individual's performance and provide performance evaluations and feedback, while *self-monitoring* suggests that everyone possesses requisite goal clarity and measurement skills, as well as access to relevant data. Thus armed, they can check their own performance and make the behavior adjustments they need to stay on goal. *Do as you are told* exemplifies the external commitment attitude. Once you are told what to do, you can do it, but please don't use your intellect or judgment, and don't be too concerned about results—that's the manager's job. On the other hand, *own your job* exemplifies the internal commitment attitude: You care about results and use your own intellect and judgment to decide how to achieve individual, team, and company success.

This final example may best clarify the key distinction between a hierarchical culture and a culture of empowerment. Individuals will do what they are told—to a fault. Even when they know a task is not being done the best way, or that it may be altogether the wrong task, they may continue to do it in a spirit of malicious compliance. Why? Because that is what they are rewarded for and what they are expected to do under hierarchical management.

In a culture of empowerment, individuals respond differently. They take the risk of challenging tasks and procedures that they feel are not in the best interest of the organization. They are driven by a sense of pride in their jobs and a feeling of ownership of the results. People think about what makes sense in the situation and act in ways that both serve the customer and achieve the goals of the organization.

The Three Keys to Empowerment

The journey to empowerment needs strong leadership to support this change. In their book *Empowerment Takes More Than a Minute*, Ken Blanchard, John Carlos, and Alan Randolph contend that to guide the transition to a culture of empowerment, leaders must use three keys: Sharing Information, Declaring the Boundaries, and Replacing the Old Hierarchy with Self-Directed Individuals and Teams.[6]

The First Key to Empowerment:
Share Information with Everyone

One of the best ways to build a sense of trust and responsibility in people is by sharing information. Giving team members the information they need enables them to make good business decisions. Sharing information sometimes means disclosing information that is considered privileged, including sensitive and important topics such as the competition's activities, future business plans and strategies, financial data, industry issues or problem areas, competitors' best practices, how group activities contribute to organizational goals, and performance feedback. Providing people with more-complete information communicates trust and a sense of "we're in this together." It helps people think more broadly about the organization and the interrelationships of various groups, resources, and goals. By having access to information that helps them understand the big picture, people can better appreciate how their contribution fits in and how their behavior impacts other aspects of the organization. All of this leads to responsible, goal-related use of people's knowledge, experience, and motivation. While this runs counter to hierarchical management, it is based on the following premise:

People without accurate information
cannot act responsibly;
people with accurate information
feel compelled to act responsibly.

In an example close to home, The Ken Blanchard Companies, like many businesses, was negatively impacted by the events of September 11, 2001. In fact, the company lost $1.5 million that month. To have any chance of ending the fiscal year in the black, the company would have to cut about $350,000 a month in expenses.

The leadership team had some tough decisions to make. One of the leaders suggested that the staffing level be cut by at least 10 percent to stem the losses and help get the company get back in the black—a typical response in most companies.

As they do before making any major decision, members of the leadership team checked the decision to cut staff against the rank-ordered organizational values of ethical behavior, relationships, success, and learning. Was the decision to let people go at such a difficult time ethical? To many, the answer was no. There was a general feeling that the staff had made the company what it was; putting people out on the street at a time like this just was not the right thing to do. Did the decision honor the high value that the organization placed on relationships? No, it did not. But what could be done? The company could not go on bleeding money and be successful.

Knowing that "no one of us is as smart as all of us," the leadership team decided to draw on the knowledge and talents of the entire staff. At an all-company meeting, the books were opened to show everyone how much the company was bleeding, and from where. This open-book policy unleashed a torrent of ideas and commitment. Small task forces were organized to look for ways to increase revenues and cut costs. This participation resulted in departments throughout the company finding all kinds of ways to minimize spending and maximize income. As the company's Chief Spiritual Officer, Ken Blanchard cheered people on by announcing they would all go to Hawaii together when the company got through the crisis. People smiled politely, although many had their doubts.

Over the next two years, the finances gradually turned around. By 2004, the company produced the highest sales in its history, exceeding its annual goal. In March 2005, the entire company— 350 people strong—flew to Maui for a four-day celebration.

When important information is shared with people, they soon act like owners. They begin to solve problems creatively, which makes celebrating the wins even more special. On the other hand, leaders who are unwilling to share information will never have their people as partners in running a successful, empowered organization.

Sharing Information Builds Trust

Another powerful benefit of information sharing is raising the level of trust in the organization. Bureaucratic organizations are typically close to bankruptcy in terms of trust—direct reports do not trust managers, and managers do not trust direct reports. As a result, people exert enormous energy trying to protect themselves from each other. It's important to share information, even if the news is bad. If no decisions have been made, share information about what is being discussed. By sharing information about market share, true costs, potential layoffs, and real company performance—in other words, opening the books for everyone to see—management begins to let people know they are trusted, and people will return that trust to managers.

One top-level manager took the risk of sharing information that had previously been seen only by top management. Although he was initially scared to share such sensitive information, people responded with a more mature understanding and a sense of appreciation for being included. "It created such a sense of ownership," the manager commented, "far more than I could have imagined. People began to come forward with ideas to save money by changing their jobs and by reorganizing departments—ideas that previously had been met with great fear when proposed by management."

Sharing Information Promotes Organizational Learning

One of the most powerful ways to share information is through organizational learning, one of the key elements of high performing organizations.[7] What we're talking about here goes beyond merely acquiring information; it means actually learning from that information and applying that knowledge to new situations.

High performing organizations **seek knowledge** by constantly scanning the environment, checking the pulse of their customers, tracking their competition, surveying the marketplace, and following global events. They collect data continuously and use it to make corrections and develop new approaches. High performing organizations also seek knowledge about internal performance. They treat mistakes and failures as important data, recognizing that they can often lead to breakthroughs. This is why Hewlett-Packard's "H-P Way" includes the statement "We reserve the right to make mistakes."[8]

High performing organizations **transfer knowledge** by encouraging dialogue, questioning, and discussion. This runs counter to traditional organizations, where people hoard information as a way to protect themselves and establish a power base. High performing organizations make information easy to access. They know that when data is not available or easily retrieved, people have a harder time learning and lose opportunities. They create structures like cross-functional teams that teach people how to transfer the knowledge they've gained, because they know that knowledge sharing is critical to success.

New-car developers at Ford Motor Company learned this the hard way when they set out to understand why the original

Taurus design team was so successful. Unfortunately, no one could tell them. No one remembered or had recorded what made that effort so special. The knowledge gained in the Taurus project was lost forever.[9]

High performing organizations continually look for ways to **incorporate knowledge into new ways of doing business**. When you don't recognize or share knowledge, you can't apply it directly to work. In the words of Michael Brown, former chief financial officer of Microsoft:[10]

The only way to compete today is to make your intellectual capital obsolete before anyone else does.

The Second Key to Empowerment: Create Autonomy Through Boundaries

In a hierarchical culture, boundaries are really like barbed-wire fences. They are designed to control people by keeping them in certain places and out of other places. In an empowered culture, boundaries are more like rubber bands that can expand to allow people to take on more responsibility as they grow and develop.

Unlike the restrictive boundaries of a hierarchical culture, boundaries in an empowerment culture tell people where they *can* be autonomous and responsible, rather than telling them what they *can't* do. Boundaries are based on people's skill level. For example, people who lack the skills to set budgets are given a boundary—a spending limit—before they are given more responsibility. In an empowerment culture, they also are given the training and skill development needed to enable greater autonomy. One of the most intriguing aspects of creating a culture of empowerment is that managers must start by creating *more* rather than *less* structure.

*Like the lines on a tennis court, the boundaries
in an empowerment culture help people keep
score and improve their game.*

A good example of boundary setting came up recently for a supervisor we know who was frustrated by the amount of time he spent performing tasks that, although important from an administrative viewpoint, did not maximize his talents and skills. One of his most frustrating tasks was ordering small tools and materials for the team each time a team member came to him with a request. In a spirit of empowerment, he taught them how to place the orders themselves and allowed them to submit small orders directly without his approval. Initially, he placed a boundary on the purchases—a cost limit of $100—but he later widened the boundary as the team's (and his) comfort level grew. Because they had the authority to order needed supplies without the delay of their supervisor's approval, the team members felt great. The cost of supplies decreased by 20 percent as people took more care in ordering only those materials they really needed.

Boundaries help people clarify the big picture as well as the little picture. As you saw in Chapter 2, "The Power of Vision," organizations need to **create a compelling vision** that motivates and guides people.

*The organizational vision is the big picture.
Boundaries help people see how their
piece of the puzzle fits into that picture.*

Declaring the boundaries translates the big picture into specific actions. It allows people to **set goals** that help the organization achieve that big picture. These goals are not viewed as ends, but rather as collaboratively set milestones of progress.

For example, at one information services company, senior leaders agreed that team members with increased information at their disposal could now identify and define some of their own goals in collaboration with their leaders. Of the five to eight performance goals that were typical for teams, the leaders instructed members to develop three to four of those goals themselves. Team members quickly came to like the idea, since it used their input and gave them a sense of ownership. The team leaders liked it, too, because team members were sharing the responsibility of identifying and defining the goals that were critical to the organization's success.

Declaring boundaries also requires that managers **clarify the new decision-making rules**. At first, team members may think that empowerment means, "We get to make all the decisions." Two reactions often follow. One is that team members are disappointed when managers continue to make strategic decisions and leave only the operational decisions to them. The other is that team members feel the urge to back off from decisions when they realize they will be held accountable for all the decisions they make—both good and bad.

Empowerment means people have the freedom to act. It also means they are accountable for results.

In a culture of empowerment, managers will continue to make strategic decisions. Team members will get involved in making more of the operational decisions as they become more comfortable assuming the risks that are inherent in the decisions. As people gradually begin to assume responsibility for decisions and their consequences, managers must gradually pull back on their involvement in decision making. The new decision-making guidelines will allow managers and team members to operate freely within their newly defined roles.

Declaring boundaries also calls managers to ***create new performance appraisal processes***. The performance appraisal process found in most companies is almost inevitably disempowering in nature and must be restructured. Focus must shift away from the *appraisal* of the team member by the manager toward *collaboration* between the team member and the manager. As a manager once told us, "The best person to assess an employee's performance and improvement is the employee himself or herself. The manager may change, the task may change, but the employee is still the focal person. What we have to do is give people enough information and clear structure to allow them to responsibly assess their own performance." Of course, this cultural shift is not easy. In Chapter 7, "Partnering for Performance," we'll discuss this transition to a new performance appraisal process in considerable detail.

As we stated earlier, declaring the boundaries requires that leaders ***provide heavy doses of training***. To master the new skills of empowerment—negotiating performance plans, decision making, conflict resolution, leadership, budgeting, and technical expertise—people need regular training. Without this continuous learning, people cannot function in an evolving culture of empowerment. They have to unlearn bureaucratic habits and learn the new skills and attitudes needed in an empowered world. Ongoing learning is an integral part of a high performing organization, not an extra perk or necessary evil.

Moving from a hierarchical culture to a culture of empowerment should be a gradual process. People cannot handle too many changes at once, or large changes in one dose. It is not possible to anticipate all the boundary changes that will be necessary in this cultural change—some things just have to be dealt with as they arise. We will discuss these issues further in Chapter 11, "Strategies for Managing a Change."

The Third Key to Empowerment: Replace the Old Hierarchy with Self-Directed Individuals and Teams

As people learn to create autonomy by using newly shared information and boundaries, they must move away from dependence on the hierarchy. But what will replace the clarity and support of the hierarchy? The answer is self-directed individuals and Next Level teams—highly skilled, interactive groups with strong self-managing skills.[11] Continual downsizing, which reduces the number of management layers and increases the spans of control for managers, is forcing companies to empower individuals and teams today. The result has been a decision-making void that must be filled if companies are to be successful.

---

*The perceived division between superior and subordinate
is no longer very useful in business organizations.
In fact, it works directly counter to success.
Success today depends on individual and team effort.*

Does success today really depend on empowered individuals and teams? In our work with organizations, we uncover stories every day that suggest the answer to this question is a resounding yes. Here are two examples.

The Power of Self-Directed Individuals

The leaders of Yum! Brands—the world's largest restaurant company, with 850,000 employees in more than 100 nations—understand the power of self-directed individuals.[12] A significant part of training at Yum! now focuses on empowering people to take care of customer problems. If a waitperson has a customer with a problem, the team member is encouraged to solve it immediately rather than talking to the manager. In fact, team members can create the way they take care of customers. That makes things a little crazy, but that's how Yum! likes it.

When Ken Blanchard spoke at a meeting of KFC (one of the companies that Yum! owns), he told the story of how Ritz-Carlton gives their frontline people a $2,000 discretionary fund to solve customer problems without checking with anyone. Yum! chairman and CEO David Novak—who is a great learner—loved the idea of giving people discretionary funds. He later told us, "Our customer mania program now includes empowering team members to solve customer complaints right on the spot. They used to have to get the restaurant general manager to deal with problems. Now they can use up to $10 to respond to a customer issue.

"Some people in our organization said, 'Hey, if we let our team members do that, we'll end up going broke because we'll be giving all our profits away.' And yet we've got the highest margin we've ever had in the company since we launched customer mania. So people aren't out there ripping us off. The half or 1 percent who were doing it before are probably still doing it. But this policy has had an impact on team members. They feel respected and empowered; consequently, our customers see us as much more responsive."

A $10 discretionary fund in a quick-service restaurant is a lot of money. In Ritz-Carlton, which is a much higher-end operation, $2,000 is a lot of money. The point is, a discretionary fund becomes a competitive advantage when individuals who are closest to the customer are empowered to solve problems.

The Power of Self-Directed Teams

The case of the Allied Signal fibers plant in Moncure, North Carolina, illustrates the power of self-directed teams. The shift leaders (formerly called forepersons) were frustrated, angry, and confused about their role in the fall of 1996. The plant had recently shifted its manufacturing operations to work group teams, provided some training, and told the shift leaders to back off and let the teams move toward self-management. They heard it as "Back off or get another job—teams are here to stay." Not only were the shift leaders frustrated, but morale among team members was also low. There was a decrease in production and an increase in cost per pound of products. Was the solution to go back to the old way of working? Some people wondered why not. The Moncure fibers plant had a history of excellent labor/management relationships, had low turnover and absenteeism, and was committed to employee involvement and continuous improvement. But leadership saw an opportunity for the organization to move to a higher level if they could figure out how to do it right.

One shift leader, Barney, and two master facilitators—Dawn and Gloria—attended a program on building high performing teams facilitated by one of the HPO SCORES researchers, Don Carew. He helped them understand that the plant would benefit greatly by further training in team skills and team leadership and that support for ongoing learning in the implementation of these skills would solve their problems. Excited and enthusiastic, they returned to Moncure and convinced the plant leaders to implement further training throughout the plant.

The researcher worked with a core team—made up of shift leaders and master facilitators—to develop customized, one-day classroom training to be given to each product team by their respective shift leader. The 24 shift leaders were trained to deliver this program in August 1997. Over the next two years, with the help of the core team as mentors, they provided the one-day initial training program to all 59 of the plant's teams. The trainings were followed by additional learning sessions based on the assessment of each team's needs.

Picture formerly disillusioned shift leaders having a whole new sense of purpose and a whole new set of skills as they took on the challenges of facilitating continuous learning for their team members, both in a classroom setting and on the shop floor. Their role had become clear: to focus on developing people and teams. As a result, the atmosphere in the plant changed from frustration to enthusiasm. Furthermore, productivity increased by 5 percent, and costs decreased by 6 percent.[13]

Dealing with the Leadership Vacuum

As they move toward empowered individuals and Next Level teams, both managers and team members will go through a stage of disillusionment and demotivation. During this time, team members often feel they lack competence, and managers are often just as lost as their people about what to do next. Even the top-level managers who initiated the empowerment process are often unclear about what to do. We call this phenomenon the *leadership vacuum*. Remember that both managers and team members are emerging from the grip of bureaucratic, hierarchical practices and assumptions. Both have been accustomed to operating in a hierarchy where managers make decisions and team members implement them. They have a lot to learn, and this learning is often fraught with periods of frustration.

Once people admit this lack of management knowledge, a dramatic transformation occurs. When managers begin to admit their confusion—but continue to hold on to a clear vision of empowerment and keep communication open and information flowing—things begin to change. Small flashes of empowerment begin to appear among individual performers and teams. One person might offer a suggestion to which others will gravitate; then other ideas will be expressed. Almost before anyone realizes what is happening, leadership emerges from an unexpected source—team members. Over time, the glimmerings of empowerment become more frequent. The very leadership vacuum that has been so uncomfortable has actually drawn out team member talent and applied it to organizational problems. In the end, the leadership vacuum enhances the empowerment of people and organizations.

The journey to empowerment requires managers and direct reports alike to challenge some of their most basic assumptions about how organizations should operate. Simply announcing the destination is insufficient. People at all levels of the organization must master new skills and learn to trust self-directed individuals and teams as decision-making entities. We will give a detailed discussion of the development of self-directed individuals in Chapter 6, "Self Leadership: The Power Behind Empowerment," through Chapter 8, "Essential Skills for Partnering for Performance" and the development of high performing teams in Chapter 9, "Situational Team Leadership." But first let's turn to Chapter 5, "Situational Leadership® II: The Integrating Concept," which explores the leader's role in empowering people.

Chapter 5

SITUATIONAL LEADERSHIP® II:
THE
INTEGRATING CONCEPT

The Founding Associates:
Ken Blanchard, Margie Blanchard,
Don Carew, Eunice Parisi-Carew,
Fred Finch, Laurence Hawkins,
Drea Zigarmi, and Pat Zigarmi

If empowerment is the key to treating people right and motivating them to treat your customers right, having a strategy to shift the emphasis from leader as boss and evaluator to leader as partner and cheerleader is imperative. But what, exactly, is the right strategy or leadership style?

For a long time, people thought there were only two leadership styles—autocratic and democratic. In fact, people used to shout at each other from these two extremes, insisting that one style was better than the other. Democratic managers were accused of being too soft and easy, while their autocratic counterparts were often called too tough and domineering.

We believe that managers who restrict themselves to either extreme are bound to be ineffective "half managers." Whole managers are flexible and able to adapt their leadership style to the situation. Is the direct report new and inexperienced about the task at hand? Then more guidance and direction are called for. Is the direct report experienced and skilled? That person requires less hands-on supervision. The truth is, all of us are at different levels of development, depending on the task we are working on at a particular time.

> To bring out the best in others, leadership must match the development level of the person being led.

Over-supervising or under-supervising—that is, giving people too much or too little direction—has a negative impact on people's development. That's why it's so important to match leadership style to development level. This matching strategy is the essence of Situational Leadership®, a leadership model originally created by Ken Blanchard and Paul Hersey at Ohio University in 1968.[1] The revised model, Situational Leadership® II, has endured as an effective approach to managing and motivating people because it opens up communication and fosters a partnership between the leader and the people the leader supports and depends on. This model can be summed up by this familiar phrase:

> Different strokes for different folks.

Situational Leadership® II is based on the beliefs that *people can and want to develop* and *there is no best leadership style* to encourage that development. You should tailor leadership style to the situation.

The Situational Leadership® II Model

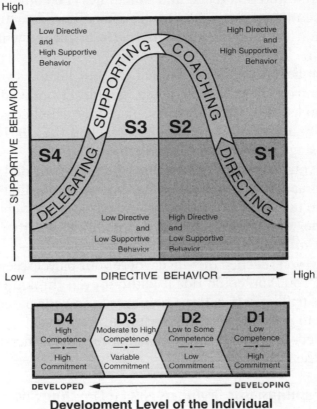

Figure 5.1   The Situational Leadership® II Model

Matching Leadership Style to Development Level

There are four basic leadership styles in the Situational Leadership® II model: *directing (S1), coaching (S2), supporting (S3),* and *delegating (S4)*. These correspond with the four basic development levels: *enthusiastic beginner (D1–low competence, high commitment), disillusioned learner (D2–low to some competence, low commitment), capable but cautious performer (D3–moderate to high competence, variable commitment),* and *self-reliant achiever (D4–high competence, high commitment)*.

Can you remember when you began learning how to ride a bicycle? You were so excited that sometimes you couldn't sleep at night, even though you didn't have a clue how to actually ride a bike. You were a classic ***enthusiastic beginner*** who needed ***direction***.

Remember the first time you fell off your bike? As you picked yourself up off the pavement, you might have wondered why you wanted to learn to ride in the first place and whether you would ever really master it. Now you had reached the ***disillusioned learner*** stage, and you needed ***coaching***.

Once you were able to ride your bike with your dad cheering you on, that confidence probably became shaky the first time you decided to take your bike out for a spin without your cheerleader and supporter close at hand. At this point, you were a ***capable but cautious performer*** in need of ***support***.

Finally, you reached the stage where your bicycle seemed to be a part of you. You could ride it without even thinking about it. You were truly a ***self-reliant achiever***, and your parents could ***delegate*** to you the job of having fun on your bike.

Now, let's see how the development levels and leadership styles apply to the workplace.

Enthusiastic Beginners Need a Directing Style

Suppose you recently hired a 22-year-old salesperson. There are three key responsibilities required of an effective salesperson besides selling: service, administration, and team contribution. Having worked in the hotel industry during the summer, your new salesperson seems to have good experience in service. Since he was the treasurer of his fraternity and captain of his college soccer team, it looks like he also has some experience in administration and team contribution. As a result, your initial training focus with him will be in the sales part of his job, where he is an ***enthusiastic beginner***. In this area, he is enthusiastic and ready to learn, despite his lack of skills. Because of his high commitment to becoming a good salesperson, he is curious, hopeful, optimistic, and excited. In this area of his job, a ***directing*** leadership style is appropriate. You teach your new hire everything about the sales process, from making a sales call to closing the sale. You take him on sales calls with you so that you can show him how the sales process works and what a good job looks like. Then, you lay out a step-by-step plan for his self-development as a salesperson. In other words, you not only pass out the test, but you also are involved in teaching him the answers. You provide specific direction and closely supervise his sales performance, planning and prioritizing what has to be accomplished for him to be successful. Teaching and showing him what experienced salespeople do—and letting him practice in low-risk sales situations—is the appropriate approach for this enthusiastic beginner.

Disillusioned Learners Need a Coaching Style

Now, suppose that your new hire has a few weeks of sales training under his belt. He understands the basics of selling but is finding it harder to master than he expected. You notice that his step has lost a little of its spring, and he looks a bit discouraged at times. While he knows more about sales than he did as a beginner and has flashes of real competence, he's sometimes overwhelmed and frustrated, which has put a damper on his commitment. A person at this stage is a ***disillusioned learner***. What's needed now is a ***coaching*** leadership style, which is high on direction and support. You continue to direct and closely monitor his sales efforts, but you now engage in more two-way conversations, going back and forth between your advice and his questions and suggestions. You also provide a lot of praise and support at this stage, because you want to build his confidence, restore his commitment, and encourage his initiative. While you consider your salesperson's input, you are the one who makes the final decisions, since he is learning on actual clients.

Capable but Cautious Performers Need a Supporting Style

Fast-forward a couple of months. Now the young man you hired knows the day-to-day responsibilities of his sales position and has acquired some good sales skills. Yet he still has some self-doubt and questions whether he can sell well *on his own*, without your help or the support of other colleagues. You believe he's competent and knows what he's doing, but he is not so sure. He has a good grasp of the sales process and is working well with clients, but he's hesitant to be out there completely on his own. He may become self-critical or even reluctant to trust his own instincts. At this stage, he is a **capable but cautious performer** whose commitment to selling fluctuates from excitement to insecurity. This is when a **supporting** leadership style is called for. Since your direct report has learned his selling skills well, he needs little direction but lots of support from you to encourage his wavering confidence. Now is the time to stand behind his efforts, listen to his concerns and suggestions, and be there to support his interactions not only with clients, but also with others on your staff. You encourage and praise, but rarely do you direct his efforts. The supporting style is more collaborative; feedback is now a give-and-take process between the two of you. You help him reach his own sales solutions by asking questions that expand his thinking and encourage risk taking.

Self-Reliant Achievers Need a Delegating Style

As time passes, your former new salesperson becomes a key player on your team. Not only has he mastered sales tasks and skills, but he's also taken on challenging clients and has been successful with them. He anticipates problems and is ready with solutions. He is justifiably confident because of his success in managing his own sales area. Not only is he able to work on his own, but he is also able to inspire others. At this stage, he is a **self-reliant achiever** in the sales part of his job. You can count on him to hit his sales goals. For a person at this level of development, a **delegating** leadership style is best. In this situation, it is appropriate to turn over responsibility for day-to-day decision making and problem solving to him by letting him run his own territory. Your job now is to empower him by allowing and trusting him to act independently. What you need to do is acknowledge his excellent performance and provide the appropriate resources he requires to carry out his sales duties. It's important at this stage to challenge your high performing salesperson to continue to grow in his sales ability and cheer him on to even higher levels of sales.

Development Level Varies from Goal to Goal or Task to Task

As we implied in the preceding example, development level is not a global concept—it's task-specific. We could have tracked the salesperson's progress in service, administration, or team contribution, and it would have been a different journey. It's important not to pigeonhole people into any particular development level. In reality, development level does not apply to the person, but rather to the person's competence and commitment to do *a specific goal or task*. In other words, an individual is not at any one development level overall. Development level varies from goal to goal and task to task. An individual can be at one level of development on one goal or task and be at a different level of development on another goal or task.

For example, Casey works in the consumer products industry. In the marketing part of her job, she is a genius when it comes to rolling out new products and opening new markets. Clearly she is a ***self-reliant achiever***, as demonstrated by the success of her past marketing plans. However, when it comes to setting up a database to track demographics and buying patterns, Casey has little experience beyond e-mail and word processing on her laptop. Depending on her motivation for the task, she could be an ***enthusiastic beginner*** or a ***disillusioned learner***.

This example shows that you not only need to use *different strokes for different folks*, but also *different strokes for the same folks*, depending on what goal or part of their job you are focused on at any given time.

To determine the appropriate leadership style to use with each of the four development levels, draw a vertical line up from a diagnosed development level to the leadership curve running through the four-quadrant model. As illustrated in Figure 5.2, the appropriate leadership style—the match—is the quadrant where the vertical line intersects the curved line.

Matching Leadership Style to Development Level

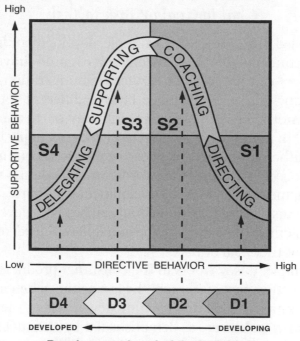

Development Level of the Individual

Figure 5.2   Matching Leadership Style to Development Level

Using this approach, the *enthusiastic beginner (D1)* would get a *directing (S1)* leadership style. The *disillusioned learner (D2)* would get a *coaching (S2)* leadership style. The *capable but cautious performer*

(D3) would get a *supporting (S3)* leadership style, and the *self-reliant achiever (D4)* would get a *delegating (S4)* leadership style. In determining what style to use with what development level, just remember this:

> *Leaders need to do what the people they supervise can't do for themselves at the present moment.*

The Importance of Meeting People Where They Are

Some people think that it's inconsistent to manage some people one way and other people in a different way. However, we don't define consistency as "treating everybody the same way." We define it as "using the same leadership style in similar situations." To those who argue that it's unfair to treat direct reports differently, we agree with U.S. Supreme Court justice Felix Frankfurter:

> *There is nothing so unequal as the equal treatment of unequals.*

Friends of ours experienced the downside of equal treatment for unequals when their son was eight years old and in the third grade. They got word from the school that he was way ahead of his class in reading but far behind in math. Initially, they thought, "How is that possible? How could a kid be so good in reading and so bad in math?" After thinking about it for a while, of course, it made perfect sense. Some kids are great in social studies but poor in science. People are good at some things and not others.

When the father of the child in question understood the reality of the situation and how it was possible, he met with one of his son's teachers. The reason we say "one of his son's teachers" is because their son was in an open-style school with 110 kids in the class and four or five teachers working with them in a large, open space.

"Look, I don't want to cause any problems," he said, "but what I'd like to know is, why is our son doing so well in reading and so poorly in math? How do you treat him differently in reading versus math?"

The teacher said, "Over here on this wall we have a group of files. Each kid has his or her own reading file. When it's time for reading, the kids go get their reading files, come back to their desks, and continue to do their reading where they left off. If they have a question, they raise their hand, and one of us comes over and sees them."

Our friend asked, "How is that working with our son?"

The teacher said, "Super. He's one of our best readers."

Our friend said, "Keep it up. You're doing a great job teaching him reading."

What leadership style were they using with this youngster in reading? They were using a ***delegating*** leadership style. He picks out his folder; he decides when he needs help. Why was it working? Because the kid was a ***self-reliant achiever*** in reading. He loved it, and he had skills.

Our friend said, "Now tell me what you're doing with our son in math."

The teacher said, "Over on the other wall we have a group of files for our math program. When it's time for math, the kids go get their folders, bring them back to their desks, and continue to do their math where they left off. If they have any problems, they raise their hands, and a teacher comes to see them."

Our friend said, "How is that working with our son?"

The teacher said, "Not very well. He's falling behind the class."

What leadership style were they using with the boy in math? They were using a ***delegating*** leadership style, the same style they were using to teach him reading. In fact, that was the teaching style generally used in this open school. The problem with using a delegating style with this youngster in math was that the kid was at a much lower development level in math than he was in reading. He was a ***disillusioned learner***. He didn't have the competency. He didn't have the interest or the confidence. The teachers were leaving him alone.

Our friend had been taught all about Situational Leadership® II, so he said to the teacher, "Didn't they ever teach you in teacher education that with the same kid on a different subject you need to use a different leadership or teaching style?" Then our friend asked all the teachers in this open classroom, "Which one of you has the reputation of being a traditional teacher?" An older woman smiled. She had been a teacher for 35 years in this school system. Our friend had heard about her. Her close supervision of kids had given her a reputation for being too tough. Recognizing that this was just what his kid needed, our friend asked her, "How would you deal with our son's math problem? He's not doing very well."

Before we tell you what she said, let us tell you a bit about this teacher. One of our associates had gone to the elementary school where this teacher taught before she moved to the open school. In this school, the teacher had 30 third graders to herself. The kids had to eat lunch in the classroom, because the school wasn't big enough to have a lunchroom. Our associate walked by her classroom one day at 12:15. The door was wide open, and 30 third graders were sitting eating their lunches in dead silence while our teacher friend was playing Beethoven on the recorder. Our associate smiled when he saw this and said to himself, "That's what I call control."

Across the hall was the other third-grade teacher. The door to the classroom was shut, but our associate could see in through a window. The place looked like a zoo. Kids were running all over the place, up on the desks, while the teacher was dancing and hugging them. It looked like a fun place to be. Would that teacher be a good reading teacher for our friend's son? Absolutely, because the boy didn't need a reading teacher. If you don't need a manager, you might as well have a nice, warm, supportive one. Would this teacher be any good teaching the youngster math? No, she wouldn't.

Now, back to the directive teacher's response to our friend. She said, "It would have been a lot easier if I'd had your son from the beginning. I think he's discouraged now, because it's harder than he thought it would be, and he's not doing well. So when it's time for math, I would go over to him and say, 'It's time for math.' Then I'd lead him by the hand over to his file. Sometimes I don't think he even gets his own file—he gets absent kids' files so he can goof them up. Then I would take him back to his desk, sit him down, and say, 'Do problems 1 through 3, and I'll be back in five minutes to check on you. If we work on this together, I know you're going to get better at math.'"

Our friend said, "You're beautiful. Would you take over his math?" She did. Do you think their son got any better with her **coaching** style? You'd better believe it. Do you think he liked it? Not particularly. It is much easier to loosen up than tighten up. He had been used to working on his own. Even though working alone was not effective, he didn't welcome the sudden shift to close supervision. Yet if people don't know what they're doing and are discouraged, somebody has to direct and coach them. Notice that our effective math teacher *clarified expectations and goals, observed and monitored performance,* and *gave him feedback.*

Luckily, there were only three months left in the school year. Why do we say luckily? Because it was difficult for this teacher to move from a **directing/coaching** style to a **supporting/delegating** style. She was great at start-up work, but once the kids got the skills, she had problems letting the students take responsibility for their own learning. After three months, our friend's son was able to get out from under her and get on with a more humanistic, supporting teacher who could work with him now that he had the skills—like the warm, friendly teacher we described earlier.

Teachers like these are absolutely super in their particular role, but you have to make sure they are working with the right kid at the right time. Both the directive teacher and the humanistic teacher would have been more effective if they could have used a variety of leadership styles. It's the same with managers and leaders. You have to be flexible enough to vary your leadership style depending on the skill level of your people; otherwise, your effectiveness will be limited.

---

*All people have peak performance potential—
you just need to know where they
are coming from and meet them there.*

The Three Skills of a Situational Leader

To become effective in using Situational Leadership® II, you must master three skills: ***diagnosis***, ***flexibility***, and ***partnering for performance***. None of these skills is particularly difficult; each simply requires practice.

Diagnosis: The First Skill

As we stated earlier, to be an effective situational leader, you must determine the development level of your direct report. But how, exactly, do you do that? The key is to look at two factors—competence and commitment.

Competence is the sum of knowledge and skills that an individual brings to a goal or task. The best way to determine competence is to look at a person's performance. How well can your direct reports plan, organize, problem-solve, and communicate about doing a particular task? Can they accomplish the stated goal accurately and on time? Competence can be gained through formal education, on-the-job training, and experience, and it can be developed over time with appropriate direction and support.

The second factor to look for when diagnosing development level is ***commitment***: a person's motivation and confidence about a goal or task. How interested and enthusiastic are your direct reports about doing a particular job? Are they self-assured? Do they trust their own ability to do the goal or task? If their motivation and confidence are high, your direct reports are committed.

Flexibility: The Second Skill

When you are comfortably able to use a variety of leadership styles, you have mastered the second skill of a situational leader: **flexibility**. As your direct reports move from one development level to the next, your style should change accordingly. Yet our research shows that most leaders have a preferred leadership style.[2] In fact, 54 percent of leaders tend to use only one style, 35 percent tend to use two styles, 10 percent tend to use three styles, and only 1 percent use four styles. To be effective, leaders must be able to use all four leadership styles.

Partnering for Performance: The Third Skill

The third skill of a situational leader is **partnering for performance**. Partnering opens up communication between you and your direct reports and increases the quality and quantity of your conversations. When we first started to teach Situational Leadership® II, managers would leave our training excited and ready to apply and use the concepts. Yet, we found that problems developed, because the people managers were applying the model to didn't understand what the managers were doing and often misinterpreted their intentions.

For example, suppose that you diagnose one of your people as predominantly a self-reliant achiever. As a result, you decide to basically leave that person alone, but you don't tell her why. After a while—when she hardly ever sees you anymore—she becomes confused. "I wonder what I've done wrong," she thinks. "I never see my manager anymore."

Suppose another one of your people is new and you decide that person needs, at a minimum, a coaching style. As a result, you're in his office all the time. After a while, he starts to wonder, "Why doesn't my boss trust me? He's always looking over my shoulder."

In both cases, you might have made the right diagnosis, but since your people don't understand your rationale, they misinterpret your intentions. Through these kinds of experiences, we realized this:

Leadership is not something you do to people,
but something you do with people.

That's where partnering for performance comes in. This skill is about gaining your direct reports' permission to use the leadership style that is a match for their development level. As you will learn in the next chapter, "Self Leadership: The Power Behind Empowerment," partnering for performance also allows people to ask their manager for the leadership style they need. Since partnering for performance involves this kind of give-and-take between leader and follower, we will wait until you fully understand Situational Self Leadership before going into depth about partnering for performance in Chapter 7, "Partnering for Performance."

Effective Leadership Is a Transformational Journey

We call Situational Leadership® II the integrating concept, because it was on this theory that The Ken Blanchard Companies was built. Over time, we realized that situational leadership applied not only when you were leading an individual, but also when you were leading a team, an organization, and, most importantly, yourself. In fact, we have found that leadership is a four-stage transformational journey that includes self leadership, one-on-one leadership, team leadership, and organizational leadership.[3]

Self leadership comes first, because effective leadership starts on the inside. Before you can hope to lead anyone else, you have to know yourself and what you need to be successful. Self knowledge gives you perspective.

Only when leaders have had experience in leading themselves are they ready to lead others. The key to **one-on-one leadership** is being able to develop a trusting relationship with others. If you don't know who you are—or what your strengths and weaknesses are—and you are not willing to be vulnerable, you will never develop a trusting relationship. Without trust, it is impossible for an organization to function effectively. *Trust* between you and the people you lead is essential for working together.

The next step on a leader's transformational journey is **team leadership**. As leaders develop a trusting relationship with people in the one-on-one leadership arena, they become trustworthy. This is great preparation for team development and building a *community*. Effective leaders working at the team level realize that to be good stewards of the energy and efforts of those committed to work with them, they must honor the power of diversity and acknowledge the power of teamwork. This makes the leadership challenge more complicated, yet the results can be especially gratifying.

Organizational leadership is the final stage in the transformational journey. Whether a leader can function well as an organizational leader—someone supervising more than one team—depends on the perspective, trust, and community attained during the first three stages of the leader's transformational journey. The key to developing an effective organization is creating an environment that *values both relationships and results*.

One of the primary mistakes that leaders make today is that when they are called to lead, they spend most of their time and energy trying to improve things at the organizational level before ensuring that they have adequately addressed their own credibility at the self, one-on-one, or team leadership levels.

As you take time at each of the leadership stops along your transformational journey, Situational Leadership® II will play a major role. The following chapter examines how the model applies to the first step of the transformational journey: self leadership.

Chapter 6

SELF LEADERSHIP: THE POWER BEHIND EMPOWERMENT

Susan Fowler,
Ken Blanchard,
and Laurence Hawkins

As we discussed in Chapter 4, "Empowerment Is the Key," the traditional hierarchy of leadership is evolving into a new order: empowerment of individuals. When self leaders can take the initiative to get what they need to succeed and leaders respond to those needs, the proverbial pyramid turns upside down, and leaders serve those who are being led. This puts the power into empowerment.

Managers must learn to let go of command-and-control leadership styles, because soon they will have no choice. In the 1980s, a manager typically supervised five people—in other words, the span of control was one manager to five direct reports. Today, companies have more mean-and-lean organizational structures, where spans of control have increased considerably. Now, it is common to find one manager for 25 to 75 direct reports. Add to that the emergence of virtual organizations—where managers are being asked to supervise people they seldom, if ever, meet face to face—and we have an entirely different work landscape emerging. The truth is that most bosses today can no longer play the traditional role of telling people what, when, and how to do everything. Managers just don't have time, and in many cases, their people know more about the work than they do. More than ever before, companies today are relying on empowered individuals to get the job done.

A number of people are taking to this empowered environment like ducks to water. But some are becoming immobilized, unsure of how to take action without being told directly what to do by their manager. What's the solution? How can you get people to grab hold and run with the ball that they're being handed? How can you help people flourish as empowered problem solvers and decision makers?

Creating an Empowered Workforce

Just as leaders must move from command-and-control to partnering for performance, so too must those who are being led move from "waiting to be told" to taking the initiative to lead themselves. If the key role of situational leaders is to become partners with their people, the new role of people is to become partners with their leaders. This is what self leadership is all about.

If empowerment is to be successful, organizations and leaders must develop self leaders in the workforce who have the skills to take initiative.

People need to be trained in self leadership. While many organizations teach managers how to delegate and "let go," there is less emphasis on developing individuals to pick up the ball and run with it. Organizations on the leading edge have learned that developing self leaders is a powerful way to positively impact the triple bottom line.

For example, one of our clients, Bandag Manufacturing, experienced the value of self leadership after a major equipment breakdown. Rather than laying off the affected workforce, the company opted to train them in self leadership. A funny thing happened. Direct reports began holding their managers account-able and asking them to demonstrate their leadership abilities. They were asking managers for direction and support and urging them to clarify goals and expectations. Suddenly, managers were studying up on rusty skills and working harder.

When the plant's ramp-up time was compared to the compa-ny's other eight plants that had experienced similar breakdowns in the past, the California plant reached pre-breakdown produc-tion levels faster than any other in history. The manufacturer studied other measures, too, and concluded that the determining factor in the plant's successful rebound was primarily due to the proactive behavior of the workers, who were fully engaged and armed with the skills of self leadership.

An organization filled with self leaders is
an organization with an empowered workforce.

Creating Self Leaders Through Individual Learning

Individual learning—one of the key elements of a high perform-ing organization—is essential to self leadership.[1] Organizations that do not encourage people to learn are less likely to be high performing, because the skills of an organization are no greater than the skills of its people. Unless the individual learns, the organization cannot learn.

In high performing organizations, people are treated as appre-ciating assets who grow more valuable with experience and knowledge. High performing organizations use formal training, mentoring, and on-the-job support to develop the skills and com-petencies of their people.

While self leaders should be responsible for their own learn-ing, they shouldn't bear the burden alone; management practices should support the development of knowledge and skills. This works best when learning activities are integrated into everyone's work. In high performing organizations, all learning is aligned with and supports the company's strategic direction.

Fortunately, examples of organizations that support individual learning and the development of self leaders are plentiful. Yum! Brands—the parent company of Pizza Hut, Taco Bell, and KFC, among others—supports Yum! University, where associates learn the technical, business, and interpersonal skills that are related to creating customer mania.[2]

Johnsonville Foods promotes continuous learning by encouraging all employees to attend any training class—regardless of its direct applicability to their current jobs.[3] GE is another excellent example of an organization that values learning. Their Work Out initiative launched in 1989 broke down barriers to learning through cross-functional work on real applications. Work Out eliminated waste and increased productivity by removing communication barriers so that employees shared knowledge and acted on it. GE continues to build on all that employees are learning through the Work Out program—the hallmark of an organization that promotes ongoing learning and the development of self leaders.[4]

Empowerment is what leaders
give to their people.
Self leadership is what people
do to make empowerment work.

The Three Skills of a Self Leader

You cannot invert the hierarchal pyramid and simply tell self leaders to take responsibility. Self leaders must be actively developed by teaching people skills and mental attitudes that foster empowerment.[5] In *Self Leadership and The One Minute Manager*,

Ken Blanchard, Susan Fowler, and Laurence Hawkins teach the three skills of self leadership: ***challenge assumed constraints***, ***celebrate your points of power***, and ***collaborate for success***.[6]

The First Skill of a Self Leader: Challenge Assumed Constraints

The first skill of a self leader is to **challenge assumed constraints**. What, exactly, do we mean by an assumed constraint?

An assumed constraint is a belief, based on past experience, that limits current and future experiences.

The classic example of an assumed constraint is illustrated by the training of circus elephants. The trainer takes a baby elephant and ties him to a stake with a big, heavy chain. Although the baby elephant pulls and tugs, he can't break the chain. Eventually he stops trying. He is now a six-ton elephant with the Barnum & Bailey circus. He could easily pull the entire stake out of the ground—plus the stage—but he doesn't even try. His inability to move beyond the length of the chain isn't real; it's an assumed constraint.

Consider how the elephant's story relates to your own work experience. Do any of the following statements sound familiar? "Why should I bother? My boss won't approve anyway. They never listen to anyone's ideas around here. A woman has never held that position before. I've never been any good at that." These are all examples of assumed constraints that might be true at some level but are not the truth that should define your experience.

Indicators that an assumed constraint may be holding you hostage are negative internal dialogue, excuses, and blaming statements. At one time or another, most of us have assumed that because we did not have direct authority or position power, we could not be leaders or influence outcomes. This is one of the most common assumed constraints in the workplace. People who have become legendary for their effectiveness—from Bill Gates to Mother Teresa—are those who go beyond assumed constraints to reach their goals. For example, Mother Teresa—a minority Albanian who spoke broken English—did not begin her amazing career with a high position and authority. She used her personal power to achieve her goal of bringing dignity to the destitute. Fame and success followed.

This is not to say that all of us aren't constrained by outside forces, whether it's a lack of time, money, or position of authority. Yet self leadership teaches that constraints are not the problem; the problem is that we think these things are the only sources of power that are available to us. Every successful person can almost name the time and date when they decided to let go of an assumed constraint.

The Second Skill of a Self Leader: Celebrate Your Points of Power

The second skill of a self leader is to **celebrate your points of power**. Everyone has points of power, although many are not aware of them. For example, in our work in public schools, we have found that students often feel that because they are not a parent, principal, teacher, or coach, they have no power. As a result, they either go underground with their feelings of frustration, or they become hostile and rebellious. This is not just a young person's problem. People of all ages struggle with the mere notion of power. They often don't recognize or acknowledge that they also have some power.

The abuse of power, the use of status and position to coerce others, and the egoism associated with people who have social and political power have turned people off to the acceptance of—let alone use of—power. Situational Self Leadership teaches people that we all have points of power. In helping people recognize and accept their points of power, we suggest that "the sole advantage of power is the ability to do more good." Self leaders can do more good for themselves, their families, their communities, their organizations, and their coworkers when they accept and tap into their power.

There are five sources of power: *position power*, *personal power*, *task power*, *relationship power*, and *knowledge power*.

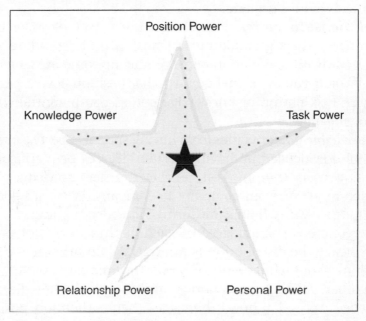

Figure 6.1   Points of Power

Position power is the most recognized point of power. It is inherent in the authority of your position. You have position power when your business card has a title printed on it that indicates you have the power to manage people or command resources. But as Ken Blanchard's dad, an officer in the Navy, always said, "The best leaders are those who have position power and never have to use it."

Personal power comes from personal attributes such as strength of character, passion, inspiration, or wisdom. Personal power is further enhanced by strong interpersonal skills, such as the ability to communicate well and be persuasive. If people like to be around you, you have personal power.

Task power stems from a task or particular job. This is power you have in being able to help others with a process or procedure they need to do or, conversely, to block or delay others from doing a task. For example, an executive secretary for a president or CEO often has the power to influence who gets added to or deleted from the executive's agenda.

Relationship power comes from the power of association with others—through building a friendship, understanding a colleague, cultivating a relationship, or knowing someone who owes you a favor. If you are somebody who has position power, personal power, task power, or knowledge power, you potentially have relationship power.

Knowledge power comes from having special expertise or skills but is also evidenced by having certain degrees or certifications indicating special training. You can often transfer knowledge power from job to job or from company to company. We're all good at something, so we all have some form of knowledge power.

Everyone has some degree of each of these forms of power, and typically the distribution is uneven. We find that few people ever think about what points of power they have. Fewer still have asked others for their perceptions on this topic. If they did, they might be surprised at how others view them—their job, position, personality, and abilities.

Getting feedback on your points of power can be an enlightening experience. Chances are good that you'll be surprised and gratified by the responses you get. With raised awareness and attention to your own power, you come to realize how to use your points of power to better advantage. You will probably also realize that while you have been taking some points of power for granted, you have been oblivious to others. The best way to increase your power base is to gather people around you who have points of power you don't have.

Don't buy into the assumed constraint that position power is the only power that works.

Once you learn what your points of power are, you are ready to expand them. If you are strong in some points of power or weak in others, don't assume that will be true the rest of your life. For example, it wouldn't hurt a person with high knowledge power due to computer expertise but low personal power due to weak interpersonal skills to take a Dale Carnegie course on *How to Win Friends and Influence People*. To assume that people will never want to be around you is a life-limiting assumed constraint. The same can be said of people who have good interpersonal skills but lack technical skills. You're naïve to think that the computer is going to go away. So get with the program and ask someone to help you learn.

Using the Power of "I Need"

You can maximize your points of power when you combine them with two powerful words: "I need." Instead of directly stating what we need, many of us get trapped in asking dumb questions, like the woman in the subway. Let us explain: A man got on a subway in New York City and discovered there was only one seat left. There was something on the seat he didn't want on his slacks, so he laid his newspaper down and sat on it. A few minutes later, a woman tapped him on the shoulder and said, "Excuse me, sir. Are you reading your newspaper?" The man thought that was one of the dumbest questions he'd ever heard. He couldn't help himself. He stood up, turned the page, sat back down on the paper, and replied, "Yes, ma'am, I am."

While that story is amusing, you might wonder if you ask any dumb questions. We all do. For example, suppose that a coworker is running around like a chicken with her head cut off, but you need some help. So you ask, "Are you busy?" That's a dumb question. Of course she's busy! So she says something like, "There just aren't enough hours in the day." You feel guilty, so you get flustered and leave her alone, not wanting to add to her burden.

The alternative to dumb questions is to simply state your needs to your coworker truthfully: "I need 15 minutes to discuss this project. If this isn't a good time, I could come back at 3:00."

What makes the "I need" phrase so powerful? When you tell somebody you *want* something, that person's first thought is usually, "We all want things we can't have." However, when you use the "I need" phrase, you're coming from a position of strength. You've thought about what it will take to succeed, and you are requesting a someone's help. Human beings love to feel needed. They love to think they can help you.

Don't be afraid to ask for what you need from people who have points of power you don't have. By being assertive in this way, you will eliminate "being a victim" from your vocabulary. Remember, if you ask for what you need, you will either win or break even. Would you be excited to go to Las Vegas if the worst you could do was win or break even? Of course—you would catch the next plane. If you ask for what you need and you get it, you win. If you ask and don't get it, you break even—you didn't have it in the first place. Most people are afraid to ask for what they need for fear of rejection. Remember, when people say no to you, they are only turning down your idea. The only person who can turn you down is you.

"I need" is compelling. This is a key phrase when you begin to collaborate for success.

The Third Skill of a Self Leader: Collaborate for Success

The third skill of a self leader is to **collaborate for success**. This is where self leaders take the initiative to get the direction and support they need to achieve their goals.

In Chapter 5, "Situational Leadership® II: The Integrating Concept," we introduced the four development levels and the appropriate leadership styles for each. Situational Self Leadership turns the model upside down, so that direct reports can now diagnose their own development levels on a particular goal or task and take the initiative to get from their managers the leadership style they need to succeed.

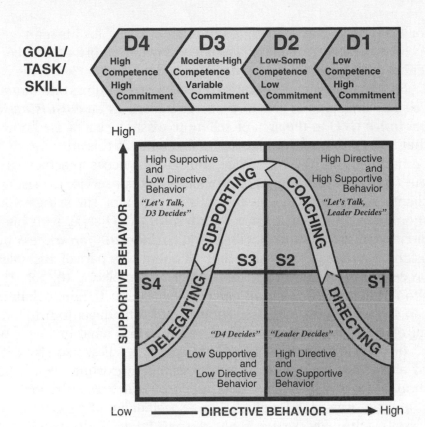

Figure 6.2   The Needs Model

To illustrate how this works, let's return to our example in Chapter 5 of the recently hired 22-year-old salesperson. Suppose that the first thing the salesperson's manager did with him was train him in Situational Self Leadership. Now when he and his manager set goals around his four key areas of responsibility—sales, service, administration, and team contribution—the young salesperson can **collaborate for success** by playing an active role in diagnosing his own development level and determining the leadership style he needs for each, rather than relying on his manager to do all the work. Not only will this increase his self-esteem and speed his journey to empowerment, but by being a good partner, he also will alleviate some of the management load for his boss. In the process, it will make it easier for his manager to invert the hierarchal pyramid and become more of a cheerleader and supporter than a director and controller.

Back to our example: Because the salesperson knows Situational Self Leadership, he is able to diagnose himself as an ***enthusiastic beginner (D1)*** in the area of selling to existing clients. He knows that he has not yet demonstrated competence in this area and that he hasn't gained the knowledge and skills he needs to achieve his sales goals. Yet the thought of providing superior service to existing clients excites him, and his commitment is high. The salesperson should recognize that he needs a ***directing (S1)*** style, with high direction and low support. He should ***collaborate for success*** by asking his manager to teach him all about this part of the sales process, from making the first contact to completing the job. He should ask his manager to visit an existing client with him so that he can see how it's done. He also should ask his manager to help him set appropriate goals and to plan and prioritize what he needs to accomplish to succeed in this area. Because the salesperson is excited about and highly committed to selling to existing clients, he shouldn't need a lot of emotional support in this area of his job.

In the area of administration—specifically, filing electronic reports—the salesperson realizes that he is a ***disillusioned learner (D2)*** in need of ***coaching (S2)***. His hotel job during the summer didn't give him a lot of computer training. After taking some beginning software classes, he thought he was on his way to computer literacy. Yet without the instructor at his side, his confidence is waning. The salesperson should admit to his manager that while he's fairly comfortable with e-mail, he's so baffled by the spreadsheet program that he finds himself mumbling to the computer monitor. Recognizing that he needs a lot of direction and support in this area, the salesperson should ***collaborate for success*** by asking his manager for more computer training so that he can dialogue with the instructor as he learns. He also should ask his manager for lots of praise and support to build his confidence on the computer and encourage him to keep learning.

In the area of cold calling, the salesperson is having some trouble. He has been well trained in this area and knows the step-by-step process for cold calling. During his training and for the first few weeks afterward, he had several successes. During the past couple of weeks, however, he's made hardly any sales through cold calls. His self-doubt has come roaring back, and he's beginning to wonder if he has what it takes to succeed in cold calling. Remembering how excited and competent he felt about cold calling just a few weeks ago, he realizes that he is a ***capable but cautious performer (D3)*** who needs a ***supporting (S3)*** leadership style. He should ***collaborate for success*** by asking his manager to listen to his concerns and questions and encourage his flagging confidence. Knowing that collaboration with a master in cold calling will give him the boost he needs, he should ask his manager to help him brainstorm and take risks.

In the area of customer service, the salesperson knows full well he's a ***self-reliant achiever (D4)***. Having worked in the hospitality industry, he brings all kinds of customer-pleasing skills to his new position, and delighting customers comes as naturally to him as breathing. He has already won the hearts of some of the company's biggest clients by anticipating their needs and delivering more than they ever dreamed of receiving. In this area, the salesperson should ***collaborate for success*** by letting his manager know that a ***delegating (S4)*** leadership style would work best for him. He should ask his manager to let him do the day-to-day decision making in this area, and he should let his manager know that the best way to support him is to trust him to do his job well, provide him with the resources he needs, and challenge him to deliver even higher levels of raving fan service.

It is important to remember that the process of collaborating for success doesn't have to be restricted to your manager. You can diagnose your development level and ask for the appropriate leadership style from any number of leaders. Remember that *a leader is anyone who can give the direction and support you need to achieve your goal.* This is the perfect time for you to challenge your assumed constraints. What are the little voices in your head that are telling you, "Why would this person want to help me?"

Now that you know about challenging assumed constraints, celebrating your points of power, and collaborating for success, in the next chapter we introduce partnering for performance, the third skill of becoming an effective situational leader. Partnering for performance formalizes the process of collaborating for success and increases the quality and quantity of discussions between leaders and the people they support and depend on. It creates a structure in which people can ask their managers for the leadership style they need and in the process create the kind of give-and-take between leader and follower that produces amazing results.

Chapter 7

PARTNERING
FOR
PERFORMANCE

Fred Finch
and Ken Blanchard

A t its best, leadership is a partnership that involves mutual trust between two people who work together to achieve common goals. When that occurs, both leader and follower have an opportunity to influence each other. Leadership shifts back and forth between them, depending on the task at hand and who has the competence and commitment to deal with it. Both parties play a role in determining how things get done.

Partnering for performance, the third skill of effective situational leaders, provides a guide for creating such side-by-side leadership relationships. It is a process for increasing the quality and quantity of conversations between managers and direct reports—the people they support and depend on. These conversations not only help people perform better, but they also help everyone involved feel better about themselves and each other. Why is that important?

We have found that the best way to improve people's job satisfaction and feelings of self-worth is to help them perform well. That requires a good formal and informal performance management system. That's exactly what partnering for performance promotes.

Establishing an Effective Performance Management System

An effective performance management system has three parts. The first is **performance planning**. After everyone is clear on the organizational vision and direction, it's during performance planning that leaders agree with their direct reports about the goals and objectives they should be focusing on. During performance planning, it's okay for the traditional hierarchy to be alive and well, because if there's a disagreement between a manager and a direct report about goals, who wins? The manager, because that person represents the organization's goals and objectives.

The second aspect of an effective performance management system is **performance coaching**. This is where the pyramid is inverted and the hierarchy is turned upside down on a day-to-day basis. Now leaders do everything they can to help direct reports be successful. This is where servant leadership kicks in. At this stage, managers work for their people, praising progress and redirecting inappropriate performance.

The third and final aspect of an effective performance management system is **performance review**. This is where a manager and direct report sit down and assess the direct report's performance over time.

Which of these three—performance planning, performance coaching, or performance review—do most organizations devote the greatest amount of time to? Unfortunately, it's performance review. We go into organization after organization, and people say to us, "You'll love our new performance review form." We always laugh, because we think most of them can be thrown out. Why? Because these forms often measure things nobody knows how to evaluate. For example, "initiative" or "willingness to take responsibility." Or "promotability"—that's a good one. When no one knows how to win during a performance review, they focus most of their energy up the hierarchy. After all, if you have a good relationship with your boss, you have a higher probability of getting a good evaluation.

Some organizations do a good job on performance planning and set very clear goals. However, after goal setting, what do you think happens to those goals? Most often they get filed, and no one looks at them until they are told it's time for performance reviews. Then everybody runs around, bumping into each other, trying to find the goals.

Of the three aspects of an effective performance management system, which one do people spend the least time on? The answer is performance coaching. Yet, this is the most important aspect of managing people's performance, because it's during performance coaching that feedback—praising progress and redirecting inappropriate behavior—happens on an ongoing basis.

To illustrate our thinking in this area, consider Ken's ten-year experience as a college professor. He was always in trouble. What drove the faculty crazy more than anything was that at the beginning of every course he gave students the final exam. When the faculty found out about that, they asked, "What are you doing?"

Ken said, "I thought we were supposed to teach these students."

The faculty said, "You are, but don't give them the final exam ahead of time!"

Ken said, "Not only will I give them the final exam ahead of time, what do you think I'll do throughout the semester? I'll teach them the answers so that when they get to the final exam, they'll get A's. You see, life is all about getting A's—not some stupid normal distribution curve."

Do you hire losers? Do you go around saying, "We lost some of our best losers last year, so let's hire some new ones to fill those low spots"? No! You hire either winners or potential winners. You don't hire people to fit a normal distribution curve. You want to hire the best people possible, and you want them to perform at their highest level.

Giving people the final exam ahead of time is equivalent to performance planning. It lets people know exactly what's expected of them. Teaching direct reports the answers is what performance coaching is all about. If you see people doing something right, you give them an "attaboy" or "attagirl." If they do something wrong, you don't beat them up or save your feedback for the performance review. Instead, you say, "Wrong answer. What do you think would be the right answer?" In other words, you redirect them. Finally, giving people the same exam during the performance review that you gave them at the beginning of the year helps them win—get a good evaluation. There should be no surprises in an annual or semi-annual performance review. Everyone should know what the test will be and should get help throughout the year to achieve a high score on it. When you have a forced distribution curve—where a certain percentage of your people have to be average or less—you lose everyone's trust. Now all people are concerned about is looking out for number one.

After learning about this philosophy, Garry Ridge, president of WD-40, implemented "Don't Mark My Paper—Help Me Get an A" as a major theme in his company. He is so emphatic about this concept that he fired a poor performer's manager rather than the poor performer when he found out that the manager had done nothing to help that person get an A.

Not all managers are like Garry Ridge. Many still believe you need to use a normal distribution curve that grades a few people high, a few people low, and the rest average. The reason these managers and their organizations are often reluctant to discard the normal distribution curve is that they don't know how they will deal with career planning if some people don't get sorted out at a lower level. If they rated a high percentage of their people as top performers, they wonder how they can possibly reward them all. As people move up the hierarchy, aren't there fewer opportunities for promotion? We believe that question is quite naïve. If you treat people well and help them win in their present position, they often will use their creativity to come up with new business ideas that will expand your vision and grow the organization. Protecting the hierarchy doesn't do your people or your organization any good.

Ralph Stayer, coauthor with Jim Belasco of *Flight of the Buffalo*, tells a wonderful story that proves this point. Stayer was in the sausage manufacturing business. His secretary came to him one day with a great idea. She suggested that they start a catalog business, because at the time they were direct-selling their sausages to only grocery stores and other distributors. He said, "What a great idea! Why don't you organize a business plan and run it?" Soon the woman who was his former secretary was running a major new division of his company and creating all kinds of job opportunities for people, as well as revenue for the company.[1]

Leadership that emphasizes judgment, criticism, and evaluation is a thing of the past. Leading at a higher level today is about treating people the right way by providing the direction, support, and encouragement they need to be their best. If you help your people get A's, your performance management system will ignite them to blow your customers away, because they will feel good about themselves and will want to return the favor to others. This gets magnified when your performance management system is integrated with partnering for performance.

Partnering and the Performance Management System

To give you a better sense of how this works, we want to share with you a game plan that will help you understand how partnering for performance fits into the formal performance management system we just described. While you can put this game plan into action with no prior training, it is much more powerful when everyone involved—both leaders and direct reports—understands Situational Leadership® II or Situational Self Leadership. This ensures that everyone is speaking the same language.

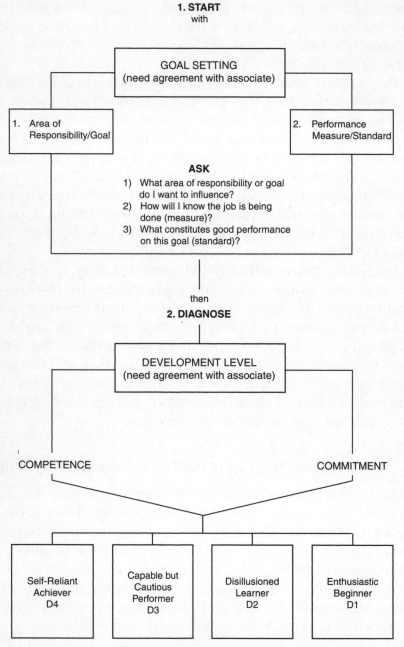

Figure 7.1   The Partnering for Performance Game Plan

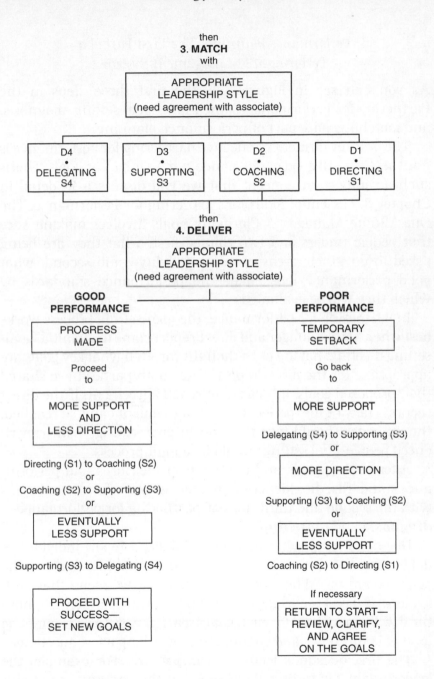

then
3. MATCH
with

APPROPRIATE
LEADERSHIP STYLE
(need agreement with associate)

D4 • DELEGATING S4	D3 • SUPPORTING S3	D2 • COACHING S2	D1 • DIRECTING S1

then
4. DELIVER

APPROPRIATE
LEADERSHIP STYLE
(need agreement with associate)

GOOD PERFORMANCE — — — **POOR PERFORMANCE**

PROGRESS MADE

TEMPORARY SETBACK

Proceed to

Go back to

MORE SUPPORT AND LESS DIRECTION

MORE SUPPORT

Directing (S1) to Coaching (S2)
or
Coaching (S2) to Supporting (S3)
or

Delegating (S4) to Supporting (S3)
or

MORE DIRECTION

EVENTUALLY LESS SUPPORT

Supporting (S3) to Coaching (S2)
or

Supporting (S3) to Delegating (S4)

EVENTUALLY LESS SUPPORT

Coaching (S2) to Directing (S1)

PROCEED WITH SUCCESS— SET NEW GOALS

If necessary

RETURN TO START— REVIEW, CLARIFY, AND AGREE ON THE GOALS

Performance Planning: The First Part of a Performance Management System

As you can see in Figure 7.1, the first three steps in the Partnering for Performance Game Plan—goal setting, diagnosis, and matching—are part of performance planning.

The first key element of effective partnering for performance is ***goal setting***. All good performance starts with clear goals. This is such an important concept that we will discuss it in detail in Chapter 8, "Essential Skills for Partnering for Performance: The One Minute Manager®." Clarifying goals involves making sure that people understand two things: first, what they are being asked to do—their areas of accountability—and second, what good performance looks like—the performance standards by which they will be evaluated.

In partnering for performance, the goal-setting process works best when both manager and direct report come to an initial goal-setting meeting, having each thought through what key goals are appropriate for the direct report. Once both parties have shared their proposed goals, it is easier to reach agreement. If the direct report is new or inexperienced, or if agreement can't be reached, the manager should take the lead in goal setting. With experienced people, goal setting should be a joint process.

After setting goals and agreeing on measures and performance standards, the essence of partnering for performance begins with the second and third steps of partnering for performance—***diagnosis*** and ***matching***.

Diagnosis starts with the leader and direct report individually diagnosing the direct report's development level for each of the goals agreed on. When we say individually, we mean that both leader and direct report go to a quiet place and separately diagnose the development level for each goal area. It is easy to determine the level of competence and commitment by asking a few questions.

The first questions focus on ***competence***. For example, the leader might say to herself, "Given that the performance of this task requires these four key skills, to what extent does this person have those skills?" At the same time, the direct report would be asking that same question about himself. Another question might focus on, "Does this person know how to do this task?"

When it comes to **commitment**, the questions focus on how excited the direct report is about working in this area. "Would it be a motivating task for this person?" the leader might ask herself. Or the direct report might ask himself, "How excited am I about taking this on?"

After both people in the partnering process have done their diagnostic homework, they should come back together and agree on who goes first. If the direct report goes first, the leader's job is to listen to that person's diagnosis. Then, before saying anything else, the leader has to tell the direct report what she heard him saying until he agrees that's what he said. When it's the leader's turn, she tells the direct report her diagnosis of his development level on each of his areas of responsibility. His job is now to listen and feed back what he heard until his manager agrees that's what she said. Why do we suggest this process? Because it guarantees that both people are heard. Without some structure like this, if one of the two people involved is more verbal than the other, that person will dominate the conversation.

After both people have been heard, they should discuss similarities and differences in their diagnoses and attempt to come to some agreement. If there is a disagreement between leader and direct report on development level that cannot be resolved, who should win? The direct report. It is not the manager's job to fight over development level. However, the manager should make the direct report accountable. This means asking him, "What will you be able to show me in this goal area in a week or two that will demonstrate that your development diagnosis was right and mine was wrong?" You want to help your people win, even if agreement has not been reached. We have found that people will work hard to prove they are right, which is exactly what you want them to do. If performance does not live up to agreed-on expectations, it will be clear to the direct report that the diagnosis should be reconsidered and more direction and/or support should be given.

Once development level is clear, both parties, if they know Situational Leadership® II, should be ready to discuss which leadership style is needed. This leads to **matching**, the third step in the partnering for performance game plan. Matching ensures that the leader provides the kind of behaviors—a leadership style—that the direct report needs to perform the task well and, at the same time, enhances his commitment.

While the appropriate leadership style to use should be clear once development level is determined, that's just the beginning. When you're partnering for performance, you don't just leave it at saying you'll use a delegating or coaching style. You have to be more specific. For the leader, this provides an opportunity for what we call "getting permission to use a leadership style."

The purpose of getting permission to use a leadership style is twofold. First, checking to make sure that the style proposed is what the direct report agrees he needs creates clarity. Second, getting permission ensures the direct report's buy-in on the use of that style and increases his commitment. For example, if a direct report is an **enthusiastic beginner** who does not have much in the way of task knowledge and skill, but is excited about taking on the task, this person obviously needs a **directing** leadership style. The leader might say, "How would it be if I set a task goal that I believe will stretch you but is attainable, and then develop an action plan for you that will enable you to reach the goal? Then, I'd like to meet with you on a regular basis to discuss your progress and provide any help you need as you get started. Does this make sense as a way for you to get up to speed as quickly as possible?" If the direct report agrees, they are off and running.

On the other hand, suppose a direct report is a **self-reliant achiever** on a particular goal and therefore can handle a **delegating** leadership style. The leader might say, "Okay. The ball is in your court, but keep me in the information loop. If you have any concerns, give me a call. Unless I hear from you, or the information I receive tells me otherwise, I'll assume everything is fine. If it isn't, call early. Don't wait until the monkey is a gorilla. Does that work for you?" If the direct report says yes, he is on his own until his performance or communication suggests differently. If, in either of the two examples—the enthusiastic beginner or the self-reliant achiever—the direct report doesn't agree, what should happen? Further discussion should take place until a leadership approach is agreed on.

As you can tell from the examples, once an appropriate leadership style is agreed on, the leader still needs to provide work direction. ***Providing work direction*** might involve establishing clear performance expectations, creating an action plan, putting in place a process for checking progress, and expressing confidence that the person can deliver on the performance plan.

As part of that process, it's important to establish a monitoring process based on the agreed-on leadership style. This is where the leader and direct report commit to holding scheduled meetings—called progress-check meetings—to discuss how performance is going. If the direct report is an enthusiastic beginner or disillusioned learner, frequent meetings should be held to ensure that the person is getting the kind of direction and support that will facilitate his continued learning and performance. If the person is a capable but cautious performer or self-reliant achiever, the meetings should be held much less frequently, and the focus should be on the leader's getting informed about what's happening and praising and recognizing progress. These meetings are a critical source of feedback.

For example, if you agree with one of your people that she can handle a delegating leadership style on a particular goal, who is in charge of your communication? She is, because in this area she is a self-reliant achiever. If she needs any help from you, it's up to her to make the contact. The only rule is to call early, not late. As a leader, you don't want any surprises. As we suggested earlier, you'd rather deal with monkeys than gorillas.

If you agree that your direct report needs a **supporting** leadership style, you might ask, "What's the best way for me to recognize and praise the progress you are making? At lunch every week or so?" If you agree to have lunch together, your role would be to listen and support her actions. If a **coaching** style is chosen, you are now in charge. You might say, "Let's schedule two meetings a week for at least two hours to work on the goal you need help with. How about Mondays and Wednesdays from 1 to 3 p.m.?" With a **directing** style, you would meet even more frequently, and maybe have the direct report attend some formal training.

Performance Coaching: The Second Part of a Performance Management System

Once it's determined, the agreed-on leadership style establishes the number, frequency, and kind of progress-check meetings leaders and their direct reports have with each other. The implementation of these meetings begins performance coaching. That's where leaders praise progress and/or redirect the efforts of their partners—their direct reports.

Leaders often assume that their work-direction conversations are so clear that there is no need for follow-up or that they are so busy that they can't take the time. If you want to save yourself time and misery, schedule and hold progress-check meetings. You will be able to catch problems before they become major and significantly increase the probability that your direct report's performance on the goal will meet your expectations. Progress-check conversations enhance the quality of your relationships, build trust and commitment, open lines of communication, and diminish the amount of time spent fighting brush fires. Without scheduling progress-check meetings, leaders could set up their people for failure.

Many managers do that very thing. They hire people, tell them what to do, and then leave them alone and assume good performance will follow. In other words, they abdicate; they don't delegate. This sets up the old leave-alone-then-zap management style. So, not having progress-check meetings—the frequency of which varies according to development level—can cause real problems. That's why one of our favorite sayings is

You can expect more if
you inspect more.

While this might sound intrusive, it's really not. As Ken Blanchard, Thad Lucinak, Chuck Thompkins, and Jim Ballard point out in *Whale Done!: The Power of Positive Relationships*, inspecting should emphasize catching people doing things right, not wrong. Praising progress and/or redirecting efforts begins by accentuating the positive. Redirection follows praising to keep progress going. If no progress is being made—in other words, if performance is not improving—leaders should move straight to redirection to stop any further decline in performance.

"Management by Wandering Around" captures the essence of performance coaching.[2] It provides additional opportunities to share information, provide feedback, and encourage and support people's efforts in between progress-check meetings. This helps you keep in touch with what's going on and identify and resolve issues that come up on a daily basis.

Using Situational Leadership® II in partnering for performance is a dynamic process. Not only does it help leaders and direct reports determine what leadership style to use—as indicated by the number, frequency, and kind of progress-check meetings—it also advises both partners how and when a shift in leadership style is appropriate. Leadership style can move forward or backward, depending on changes in the direct report's competence, commitment, and performance. When they **deliver** the appropriate leadership style, managers are taking the fourth step in the partnering for performance game plan. Let's take a look at the model again and see what happens when performance is improving.

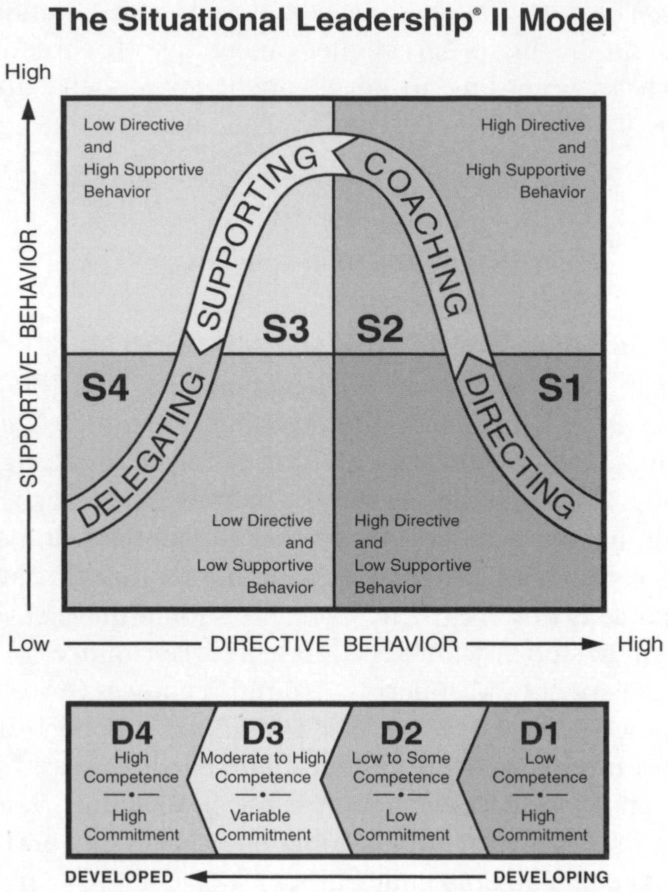

The Situational Leadership® II Model

Figure 7.2   Situational Leadership® II Leadership Styles

Improving Performance

As you re-examine Figure 7.2, you might be wondering what the curve running through the four styles means. We call it a performance curve, and for good reason.

> *Performance is what triggers a change in leadership style.*

As development level moves from ***enthusiastic beginner*** (D1) to ***self-reliant achiever*** (D4), the curve shows how a manager's leadership style moves from ***directing*** (S1) to ***delegating*** (S4), with first an increase in support (S2), and then a decrease in direction (S3), until eventually there's also a decrease in support (S4). At ***self-reliant achiever*** (D4), the person can direct and support more and more of his or her own work. Your goal as a manager, then, should be to help your direct report improve performance by changing your leadership style over time.

To help you as a leader do that, *imagine the performance curve is a railroad track*. Each of the four leadership styles depicts a station along the performance curve. If you start with an ***enthusiastic beginner*** (D1) using a ***directing*** style (S1), and you want to eventually get to ***delegating*** (S4), appropriate for a ***self-reliant achiever*** (D4), what two stations do you have to stop at along the way? ***Coaching*** (S2) and ***supporting*** (S3).

You'll notice that no railroad tracks go straight from ***directing*** (S1) to ***delegating*** (S4). What happens to a fast-moving train if it goes off the tracks? People get hurt. It is important for managers not to skip a station as they manage people's journey to high performance. By staying on track and stopping at all the stations, you will lead your direct reports to perform well on their own, with little or no supervision. Lao Tzu said it well:

> *When the best leader's work is done, the people say,*
> *"We did it ourselves!"*

A number of us were involved in an experiment years ago when we were studying and/or teaching at the University of Massachusetts. We worked with four instructors teaching four different sections of a basic course in management. We asked the first two instructors how they taught. Their response was, "We either lecture or lead discussions." We said, "Good. Keep it up." What two leadership styles are those? Directing and coaching. These two traditional instructors became our control group.

We taught the other two instructors Situational Leadership®
II and showed them how, over time, they could change their
teaching style. The course met for three hours twice a week for
eight weeks. The first two weeks that the students came to class,
the room was set up lecture-style, with a podium up front. We
told the instructors they had four three-hour classes to teach the
students everything they knew about the subject. It was the
instructors' job to fill the students' "empty barrels."

When the students came in the second two weeks, the classroom was set up in a half-moon style, like a business case class.
There was no podium. We told the instructors no longer could
they lecture—now all they could do was lead a discussion on a
concept or case. We forced them to move to a coaching leadership
style.

The third two weeks when the students came to class, the
room was set up in a circle with a seat designated for the instructor. Now we told the instructors they could no longer lecture or
lead a discussion—they could only make two kinds of comments.
One could be a process comment like "Has everybody had a
chance to speak?" Or they could make a supportive comment like
"This is a really interesting class." Now the instructors were being
asked to move to a supporting leadership style.

When the students came in for the last two weeks, the instructors told them they were writing an article for a business journal
and that during the next four classes they would be next door
working on that article. If the students needed them, they knew
where the instructors were. So, we moved the instructors out of
the classroom and forced them into a delegating leadership style.

On the last day of class, a secretary came into all four classes
and wrote a note on the whiteboard. "The instructor is sick
tonight and won't be here. Carry on as usual."

What do you think happened to the students in the first two
classes, where the instructors only lectured or led discussions?
Within five minutes, they were gone. Without the instructor
there, they didn't know what to do.

In the classes with the changing leadership style, nobody left. Students made comments like "The instructor hasn't been here for the last three classes. Big deal. What did you think about that case?" One of the two classes even stayed a half hour beyond the scheduled time.

At the end of the semester, all four classes were given the same content examination, as well as an attitudinal questionnaire that essentially asked them how well they liked the class. Records of absenteeism and tardiness also had been kept. The experimental classes with the changing teaching style outperformed the other two classes. The students knew more, they liked the course better, and they weren't late and absent. How was that possible when their instructors weren't even there for the last four classes? Because the instructors stayed on the railroad tracks and gradually changed their teaching style from directing to coaching to supporting to delegating, the students over time moved from dependence to independence, from enthusiastic beginners to self-reliant achievers.

Declining Performance

What causes decreases in performance? We rarely find decreases in performance resulting from a decline in competence. People either know how to do something or they don't. Unless you can cite cases of Alzheimer's at work, people generally don't lose their competency if they had it in the first place or were trained to have it. Therefore, changes in performance occur either because the job and the necessary skills to perform it have changed, or because people have lost their commitment.

> *Dealing with de-commitment—a change in motivation or confidence—is one of the biggest challenges facing managers.*

Throughout this section, we have focused on helping leaders more effectively grow and develop their people toward higher levels of performance and satisfaction. The focus has been on how to provide leadership in ways that prevent bad things from happening. Unfortunately, leaders face numerous situations where bad things that cause de-commitment have already happened.

For the most part, leaders avoid dealing with their de-committed people, largely because it is such an emotionally charged issue and they don't know how. When they do address it, they usually make matters worse: They turn the not engaged into the actively disengaged. The core perception on the part of these de-committed people is that either their leader or the organization has treated them unfairly.

We believe that the primary reason for loss of commitment is the behavior of the leader and/or the organization. More often than not, something the leader or organization has done or failed to do is the primary cause of the eroded commitment.

De-committed people are not provided with the kind of leadership that matches their needs—they are under- or over-supervised. De-commitment has numerous other potential causes: lack of feedback, lack of recognition, lack of clear performance expectations, unfair standards, being yelled at or blamed, reneging on commitments, being overworked and stressed out.

De-commitment is made even more difficult because in most cases the situation has gone global—the loss of commitment affects most, if not all, of the person's job functioning. The person is unhappy about everything and everyone.

So we have a pervasive problem in organizations that is either a major productivity issue (the not engaged) or a major productivity issue that is festering (the actively disengaged). People often assume that de-commitment occurs mainly at the bottom of the organization, with individual contributors. Not so. It occurs at every organizational level.

Current literature and training programs for addressing what is called "handling performance problems" are overwhelmingly focused on frontline leaders. This literature and these programs assume that the frontline employee is the problem. The language itself—"handling performance problems"—implies that the person with the problem *is* the problem. The literature and training programs emphasize issues such as employees' unacceptable performance or behavior, documenting performance problems, developing organizational policies to deal with them, employee counseling, removing poor performers, corrective counseling, and discipline.[3]

In general, these are lose-lose strategies that intensify de-commitment and that should be used only as a last resort. This approach is commonly called "blaming the victim." A process that does not address all the causes of the problem is guaranteed not to work, particularly if the person who is blaming the performer has a hand in causing it. If the leader and/or organization have a role in causing the problem, their role has to be identified and resolved as part of the solution.

Placing Blame: Not a Good Strategy

First, let's assume that either the leader or the organization has contributed to the cause of an individual's de-commitment. This is not always the case, but the evidence suggests that it is in the substantial majority of instances where de-commitment has occurred. Next, let's assume that the issue has been going on for some time. Again, evidence supports this assumption. When we ask leaders in organizations to identify the people they lead who have "performance problems" and to tell us how long this has been going on, the responses range from six months to ten years. These responses alone identify the leader as part of the problem: the issues are not being addressed.

Again, dealing with de-commitment is a difficult and usually highly emotionally charged undertaking. If the situation has been going on for some time, there is probably a high level of emotional tension in the relationship between the leader and the direct report. The leader has been observing the performance and/or behavior and has been getting angrier and more frustrated. The direct report has been stewing about something that caused his lack of performance or inappropriate behavior and is getting angrier and more frustrated. The leader blames the direct report, and the direct report blames the leader and/or the organization. Not much fun here.

It requires a sophisticated set of interpersonal skills *and* the ability not to let your ego get in the way to effectively address the problem. If you are not willing to own up to any behavior on your or the organization's part that has contributed to the cause of the problem, resolution is unlikely.

Dealing with De-Commitment

De-commitment occurs when there is a gap between the direct report's performance and/or behavior and the leader's expectations. These gaps occur for two primary reasons. First, a gap occurs when the person has demonstrated the ability to perform or behave appropriately, and now his performance has declined or his behavior has changed in a negative way. Second, a gap occurs when the person is unwilling to gain knowledge and/or skills that would lead to improved performance or behavior.

We see three possible strategies for addressing de-commitment:

1. Keep on doing what you've always done.
2. Catch it early.
3. Go to a supporting leadership style (high supportive/low directive leader behavior).

The first alternative—keep on doing what you've always done—will get you what you've always gotten: escalating anger, frustration, and no resolution.

The most effective alternative is to catch de-commitment early—the first time it is observed, before it gets out of control and festers. Early detection makes it easier for both you and your direct report to identify the causes and resolve them.

Just as improvements in performance prompt forward shifts in style along the curve, decreases in performance require a shift backward in leadership style along the performance curve. If a person you are delegating to starts to decline in performance, you want to find out why. So, you would move from a delegating style to a supporting style, where you listen and gather data. If both of you agree that the direct report is still on top of the situation, has an explanation for the decline in performance, and can get performance back in line, you can return to a delegating leadership style. However, if you both agree that this performance situation needs more attention from you, you now can go to a coaching style where you can provide closer supervision. Seldom, if ever, do you have to go all the way back to a directing style.

The third alternative for addressing de-commitment when the problem has been going on for some time is to cautiously go to a supporting leadership style. That may seem inappropriate to impatient managers who would like to get off the railroad tracks and head straight back to a directing leadership style. Let's explore why and how a supporting leadership style is a better choice. As you examine the following four steps, you will appreciate why we said to "cautiously" go to a supporting leadership style.

STEP 1: PREPARE

Preparation should involve selecting a specific performance or behavior that you believe you have a chance of jointly dealing with. Do not attempt to address everything at once. You can say that you will start on part of a bigger issue, but keep it manageable.

Once you have pinpointed the performance or behavior you want to focus on, gather all the facts that support the existence of the performance or behavior from your point of view. If it is a performance issue, quantify the decline in performance. If it is a behavior issue, limit your observations to what you have seen. Don't make assumptions or bring in the perceptions of others. This is a sure way to generate defensiveness, and you are unlikely to be able to specifically identify these "others" anyway. The "others" usually don't want to be named. Also, use the most recent information possible. The further back in time you go, the greater the likelihood of getting into an argument about whether the information is real.

Next, identify anything you or the organization might have done to contribute to the de-commitment. Be honest. Owning up is the most important part of moving toward resolution.

Ask yourself questions to determine your role in the situation. Were performance expectations clear? Have you ever talked to the person about his or her performance or behavior? Does the person know what a good job looks like? Is anything getting in the way of performance? Have you been using the right leadership style? Are you giving feedback on the performance or behavior? Is the person getting rewarded for inappropriate performance or behavior? (Often people in organizations are rewarded for poor behavior—that is, nobody says anything.) Is the person getting punished for good performance or behavior? (Often people get punished for good performance or behavior—that is, they do well and someone else gets the credit.) Do policies support the desired performance? For example, is training or time made available to learn needed skills?

Once you have done a thorough job of preparing, you're ready for Step 2.

STEP 2: SCHEDULE A MEETING, STATE THE MEETING'S PURPOSE, AND SET GROUND RULES

Scheduling a meeting is vital. It is important to begin the meeting by stating the meeting's purpose and setting ground rules to ensure that both parties will be heard in a way that doesn't arouse defensiveness. De-committed people with serious performance or behavior issues are very likely to be argumentative and defensive when confronted. For example, you might open the meeting with something like this:

"Jim, I want to talk about what I see as a serious issue with your responsiveness to information inquiries. I would like to set some ground rules about how this discussion proceeds so that we can both fully share our perspectives on the issue. I want us to work together to identify and agree on the issue and its causes so that we can set a goal and develop an action plan to resolve it.

"First, I would like to share my perceptions of the issue and what I think may have caused it. I want you to listen, but not respond to what I say, except to ask questions for clarification. Then, I want you to restate what I said, to make sure you understand my perspective and I *know* you understand it. When I am finished, I would like to hear your side of the story, with the same ground rules. I will restate what you said until you know I understand your point of view. Does this seem like a reasonable way to get started?"

Using the ground rules you have set, you should begin to understand each other's point of view on the performance issue at hand. Making sure that both of you have been heard is a wonderful way to reduce defensiveness and move toward resolution.

Once you have set ground rules for your meeting, you are ready for Step 3.

STEP 3: WORK TOWARD MUTUAL AGREEMENT ON THE PERFORMANCE ISSUE AND ITS CAUSES

The next step is to identify where there is agreement and disagreement on both the issue and its causes. Your job is to see if enough of a mutual understanding can be reached so that mutual problem solving can go forward. In most conflict situations, it is unlikely that both parties will agree on everything. Discover if there is sufficient common ground to work toward a resolution. If not, revisit those things that are getting in the way, and restate your positions to see if understanding and agreement can be reached.

When you think it is possible to go forward, ask, "Are you willing to work with me to get this resolved?"

If you still can't get a commitment to go forward, you need to use a directing leadership style. Set clear performance expectations and a timeframe for achieving them; set clear, specific performance standards and a schedule for tracking performance progress; and state consequences for nonperformance.

Understand that this is a last-resort strategy that may resolve the performance issue but not the commitment issue.

When you get a commitment to work together to resolve the issue, it is normal to feel great relief and assume that the issue is resolved. Not so fast.

If you or the organization has contributed to the cause of the problem, you need to take steps to correct what has been done. Anything you have done to cause or add to the problem needs to be addressed and resolved. Sometimes, you have no control over what the organization has done, but just acknowledging the organization's impact often releases the negative energy and regains the other party's commitment.

If you finally get a commitment to work together to resolve the issue, you can go to Step 4 and partner for performance.

STEP 4: PARTNER FOR PERFORMANCE

Now, you and the direct report need to have a partnering for performance discussion where you jointly decide the leadership style you will use to provide work direction or coaching. You should set a goal, establish an action plan, and schedule a progress-check meeting. This step is crucial.

Resolving de-commitment issues requires sophisticated interpersonal and performance management skills. The first try at one of these conversations is not likely to be as productive as you would like. However, if you conduct the conversation in good faith, it will reduce the impact of less-than-perfect interpersonal skills and set the foundation for a productive relationship built on commitment and trust.

Performance Review: The Third Part of a Performance Management System

The third part of an effective performance management system is **performance review**. This is where a person's performance over the course of a year is summed up. We have not included performance review in the traditional sense in our partnering for performance game plan. Why? Because we think effective performance review is not an annual event, but an ongoing process that takes place throughout the performance period. When progress-check meetings are scheduled according to development level, open, honest discussions about the direct report's performance take place on an ongoing basis, creating mutual understanding and agreement. If these meetings are done well, the year-end performance review will just be a review of what has already been discussed. There will be no surprises.

Partnering as an Informal Performance Management System

What we have been talking about so far is how partnering for performance could fit in with a formal performance management system. Unfortunately, most organizations don't have a formal performance management system. Organizational goals are usually set, but often no system is established to accomplish them. As a result, the management of people's performance is left to the discretion and initiative of individual managers. While annual performance reviews are usually done, they tend to be haphazard at best in most organizations. Managers working in that kind of environment can implement partnering for performance on an informal basis in their own areas, even when it comes to performance review. As we stated earlier, we believe that effective performance review is an ongoing process that should take place throughout the performance period, not just once a year. If managers do a good job with an informal performance review system, perhaps through their good example, a formal performance management system will emerge organization-wide, with partnering for performance as a core element.

One-on-Ones: An Insurance Policy for Making
Partnering for Performance Work

When they learn about partnering for performance, people like the concept. Yet as the saying goes, the road to hell is paved with good intentions. How can people close the gap between *learning* about partnering for performance and really *doing* it?

Margie Blanchard and Garry Demarest developed a one-on-one process that requires managers to hold 15-to-30-minute meetings a minimum of once every two weeks with each of their direct reports.[4] These are not progress-check meetings but relationship enhancement meetings. Since managers have more people to worry about than an individual contributor, the onus is on the direct report to schedule these meetings as well as set the agenda. This is when people can talk to their managers about anything they want—it's their meeting. While performance and goals may come up, people are free to share whatever is on their hearts and minds. These meetings allow managers and direct reports to get to know each other as real human beings, with hopes and fears.

In the old days, most businesspeople had a traditional military attitude that said, "Don't get close to your direct reports—you can't make hard decisions if you have an emotional attachment to your people." In today's competitive environment, rival organizations will come after your best people. Retention of key people is a competitive edge.

Too often, talented people report that their executive recruiter knows and cares more about their hopes and dreams than their manager does.

Don't let this be said about you. One-on-one meetings not only deepen the power of partnering for performance, they also create genuine relationships and job satisfaction.

Performance planning, performance coaching, and perform-ance review provide a great foundation to lead people effectively one-on-one. In the next chapter, we'll reveal the final secrets for leading people.

Chapter 8

ESSENTIAL SKILLS FOR PARTNERING FOR PERFORMANCE: THE ONE MINUTE MANAGER®

Ken Blanchard
and Fred Finch

Over the years, as we've been developing our concepts and theories, we have been firm believers in the 80/20 rule. Eighty percent of the results that leaders need to get in working with their people will come from about 20 percent of the leadership activities they could do. The three secrets of *The One Minute Manager*[1] are a perfect example. In this book, Ken Blanchard and Spencer Johnson focus on three basic concepts: one minute goals, one minute praisings, and one minute reprimands or redirection. While these three skills probably represent only 20 percent of the activities that managers could engage in, if done, they will provide them with the outcome they desire (the 80 percent). These three skills are core to effective partnering for performance.

One Minute Goal Setting

Without clear goals, Situational Leadership® II doesn't work. Why? Because development level is task-specific. As we've indicated, people are not globally enthusiastic beginners, disillusioned learners, capable but cautious performers, or self-reliant achievers. It all depends on which goal area of their job you're talking about.

The effective use of a goal-setting process is the foundation for high levels of performance, job satisfaction, and feelings of self-worth. In fact, according to research, goal setting is the single most powerful motivational tool in a leader's toolkit.[2] Why? Because goal setting operates in ways that provide purpose, challenge, and meaning. Goals are the guideposts along the road that make a compelling vision come alive. Goals energize people. Specific, clear, challenging goals lead to greater effort and achievement than easy or vague goals do.

Of course, people must have the knowledge, skills, and commitment necessary for goal achievement. That's what Situational Leadership® II focuses on. When dealing with enthusiastic beginners and disillusioned learners, it's probably better to set learning goals than outcome goals. For example, it is better for beginning golfers to hit balls into a net than on a driving range, because if the outcome of their efforts is evident, they could get discouraged after every shot. When they hit into a net, all they are focused on is whether they are learning how to swing properly. When these golfers begin to demonstrate a competent swing, they can go out onto the driving range.

If all good performance starts with a clear goal, how do you know a clear goal when you have one? For a goal to be clear, people need to know what they are being asked to do (their areas of accountability) and what good performance looks like (the performance standards by which they will be evaluated).

Areas of Accountability

To obtain desired performance from its people, an organization must first have a well-defined accountability system. For example, when people are asked what they do and their managers are asked what their people do, they both typically give widely divergent answers, particularly if the group is asked to prioritize their list of responsibilities. As a consequence, individuals in organizations often get punished for not doing what they didn't know they were supposed to do in the first place.

One of the biggest obstacles to productivity improvement stems from this problem of unclear organizational expectations and accountability. At times, the people management deems most responsible for a specific activity may be completely unaware of their role. For example, a group of restaurant managers concerned about sales were asked, "Who is responsible for generating sales in your organization?" They said the waiters and waitresses were. But when the waiters and waitresses were asked what their primary responsibilities were, their reply was consistently "Serving food and taking orders." They made no reference to selling. So, although it may seem very basic, managers need to make sure their people know what is expected of them.

Performance Standards

People must also know what good performance looks like. Performance standards provide that information. Performance standards help managers and direct reports more easily monitor performance, and they serve as a basis for evaluation. Whether an organization has clear performance standards can be determined by asking people, "Are you doing a good job?" Most people will respond by saying either "I don't know" or "I think so." If they answer "Yes, I think so," a revealing follow-up question would be "How do you know?" Typical responses are "I haven't been chewed out by my boss lately" or "No news is good news." Such answers imply that people receive little feedback on their performance until they make a mistake. This is a sad state of affairs. That habitual practice by managers leads to the most commonly used management style in the United States: leave-alone-then-zap. This style of management can also be called "sea-gull management." When a mistake is made, seagull managers fly in, make a lot of noise, dump on everyone, and fly out. Since this is the predominant style of management in organizations, it is no wonder that motivating people is a major organizational problem today.

Scott Meyers, a longtime consultant in the field of motivation, made the same point using a novel analogy.[3] Meyers was struck by the number of unmotivated people in organizations. Yet, he had never seen an unmotivated person after work. Everyone seemed to be motivated to do something.

One night when Meyers was bowling, he saw some of the "problem" employees from the last organization where he worked. One of the least motivated people—someone he remembered all too well—took the bowling ball, approached the line, and rolled the ball. The employee started to yell and jump around. Why do you think he was so happy? The answer was obvious to Meyers: The employee got a strike. He knew he had performed well—he had knocked down all the pins.

Goals Need to Be Clear

The reason people are not yelling in organizations, Meyers contended, is that, in part, it is not clear what is expected of them. To continue his bowling analogy, when people approach the alley, they notice there are no pins at the end; that is, they don't know what their goals are. How long would you want to bowl without pins? Yet, every day in the world of work, people are bowling without any pins, and, as a result, they cannot tell how well they are doing. Managers know what they want their people to do; they just don't bother to tell them. They assume people know. Never assume anything when it comes to goal setting.

Reaching Goals Requires Feedback

When managers assume that their people know what's expected of them, they are creating a second ineffective form of bowling. They put the pins up, but when the bowler goes to roll the ball, he notices there is a sheet across the alley. So when he rolls the ball and it slips under the sheet, he hears a crack but doesn't know how many pins he knocked down. When asked how he did, he says, "I don't know, but it felt good."

It's like playing golf at night. A lot of our friends have given up golf. When we ask them why, they say, "The courses are too crowded." When we suggest they play at night, they laugh, because who would ever play golf without being able to see the flags?

It's the same with watching football. How many people in this country would sit in front of their TVs on a Saturday or Sunday afternoon or a Monday night and watch two teams run up and down the field if there was no way to score?

To move toward goals, people need feedback on their performance.

The number one motivator of people is feedback on results.

Another way of emphasizing this is the slogan former colleague Rick Tate often used: "Feedback is the Breakfast of Champions." Can you imagine training for the Olympics with no one telling you how fast you ran or how high you jumped? The idea seems ludicrous, yet many people operate in a vacuum in organizations, not knowing how well they are doing on their jobs.

Money motivates people only if it is feedback on results. Have you ever gotten a raise that you were pleased with, only to find out that somebody else who you don't think works as hard as you got the same or even a better raise? Not only was that increase in money not *motivating*, it became *demotivating* once you knew it had nothing to do with results. Suddenly, it didn't matter how hard you worked.

Once managers are convinced that the number one motivator of people is feedback on results, they usually set up a third form of bowling. When the bowler goes to the line to roll the ball, the pins are up and the sheet is still in place, but now there's another ingredient in the game: a supervisor standing behind the sheet. When the bowler rolls the ball, he hears the crash of the falling pins. The supervisor holds up two fingers and says, "You knocked down two." In fact, most bosses would not phrase the feedback so positively; they would say, "You missed eight."

Performance Reviews Can Undermine Performance

Why don't managers lift the sheet so that everyone can see the pins? Because organizations have a strong tradition known as *the performance review*. We call it NIHYYSOB ("Now I have you, you S.O.B."). Sadly, many managers use the performance review as a once-a-year opportunity to get even with their people.

As we indicated in the last chapter, the performance review process is often used to spread people over a normal distribution curve, thereby categorizing them and distorting their performance. Having a set budget or percentage for a group's salary increases often encourages this practice. In most organizations, if six or seven people report to you, the practice of rating them all high—even if they all deserve it—is discouraged. For example, it doesn't take managers very long to realize that if they rate all their people high, they subsequently get rated low by *their* managers. The only way they can get rated high is if they rate some of their people low.

One of a manager's toughest jobs is deciding who gets the low ratings. Most Americans grow up with this win-lose mentality, in which some people in every group must lose. It pervades our educational system. For example, a fifth-grade teacher giving a test on state capitals would never consider making atlases available during the test to allow the students to look up the answers. Why? Because all the children would get 100 percent. Can you imagine what would happen to American education if kids who had to take vocabulary tests were allowed to keep dictionaries on their desks? There would be an uproar!

Limit the Number of Goals

Three to five goals are the ideal number on which peak performers can concentrate, according to most research.[4] You want to limit the number of goals people have to focus on and identify the few key activities that will have the highest impact and yield the greatest results. Once these goals are established, they should be written down so that they can be frequently used to compare actual behavior against targeted behavior.

Often, goal setting is considered a paperwork activity—a necessary evil in getting the job done. When this is the case, goals are filed and people go off and do whatever they want until a performance review draws near. With one minute goal setting, the philosophy is that you should keep your goals close at hand and be able to read each in a minute or less.

Good Goals Are SMART Goals

Although most managers agree with the importance of setting goals, many do not take the time to clearly develop goals with their people and write them down. As a result, people tend to get caught in the "activity trap," where they become busy doing things, but not necessarily the right things. To focus on what *is* important, you should set SMART goals with your people. SMART is an acronym for the most important factors in setting quality goals:

Specific and measurable. You don't say to somebody, "I want you to improve." You have to be specific about the area that needs improvement and what good performance looks like. Being specific reinforces the old saying, "If you can't measure it, you can't manage it." Therefore, goals have to be specific, observable, and measurable. If somebody says, "But my job can't be measured," offer to eliminate it to see if anything will be missed.

Motivating. Not every job people are asked to do will be super-exciting, but having motivating goals helps. Sometimes all people need to know is why the task is important. The "why" explains how the person's task fits in with overall job performance and the goals and objectives of the unit, division, organization, and customer. It clarifies how the task supports higher-level outcomes. People want to know that what they do makes a difference. That's motivating.

Attainable. It's a false assumption that to motivate people you have to set goals that are unattainable. What really motivates people is to have moderately difficult but achievable goals. This has been proven time and time again by setting up a version of the old ring toss game. People are asked to throw rings at a stake from any distance they choose. Unmotivated people, it has been found, stand either very close to the stake, where the goal is easily accomplished, or far away, where their chances for success are minimal. People who set goals that are too easy or too difficult don't want to be judged or held accountable. High achievers, based on classic research on achievement motivation conducted by David McClelland, find the appropriate distance from the stake through experimentation.[5] If they throw the rings from a certain spot and make most of their tosses, they move back. Why? It's too easy a goal. If they miss most of their tosses, they move forward. Why? It's too difficult a task. McClelland found that high achievers like to set moderately difficult but attainable goals—that is, goals that stretch them but are not impossible. That's what we mean by attainable.

Relevant. As we stated earlier, we believe in the 80/20 rule. Eighty percent of the performance you want from people comes from the 20 percent of the activities they could get involved in. Therefore, a goal is relevant if it addresses one of the 20-percent activities that make a difference in overall performance.

Trackable and time-bound. As a manager, you want to be able to praise progress or redirect inappropriate behavior. To do that, you must be able to measure or count performance frequently, which means you need to put a record-keeping system in place to track performance. You need to set interim goals so that you can praise people's progress along the way. That sets up day-to-day coaching. If a goal consists of completing a report by June 1, the chances of receiving an acceptable, even outstanding, report will increase if interim reports are required. Remember, good performance is a journey, not a destination. The goal is a destination. What managers have to do and what partnering for performance emphasizes is managing the journey.

One Minute Praisings

Once your people understand what they are being asked to do and what good behavior looks like, you are ready for the second key to obtaining desired performance: the one minute praising. Praising is the most powerful activity a manager can do. In fact, it is the key to training people and making winners of everyone working for you. A praising focuses on reinforcing behavior that moves people closer to their goals.

---

*Of all the keys of the One Minute Manager,
one minute praisings are the
most powerful.*

Look around your organization and see if you can "catch people doing something right." When you do, give them a one minute praising that is immediate and specific and states your feelings.

Be Immediate and Specific

For a praising to be effective, it must be *immediate and specific*. Tell people exactly what they did right as soon as possible. For example, "You submitted your report on time Friday, and it was well written. In fact, I used it in a meeting today, and that report made you and me and our whole department look good." Use examples such as "I see productivity in your department is up ten percent" or "Your report helped us win the contract with the Jones Company." Comments that are too general, such as "I appreciate your efforts," "Thank you very much," "I don't know what I'd do without you," and "Keep up the good work," are less likely to seem sincere and thus are unlikely to be effective. Instead of praising people at random, first find out what they have done right. A manager should take time to observe people's behavior and specifically praise improvements that are noticed. These informal interactions should be in addition to your progress-check meetings.

State Your Feelings

After you praise people, tell them how you feel about what they did. Don't intellectualize. State your gut feelings: "Let me tell you how I feel. I was so proud after hearing your financial report presentation at the Board of Directors meeting. I want you to know how good I feel about your being on our team. Thanks a lot." Although praisings do not take very long, they can have lasting effects.

Praisings Are Universally Powerful

Praisings drive all effective human interaction. These same concepts apply to any relationship, not only making people better managers, but also making them better parents, spouses, friends, and customers. Consider marriage, for example. In the United States, more second marriages break up than first marriages.[6] This is grimly amusing, because some people argue that success in marriage is a matter of selection—that if you could only get a second chance, you could do much better. What all this confirms is that if you had problems in one relationship, you'll probably have problems in your next relationship—*unless* you learn the basics of human interaction.

Have you ever seen a couple in love in a restaurant? When one is talking, the other is very attentive—listening, smiling, supporting. They don't seem to care if their meal ever comes.

In contrast, have you ever seen a couple in a restaurant who are not really happy together? They become impatient and agitated if their meal isn't served promptly. They may look as if they have nothing to say to each other. They may not say four sentences in two hours. Perhaps the man finally says, "How's your meal?" And the woman counters with, "Fine. How's yours?" That is the extent of their conversation. Their marriage is dead, but nobody buried it.

How do two people go from being excited over each other's words to having nothing to say? It's really quite simple. Good relationships are all about the frequency with which you catch each other doing something right.

When you first fall in love, everything is right. You seldom see the faults or limitations of your loved one. Love is blind—you see only the positive. When you decide to get married or commit to some permanency in your relationship, you often start to see things wrong with each other. You begin to say such things as "I didn't know you thought that" or "I can't believe you would do something like that." Your emphasis shifts to what's wrong with the other person, rather than what's right. The ultimate demise of a loving relationship is when you do something right and you get yelled at anyway because you didn't do it right enough. You hear things like "I shouldn't have to ask" or "You should have done it earlier."

Being Close Counts

This discussion brings up one of the important points to remember about praising: Don't wait for exactly the right behavior before praising someone. Catch people doing things approximately right. We want exactly right behavior, but if we wait for exactly right behavior before we recognize it, we'll probably never get it. We have to remember that exactly right behavior is made up of a whole series of approximately right behaviors. We all know that with animals and little people—we just forget it with big people.

For example, suppose you want to teach a child who is learning to speak to say, "Give me a glass of water, please." If you wait until the child says the whole sentence before you give her any water, the child will die of thirst. So you start off by saying, "Water! Water!" All of a sudden one day the child says "waller." You jump all over the place, hug and kiss the child, and get Grandmother on the phone so that the child can say, "Waller, waller." It wasn't "water," but it was close.

You don't want a kid going into a restaurant at the age of 21 asking for a glass of waller, so after a while you only accept the word "water," and then you go on to "please." So in training someone, you should emphasize catching that person doing something right—in the beginning, approximately right—and then gradually move him or her toward the desired behavior.

Bob Davis, former president of Chevron Chemical, has as one of his favorite mottos: "Praise progress—it's at least a moving target." What we need to do in all our interactions at work and at home is accentuate the positive and catch people doing things right, even if it's only approximately right. Let's look at child rearing for some examples.

Teenagers are a problem for many parents. Why? Before kids become teenagers, their parents think they are cute, and when cute kids do something wrong, they are usually forgiven. Cute kids are caught doing things approximately right. But the minute they become teenagers, the game changes. Their parents now will accept only perfection. They yell things like "Where have you been?" "Why didn't you do this?" "That sure was a stupid mistake." It doesn't take teenagers long to decide that they don't like hanging around at home. Why? Because their parents catch them doing things wrong more frequently than they catch them doing things right.

Why are some children so different from others? For example, "Mary is a model child. She does well in school, helps around the house, and is polite and friendly to adults. But Harry is nothing but trouble." Chances are good that Mary has been caught doing a lot of things right, whereas Harry has been caught doing things wrong.

If you are having difficulty with a spouse, child, team member, boss, or friend, how do you turn it around? You have to first ask yourself, "Do I want this relationship to work?" When you are looking for an answer, examine your gut feelings. If deep down you don't want to make the relationship work, you won't. Why? Because you have control of the qualifier—the "Yes, but." If you want to make the relationship work, you will catch the other person doing things right or approximately right. But if you don't want to make it work for whatever reason, you can easily undermine another person's best efforts to please you. No matter what that person does right, you will say, "Yes, but you didn't do this or that right."

Make Time for Praisings

We ask people all the time, "How many of you are sick and tired of all the praisings you get at work or at home? You wish they would lay off." Everybody laughs, because most of us do not naturally think of cheering each other on. Yet we all know people who carry around in their wallet or pocketbook a praising note they got years ago. It seems "gotcha" comes more easily to most of us than "well done." How do we break this pattern? Maybe we need to be more intentional about it.

You should set aside at least two hours a week for cheering people on. Write it on your calendar just as you do any other appointment. Then, use the Hewlett-Packard philosophy we discussed in the last chapter, Management by Wandering Around. Wander around your operation, catch people doing things right or approximately right—and tell them about it. Do the same with your spouse, children, and friends. At home, you may not need two hours a week, but ten minutes surely wouldn't hurt. Are you doing that much?

Try praising. You'll like catching people doing things right. It will put a spring in your step and a sparkle in your eye. And just imagine what it will do for the people you catch.

Reprimanding Versus Redirection

If one minute praisings are focused on catching people doing things right and accentuating the positive, the question that inevitably arises is, "That's all well and good. What do you do if somebody's performance is not up to snuff?"

Although the label for the third secret of the One Minute Manager is the one minute reprimand, there are actually two strategies for dealing with poor performance: one minute reprimands and redirection. A reprimand works best with people who have "won't do" or attitudinal problems. These people are winners, and they know how to do what they are being asked to do, but for some reason they're not doing it. Redirection is appropriate for people with "can't do" or experience problems. These people are learners and therefore do not yet know how to do what they are being asked to do.

If there are two different strategies for dealing with poor performance, then why is the one minute reprimand highlighted in *The One Minute Manager*? Because people generally are not very good at giving negative feedback to normally good performers. While that is still true, Ken is quick to admit that today he would probably highlight redirection. Why? Because things are changing so fast now in most fields that people's competency to do a job is often short-lived.

Ongoing learning is necessary for all of us to keep up today. As a result, there are far fewer situations where a one minute reprimand is more appropriate than redirection. That's one of the main reasons why Ken got excited about writing *Whale Done!: The Power of Positive Relationships* with one of his old writing buddies, Jim Ballard, and with Thad Lacinak and Chuck Tompkins, two long-time killer whale trainers at SeaWorld.[7] It doesn't take much intelligence to realize that it wouldn't make sense to punish a killer whale and then tell its trainers to get in the water with it. Thad and Chuck, who've been training killer whales at Sea World for over thirty years, point out that there is no negative interaction between killer whales and trainers. When a whale does something right or approximately right, a praising follows. That's why, when a whale successfully performs a trick and returns to the stage, it is greeted with a bucket of fish, a rub on its tongue, or a big hug. If the trick wasn't up to standards, when the whale returns to the stage, the trainers don't yell at it or punish it in any way. They simply give a hand signal that says to the whale, "Let me see that again." If trainers can't be positive with a whale, redirection comes into play.

Because there is a distinct difference between redirection and a reprimand, let's take a look at each separately.

One Minute Reprimands

As we said earlier, a reprimand is appropriate only for someone who has the skills to do the job but for some reason lacks the commitment. Keeping that in mind, consider the four keys to giving a reprimand:

- First, as with one minute praising, ***reprimand as soon as possible*** after an incident. Do not save up your feelings. If you "gunnysack" and store up your feelings, when you finally let go of them, they are apt to be out of proportion to the event that triggered your emotional release. The mistake—and the situation—will seem much worse than it really is. This is often the case when leaders lose their cool and start screaming at people. The longer you wait to give someone negative feedback, the more emotional it becomes. Give negative feedback as soon as possible. Doing so causes fewer problems.

• Second, **be specific**. Tell people specifically what they did wrong—for example, "John, you didn't get your report in on time Friday" or "I notice your sales were down 20 percent this quarter."

• Third, **share your feelings** about what was done. "Let me tell you how I feel about the late report, John. I'm angry because everyone else got their reports in on time, and not having your report delayed my analysis of our market position. It really frustrated me!" Don't intellectualize about what the person did wrong. It is more important to just focus on how you feel. Describe your feelings sincerely and honestly.

• Fourth—and this is probably the most important step— **reaffirm** the person. In the case of the late report, you might say: "Let me tell you one other thing. You're good. You're one of my best people. That's why I was angry about your late report. It's so unlike you. I count on you to set an example for others. That's why I won't let you get away with that late-report behavior. You're better than that."

Reprimand the Behavior, Not the Person

Many people can't understand why you would praise people after you have reprimanded them. You do it for two very important reasons. First, you want to separate people's behavior from them as individuals. That is, you want to keep the people but get rid of their poor behavior.

> *By reaffirming people after you have*
> *reprimanded them, you focus on their*
> *behavior without attacking them personally.*

Second, when you walk away after reprimanding, you want people to think about what they did wrong, not about how you treated them. If no reaffirmation is done, people who are reprimanded tend to direct their energy back to you, the reprimander. Why? Because of how they were treated. For example, many reprimands not only don't end with a praising, but end with a comment such as "And let me tell you one other thing..." and then the individual is given one last shot: "If you think you'll get that promotion, you have another thing coming."

Then, when you walk away, the one who has been reprimanded often turns to a coworker and, instead of discussing his poor performance, talks about the incident and the manager's poor behavior. That person is psychologically off the hook with his poor performance, and the manager becomes the villain.

However, if you end a reprimand with a praising, the person you reprimand is less likely to turn to a coworker and complain about you after you walk away, because you just told him how good he was. Now that person has to think about what he did wrong, not about your leadership style.

> *Many problems in life stem not from*
> *making mistakes, but from*
> *not learning from our mistakes.*

Whenever we do not learn from our mistakes, it is often because we are attacked for those mistakes. We are called names and generally are downgraded by other people who discover our mistakes—good old seagull managers.

When our self-concept is under attack, we feel the need to defend ourselves and our actions, even to the extent of distorting the facts. When people become defensive, they never hear the feedback they are getting. As a result, little learning takes place. The effective use of the one minute reprimand with someone who makes a mistake should eliminate this defensive behavior.

Remember, people are okay.
It is just their behavior that is
sometimes a problem.

The proper use of the one minute reprimand helps communicate important information necessary to get poor performance back on track.

Redirection

When people's performance isn't up to standards and they are still learning, redirection is more appropriate than a reprimand.

An effective redirection response has several key aspects:

- When people who are still learning do something wrong, the first thing you have to do is make sure they know that they have made a mistake or that a problem exists. Be specific. Share what happened clearly and without blame. For example, if a customer did not receive the correct order, the person responsible in the shipping department needs to know that.

- Second, the person being redirected needs to know the negative impact that the error caused. You might say, "One of our best customers was really upset. She needed that order for a sales presentation, and the fact that it didn't arrive on time resulted in a less-than-stellar presentation."

- Third, the manager in this situation, if appropriate, should take the blame for not making the task clear. Maybe the order was not clear. "That's my responsibility—that you get the best information possible so you can do your job right."

- Fourth, go over the task in detail and make sure it is clearly understood. "To rally from this mistake, we need to over-night exactly what the customer ordered. If necessary, we might have to get someone to hand-deliver the order. We must do everything we can to make this situation right. Let's double-check the order so that we're all on the same page."

- The final aspect of a redirection response is to express your continuing trust and confidence in the person. "I appreciate your enthusiasm and desire to learn. I still have confidence that you can be a standout in this department."

As is evident, these steps are similar to the one minute reprimand. The big difference is that redirection focuses on teaching as the person is still learning, while the reprimand is focused on getting people back to using the skills they already have. In both cases, the goal is not to tear people down, but to build them up in a way that they will return to top performance with a reprimand or continue to learn with redirection.

Praisings and Redirection Are Key to Partnering for Performance

The fourth step in partnering for performance is delivering the appropriate leadership style. Again, as a leader you are constantly looking for opportunities to move your leadership style forward so that you can eventually get to delegating. As people's performance increases, praising their progress is key to supporting their efforts. If at any time their performance stalls or moves backward, rather than reprimanding or punishing them, the best strategy is to redirect and get them back on course. As managers manage by wandering around, it behooves them to praise progress and/or redirect. That is how you teach your people the right answers, so that when they get to the final exam—the performance review—they have the best opportunity to get an A.

Where does that leave reprimands? Again, reprimands can be helpful when performance is declining because of an attitude problem, not a skill problem.

A reprimand can play a key role when de-commitment is detected early. As we discussed in the last chapter, when you have been using a delegating style with a high performer and performance begins to decline, you should quickly move back on the railroad tracks to a supporting style and gather information about the nonperformance. If you find the de-commitment is purely an attitude problem and has nothing to do with you or the organization, a well-delivered reprimand might be just the answer you need to get performance back on track.

The follow-up book to *The One Minute Manager*, *Putting the One Minute Manager to Work* by Ken Blanchard and Robert Lorber, shows practicing managers how to apply the three secrets—one minute goals, one minute praisings, and one minute reprimands or redirection—to improve performance on an ongoing basis.[8]

The Fourth Secret of the One Minute Manager

Shortly after Ken Blanchard and Spencer Johnson's *The One Minute Manager* came out, a top manager wrote to Ken and expressed how much he enjoyed the three secrets of the one minute manager. But he suggested that managers aren't always right. He insisted that managers make mistakes all the time. "I think the fourth secret of the one minute manager should be the one minute apology," he said.

That resonated with Ken, because his mother always said, "Two phrases that are not used enough in the world that could make it a better place are 'Thank you' and 'I'm sorry.'" One minute praising covered thank you, but the three secrets didn't cover I'm sorry. That's when Ken and Margret McBride decided to write *The One Minute Apology: The Way to Make Things Better*.[9]

The One Minute Apology

As with praisings, reprimands, and redirection, the one minute apology has several key aspects:

- A one minute apology *begins with surrender*. It starts with your being truthful and admitting to yourself that you've done something wrong and need to make up for it. The key here is a willingness to take full responsibility for your actions and any harm done to anyone else. Urgency is needed, and you should be very specific about what you did and how bad you feel about it.

- A one minute apology *ends with integrity*. This involves recognizing that what you did or failed to do is wrong and inconsistent with who you want to be. In the process, it is important that you reaffirm that you are better than your poor behavior and forgive yourself.

- Once these two things are done, your focus should be on the other person and how you can make amends for the harm you caused.

- Finally, nobody will ever listen to your apology if you do not commit to yourself and others to not repeat what you did wrong and express your determination to keep this commitment by changing your behavior.

What does an apology look like? Suppose at a meeting you kept interrupting a colleague, not permitting her to finish a thought. When another one of your associates pointed this out after the meeting, you had a big ah-ha, realizing that what you did was wrong and not beneficial to your team.

As soon as possible, go to the offended person and say something like "I got some feedback about how I kept interrupting you at the meeting today and not letting you finish. I want to apologize, because I recognize the truth in that feedback, and I feel bad.

When I looked in the mirror, the culprit was looking back at me. I feel awful. That's not who I want to be in the world. In fact, I think I'm better than that. I promise I will never do that again, and I wonder how I can make amends for what I did today."

History would have been rewritten if President Nixon had quickly apologized for Watergate when what happened became clear. The same holds true for President Clinton and the Monica Lewinsky incident. When President Kennedy took full responsibility for the Bay of Pigs debacle, even the press didn't have much more to talk about.

A one minute apology can be an effective way to correct a mistake you have made and restore the trust needed for a good relationship. Adding the one minute apology to goal setting, praising, reprimanding, and redirection makes partnering for performance a real give-and-take process where admitting your vulnerability can be more of a rule than an exception. Effective one-on-one leadership relationships depend on trust, and trust can occur only when we can get out of our own way and be authentic as we work with our people.

Do the leadership tools we've been discussing apply to only one-on-one relationships? Absolutely not. In the next chapter, you'll see how Situational Leadership® II facilitates the development of high performing teams. The skills you have been learning to effectively partner for performance can certainly help your team leadership.

Chapter 9

SITUATIONAL
TEAM LEADERSHIP

Don Carew,
Eunice Parisi-Carew,
and Ken Blanchard

Teams have become a major strategy for getting work done. We live in teams. Our organizations are made up of teams. We move from one team to another without giving it a thought. Consider the amount of time we spend in team settings—task forces, committees, temporary teams, cross-functional teams, and management teams. The percentage of time we spend on teams is huge. As you move up the managerial ladder, it gets even bigger. Managers typically spend between 30 and 99 percent of their time in a meeting or team setting. In *High Five!: The Magic of Working Together*, Ken Blanchard, Sheldon Bowles, Don Carew, and Eunice Parisi-Carew show that being effective in today's organizations is a team game, and without collaboration and teamwork skills, you are unlikely to be successful.[1]

Why Teams?

Teams can execute better and faster and change more easily than traditional hierarchical structures. They have the power to increase productivity and morale or destroy it. When working effectively, a team can make better decisions, solve more complex problems, and do more to enhance creativity and build skills than individuals working alone. The team is the only unit that has the flexibility and resources to respond quickly to changes and new needs that have become commonplace in today's world.

The business environment today has become increasingly competitive, and the issues it faces have become increasingly complex. As we emphasized in Chapter 4, "Empowerment Is the Key," this challenging environment has caused organizations to realize that they can no longer depend on hierarchical structures and a few peak performers to maintain a competitive advantage. The demand now is for collaboration and teamwork in all parts of the organization. Success today comes from using the collective knowledge and richness of diverse perspectives. Consequently, there has been a conscious movement toward teams as a strategic vehicle for getting work accomplished. They have become the vehicle for moving organizations into the future and for delivering quality products and services.

Teams are not just nice to have. They are hard-core units of production. However, they do provide a sense of worth, connection, and meaning to the people involved with them. Consider a story from a GE appliances manufacturing plant. After deciding to go to a team-based management structure, the plant created management teams and asked Don Carew to provide some intensive training in team development, skills, and leadership. After the first two days of training, a member of one of the teams—the assembly line representative—approached Don and said, "I want to thank you."

"You're welcome," Don replied. "But why are you thanking me?"

"Because," said the team member, "this is the first time in the 25 years I've worked in this plant that I've felt important."

Imagine how devastating it would be to your self-esteem to be ignored for 25 years.

It's a fact that people's health and well-being are directly affected by the amount of involvement they have in the workplace. A study of 12,000 male Swedish workers over a 14-year period revealed that workers who felt isolated and had little influence over their jobs were 162 percent more likely to have a fatal heart attack than were those who had a lot of influence in decisions at work and who worked in teams.[2] Data like this—combined with the fact that teams can be far more productive than individuals functioning alone—provides a compelling argument for creating high-involvement workplaces and using teams as the central vehicle for getting work done.

Virtual teams are becoming increasingly central to success. These teams face special challenges in building trust, developing effective communication, and managing attentiveness. However, there is no reason that time and distance should keep people from interacting as a team.[3] With proper management and the help of technology, virtual teams can be every bit as productive and rewarding as face-to-face teams.

Why Teams Fail

Teams are a major investment of time, money, and resources. The cost of allowing them to falter or underproduce is staggering. Even worse, a team meeting that is considered a waste of time has wide ranging effects. The energy does not dissipate as you leave, but spills into every aspect of organizational life. If people leave a meeting feeling unheard, or if they disagree with a decision made in the team, they leave angry and frustrated. This impacts the next event. The opposite effect happens when meetings feel productive and empowering—the positive energy spreads.

Based on research over the past ten years, Don Carew and Eunice Parisi-Carew found that teams fail for a number of reasons, from lack of a clear purpose to lack of training. Following are the top ten reasons they have found for a team failing to reach its potential. Being aware of these pitfalls is important so that you can avoid them in the teams in which you participate.

Top 10 Reasons Why Teams Fail

1. Lack of a sufficient charter that defines the team's purpose and how it will work together to achieve that purpose
2. Inability to decide what constitutes the work for which they are interdependent and mutually accountable
3. Lack of mutual accountability
4. Lack of resources to do the job, including time
5. Lack of effective leadership and lack of shared leadership
6. Lack of norms that foster creativity and excellence
7. Lack of planning
8. Lack of management support
9. Inability to deal with conflict
10. Lack of training on all levels on group skills

Our purpose in this chapter is not to focus on the reasons some teams fail or don't realize their potential, but rather to identify what makes teams great and to provide a pathway for helping them get there.

Characteristics of a High Performing Team

We define a team as *two or more persons who come together for a common purpose and who are mutually accountable for results.* This is what makes the difference between a team and a group. Often, work groups are called teams without developing a common purpose and shared accountability. This can lead to disappointing results and a belief that teams do not work well. A collection of individuals working on the same task are not necessarily a team. They might have the potential to be a high performing team once they clarify their purpose and values, strategies, and accountabilities.

Some teams achieve outstanding results no matter how difficult the objective. They are at the top of their class. These teams include a sports team that overcomes all odds to win a championship, a group of scientists that achieves a startling breakthrough, a volunteer group that raises an unprecedented amount of money for charity, or a product development team that comes up with a unique and innovative idea. High performing teams cross all walks of life and vary in size, complexity, and purpose.

What makes these teams different? What sets them apart and makes them capable of outperforming their peers? Although each team is unique, they all have characteristics that are shared by all outstanding teams regardless of their purpose or pursuits.

Building highly effective teams,
like building a great organization,
begins with a picture of
what you are aiming for—a target.

As we've said, if you don't know where you are headed, any road will get you there. So, it is imperative to know what a high performing team is and the elements that characterize it. We have identified seven key characteristics of all high performing teams, represented by the acronym **PERFORM.**

Purpose and values. A high performing team shares a strong sense of purpose and a common set of values. They have a compelling vision. If a team is faltering, start here to get buy-in. It is from purpose and values that mutually agreed-on goals are derived, roles are defined, and strategies are developed. As we discussed in Chapter 2, "The Power of Vision," if a team does not know who they are (purpose), where they are going (picture of the future), and what will guide their journey (values), the team will not develop. Purpose and values are the glue that holds the team together and forms the foundation of a high performing team.

Empowerment. Members of a high performing team are confident in the team's ability to overcome obstacles. They share information and knowledge and help each other. Policies, rules, and procedures enable the group to perform the task easily. Information is readily available, and people have the skills they need or at least know where to get them. They are provided opportunities for growth and performance. They have authority to act and make decisions and choices with clear boundaries. They have the autonomy, opportunity, and ability to experience their personal and collective power.

Relationships and communication. A high performing team is committed to open communication. People feel they can take risks and share their thoughts, opinions, and feelings without fear. They don't have to love each other but must respect, value, and care about each other. Listening is considered as important as speaking. Differences are truly valued. They embrace the belief that it is from differences that creativity is derived. If differences turn to conflict, the team is skilled in dealing with it in a way that maintains human dignity. Through honest, caring feedback, people are aware of their strengths and weaknesses and their impact on others, and they act in ways that build trust and acceptance. People are committed to each other both personally and professionally. They care and depend on each other. Cohesion is high.

Flexibility. High performing team members are interdependent and realize that all are responsible for team performance, development, and leadership. In a high performing team it is often difficult to determine who the leader is, because leadership shifts based on the needs at the time. The team engages in both hard work and fun. Feelings as well as opinions are valued. Members recognize the inevitability of change and adapt to changing conditions.

Optimal productivity. High performing teams generate optimal productivity, reflected in the amount and quality of the work they accomplish. A high performing team is committed to producing significant results. Productivity is the bottom line. Without results, little else matters. There is a commitment to high standards and quality. Team members take great pride in meeting deadlines, achieving goals, and getting the job done. They hold each other accountable and strive for continual improvement. They have developed effective decision and problem-solving methods to enhance creativity and participation. Everyone carries his or her weight, and everyone takes pride in team accomplishment.

Recognition and appreciation. A high performing team experiences continual positive feedback and recognition on the part of team members, the team leader, and the organization. Recognition and appreciation are powerful ways to motivate and enhance performance. The quickest way to demoralize a team and render it ineffective is for the team to produce and deliver results but not hear anything from the powers that be. Recognition reinforces behavior, builds esteem, and enhances a feeling of value and accomplishment. Both personal and team recognition are important.

Morale. Morale is the result of all of the above. If the other PERFORM elements are in place, morale is high. Members are enthusiastic about their work; they are proud of their results and feel pride in belonging to the team. The team is confident and optimistic about the future, and trust among members is high. There is a strong team spirit and a sense of unity.

PERFORM Across the Organization

Teams do not exist in a vacuum. They exist in an organizational context. For teams to be successful in organizations, the elements of PERFORM have to be present on every level (see Figure 9.1).

PERFORM ACROSS THE ORGANIZATION

	INDIVIDUAL LEVEL	TEAM LEVEL	MANAGEMENT LEVEL	ORGANIZATIONAL LEVEL
P — *Purpose and Values*	• Identifies clear goals, aligned with team purpose • Lives by team values and norms • Commits to team purpose	• Develops a common team purpose, aligned with the organizational purpose • Develops clear goals and standards • Shares common values	• Provides appropriate direction and resources to enhance team's purpose • Articulates "big picture" to help link daily tasks to organizational purpose	• Has articulated clear vision, values, and critical success factors
E — *Empowerment*	• Commits to continuous improvement and development of skills and knowledge • Offers new ideas and seeks out necessary resources	• Follows practices that support participation and risk taking	• Provides opportunities for team to perform • Provides resources and training for individual and team • Rewards informed risk taking and creativity	• Readily shares information • Supports teams through policies and procedures • Has orientation, training systems, and management support that foster learning and growth of individuals and teams
R — *Relationships and Communication*	• Shares knowledge and skills • Listens for understanding • Values differences • Values well-being of others	• Encourages different perspectives • Encourages open feedback • Openly discusses how the team is working together	• Values individual and team contributions • Fosters a climate of trust • Shares all relevant information • Models open communication and feedback	• Makes all information available • Values differences • Advocates open communication systems
F — *Flexibility*	• Provides leadership when appropriate • Considers a variety of approaches • Focuses on task as well as team development	• Encourages variety of approaches • Shares leadership • Encourages cross-training	• Supports new or different ideas • Advocates flexibility within the organization • Provides leadership for strong team culture	• Encourages creativity and innovation • Seeks individual and team ideas • Is highly responsive, has flexible and adaptive systems
O — *Optimal Productivity*	• Commits to high standards and to measuring progress • Understands and uses effective problem solving and decision making	• Meets goals and standards • Uses systematic problem solving and decision making practices	• Provides linkage with organizational outcomes • Monitors progress • Establishes boundaries and supports team decisions	• Articulates critical success factors clearly • Makes technical and material resources available • Aligns systems, policies, and practices with vision, values, and desired outcomes • Clarifies performance standards
R — *Recognition and Appreciation*	• Values and recognizes others' contributions • Recognizes and appreciates team efforts	• Celebrates individual and team contributions	• Values and recognizes individual and team accomplishments	• Rewards and celebrates team successes • Ensures that recognition, performance management, and compensation systems support teamwork
M — *Morale*	• Feels valued and respected • Is enthusiastic about being on team • Has pride in contributing • Is committed to continuous improvement	• Celebrates successes • Searches for continuous improvement	• Supports continuous improvement • Celebrates accomplishments	• Recognizes success • Provides resources • Encourages continuous improvement and renewal

Figure 9.1   PERFORM Across the Organization

PERFORM *in Action*

After reviewing the characteristics of high performing teams through the PERFORM model, most people's reaction is "Duh." If a team really had those characteristics, you'd better believe it would be effective. Let's give a couple of examples.

Ken was invited to a Boston Celtics practice during the heyday of Larry Bird, Robert Parish, and Kevin McHale. Standing on the sidelines with Coach KC Jones, Ken asked, "How do you lead a group of superstars like this?" KC smiled and said, "I throw the ball out and every once in a while shout 'Shoot!'" In observing Jones as a leader, Ken noticed he didn't follow any of the stereotypes of a strong leader. During time-outs, the players talked more than KC did. He didn't run up and down the sidelines yelling things at the players during the game; most of the coaching was done by the team members. They encouraged, supported, and directed each other.

This team really knew how to PERFORM. Everyone knew the team's *purpose and values*. They were *empowered* to get the job done. They had great *relationships* and communicated well with each other. They were *flexible* and changed plans as the need arose. They certainly got *optimum* performance. *Recognition* and support for each other was a way of life, and high *morale* was evident to everyone who watched them play.

When this low-key leader, KC Jones, retired, all the players essentially said he was the best coach they'd ever had. Why? Because he permitted everyone to lead, and that's what a team is all about.

Don Carew observed an extraordinary example of team leadership when he was working with Jim Despain and the leaders and employees of Caterpillar's Track Type Tractors (TTT) division in East Peoria, Illinois between 1994 and 1997.[4] The TTT division was in deep trouble in the early 1990s. It was losing millions of dollars a year, was the lowest-performing division in Caterpillar, and had been involved in a bitter strike. It had a culture as unyielding as the bulldozers it built, and working there was extremely undesirable. A round of downsizing and layoffs had only made things worse. Trust between management and hourly workers was at an all-time low and grievances at an all-time high.

Caterpillar's chairman had made it clear that things would have to be turned around at the division, and Despain agreed. Jim and his executive team, along with the 277 managers, examined the obstacles and possible solutions and decided to tackle one major problem category: the division culture. Together they developed a set of nine values and behaviors that would become the basis for a new culture—a culture that would transform the TTT division into a special place to work, restore the division to profitability, and make it the global leader in their industry. The nine values included trust and mutual respect as the foundation, with teamwork, empowerment, risk taking, and a sense of urgency as the pillars supporting continuous improvement, commitment, and customer satisfaction.

The Blanchard team, working with the executive team and an internal change team, redefined the role of TTT's leaders. Their new role was to be responsible for developing people, fostering a positive work environment, building and supporting teams, and empowering others. They created an extensive leadership development process that would help leaders at all levels behave in ways that would accomplish those ends and be consistent with the values. During 1995, there was a relentless focus on communicating the values, training and developing leaders and team members, and implementing teamwork across the organization.

By the end of 1996, the results were dramatic. A $250 million turnaround had occurred in less than three years. The company had returned over $100 million in profit. Quality as measured by customers improved by 16 times. Employee satisfaction moved from being the lowest in Caterpillar to being the highest. Frequent comments from employees suggested that if TTT ever went back to the old culture, they would leave. All of this was achieved by people at all levels working together in teams and by the organization creating the conditions that supported teamwork, collaboration, mutual respect, and trust.

Need we review the PERFORM model again? It was all there: clear purpose and values, empowerment, relationships and communication, flexibility, optimal performance, recognition, and morale.

Knowing where you are headed is the first step on the journey to high team performance. But just calling together a team and giving it a clear charge does not mean the team will be high performing. As we've said, team leadership is much more complicated than one-on-one leadership. Yet managers typically spend more time preparing for a meeting with one of their people than they do with their team. Often people just don't get it: Managing a high performing team takes considerable effort. It requires certain beliefs and attitudes, as well as team knowledge and skills.

Team Beliefs and Attitudes

Building and maintaining high performing teams requires two beliefs:

No one of us is as smart as all of us,
and people have a right to be involved in
decisions that affect them.

It is also essential that team members adopt community-building attitudes and perspectives.

First, team members must ***develop a learning attitude***. Everything that happens in the team is "grist for the mill." There are no failures—only learning opportunities.

Second, the team must ***build a trust-based environment***. Trust is built by sharing information, ideas, and skills. Building trust requires that team members cooperate rather than compete, judge, or blame. Trust is also built when team members follow through on their commitments. It is critical that team members communicate openly and honestly and demonstrate respect for others.

Third, the team must ***value differences***. Team members should encourage and honor differences. Different viewpoints are the heart of creativity.

Fourth, people must ***view the team as a whole***. By seeing the team as a living system rather than a collection of individuals, team members begin to think in terms of "we" rather than "you" and "me."

Team Knowledge and Skills

Working in teams also requires leaders to acquire new knowledge and skills that they may not have developed earlier. Yet, if they hope to build high performing teams, they'd better learn these skills. Just as in working with people one-on-one, it really helps team leaders if their people know what they know. Team members need to learn the same critical knowledge and skills as their team leader. For some people, that's revolutionary; when they're part of a team, they expect to be "done to." Thinking of a team as a partnership between team leader(s) and members is foreign to many.

The knowledge and skills required by all team members include the ability to observe and understand what is occurring in a team at any point in time and to intervene in ways that help the team grow and develop. Team members must ***become participant observers***. To work well in a team environment, members should develop the skill of participating and, at the same time, observing. This practice, akin to being in a movie at the same time you are watching the movie, can give team members valuable perspective. That requires knowledge about both content (what is getting done at the meeting) and process (how that is happening).

When you ask most team leaders after a meeting how it went, they want to talk about the number of agenda items they got through and the decisions that were made. They are focused only on content. Very seldom do they comment on or even seem to care about how the team interacted. They are "process clueless." We have all been part of teams or committees where we dread going to meetings. Sometimes, this is driven by an egotistical leader who loves to hear his or her own voice, is not open to feedback, and wants everyone to endorse his or her agenda for everything. If you really want to find out what's going on with teams like that, go in the halls or restrooms after a meeting, where everyone is holding "I should have said" meetings.

You can see the dilemma that many team leaders face. If you don't have the ability to observe and understand what is occurring in a team at any point in time, how in the world would you know how to intervene in ways that help the team grow and develop?

Situational Leadership® II and High Performing Teams

Building a high performing team is a journey—a predictable progression from a collection of individuals to a well-oiled system where all the PERFORM characteristics are evident.

As we mentioned earlier, Situational Leadership® II applies whether you are leading yourself, another individual, a team, or an organization. What changes are the complexity and the diagnostic dimension being analyzed to determine the appropriate leadership style. In team leadership, the focus is on Stages of Team Development.

The three keys to effective team leadership are **diagnosis**, or the ability to assess the team's needs and stage of development; **flexibility**, or the ability to use a variety of leadership behaviors; and **matching**, or the ability to use leadership behaviors that meet the team's development needs.

Stages of Team Development

All teams are unique and complex living systems. The whole of a team is different from the sum of its members. Knowing the characteristics and needs of a high performing team is critical. It gives us a target to shoot for. However, we all know that teams don't start with all of the PERFORM characteristics in place. Research over the past sixty years has consistently demonstrated that regardless of their purpose, teams, like individuals, go through a series of developmental stages as they grow.

All of these comprehensive research efforts were surprisingly consistent in their conclusions.[5] They all identified either four or five stages of development and were very similar in their descriptions of the characteristics of each stage. After a comprehensive review of more than 200 studies on group development, Lacoursiere identified five stages of team development (see Figure 9.2), which we will examine in detail in a moment:

1. Orientation
2. Dissatisfaction
3. Integration
4. Production
5. Termination

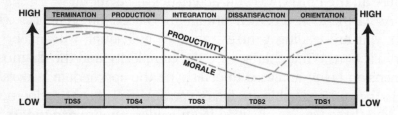

Figure 9.2   The Stages of Team Development Model[6]

Understanding these development stages and the characteristics and needs of a team in each stage is essential for team leaders and team members if they are going to be effective in building successful, productive teams.

That's what **_diagnosis_** is all about. The ability to determine a team's stage of development and assess its needs requires stepping back and looking at the team as a whole, rather than focusing on individual behaviors and needs.

Productivity and Morale

Two variables determine the team development stage: productivity and morale. **Productivity** is the amount and quality of the work accomplished. It depends on members' ability to collaborate, their knowledge and skills, clear goals, and access to needed resources. **Morale** is the team's confidence, motivation, and unity in achieving the purpose. The Stages of Team Development Model clearly illustrates how productivity and morale vary as the team progresses through the stages of development.

When a group first comes together, they can't accomplish very much. They don't even know each other. Over time, as they learn to work together, their performance should gradually increase. If that is not the case, something is seriously wrong. Either they have a leadership problem, or the skills necessary to perform well are not present in the group.

Morale, on the other hand, starts out high and takes a sudden dip. People are usually enthusiastic about being on a new team, unless they've been forced to join. The initial euphoria dissipates quickly when the reality of the difficulty of working on a team comes into play. Now you might hear people say, "Why did I agree to be on that team?" As differences are explored and people begin to break through initial frustrations and working together becomes easier, the team begins to achieve results, and morale begins to rise again. Ultimately, both morale and productivity are high as a group becomes a high performing team.

Why are high morale and high productivity the ultimate goals? The answer is quite simple. High morale with no performance is a country club, not a team. On the other hand, a high performing team with low morale will eventually stumble, and performance will fade. In other words, either one by itself cannot maintain high performance.

Diagnosing the level of productivity and morale is a clear way to determine a team's development stage and understand team needs at any point in time.

Team Development Stage 1 (TDS1): Orientation

Most team members, unless coerced, are fairly eager to be on the team. However, they often come with high, unrealistic expectations. These expectations are accompanied by some anxiety about how they will fit in, how much they can trust others, and what demands will be placed on them. Team members are also unclear about norms, roles, goals, and timelines.

In this stage, there is high dependence on the leadership figure for purpose and direction. Although there is some testing of boundaries and the central figure, behavior is usually tentative and polite. Morale is moderately high and productivity is low during this stage.

Two of us were asked to serve on a task force to study and modify the compensation system for our consulting partners. At the first meeting, we were excited and anxious to see who else was on the task force. There had been many complaints about the system, and we were eager to make positive changes. There was some apprehension about if "they" would really listen. We also wondered how much time this was really going to take, who would be in charge of the team, and how we would fit in with other members. We had no idea about how to proceed or even what our goals should be. We looked to the team leader to steer us in the right direction. These feelings of excitement, anxiety, and dependence on the leader are normal for team members at Stage 1.

The challenge at the orientation stage is to get the team off on the right foot by developing a strong team charter and building relationships and trust.

The duration of this stage depends on the clarity and difficulty of the task, as well as clarity about how the team will work together. With simple, easily defined tasks, the orientation stage may be relatively short—5 to 10 percent of the team's life. On the other hand, with complex goals and tasks, the team may spend 30 to 60 percent of its time in this stage.

Team Development Stage 2 (TDS2): Dissatisfaction

As the team gets some experience under its belt, morale dips as team members experience a discrepancy between their initial expectations and reality. Reluctant team members start out in Stage 2. The difficulties in accomplishing the task and in working together lead to confusion and frustration, as well as a growing dissatisfaction with dependence on the leadership figure. Negative reactions to each other develop, and subgroups form that can polarize the team. The breakdown of communication and the inability to solve problems result in lowered trust. Productivity increases somewhat but may be hampered by low morale.

Back to that compensation task force we mentioned earlier: While we started off with enthusiasm, we quickly realized how much hard work would be involved, the task's controversial nature, and the possibility that recommendations we would make might not be accepted. We began to experience some strong negative feelings among members, and subgroups began to form. Frustration with the team leader began to develop. We started to wonder whether this was worth our time. These feelings of questioning, doubt, and frustration are typical of team members during Stage 2.

The challenge in the dissatisfaction stage is helping the team manage issues of power, control, and conflict and to begin to work together effectively.

The amount of time spent in this stage depends on how quickly issues can be resolved. It is possible for the team to get stuck at the dissatisfaction stage and continue to be both demoralized and relatively unproductive.

Team Development Stage 3 (TDS3): Integration

Moderate to high productivity and variable or improving morale characterize a team at the integration stage. As issues encountered in the dissatisfaction stage are addressed and resolved, morale begins to rise. The team develops practices that allow members to work together more easily. Task accomplishment and technical skills increase, which contributes to positive feelings. There is increased clarity and commitment to purpose, values, norms, roles, and goals. Trust and cohesion grow as communication becomes more open and task-oriented. There is a willingness to share leadership and control.

---

*You will never, never, never have a
high performing team unless leadership
and control are shared.*

Team members learn to appreciate the differences among themselves. The team starts thinking in terms of "we" rather than "I." Because the newly developed feelings of trust and cohesion are fragile, team members tend to avoid conflict for fear of losing the positive climate. This reluctance to deal with conflict can slow progress and lead to less-effective decisions.

Back to our compensation task force: As our task force began to resolve the frustrations we had experienced in Stage 2, we began to listen more carefully and came to appreciate different points of view. We developed some initial strategies for accomplishing the task and clarified our roles and goals. In spite of the task's difficulty, working with the team now became more fun. People were getting along, and at every meeting we were more clearly seeing what needed to be done. We even began to see the possibility of some success down the road. These feelings of increasing satisfaction and commitment and the development of skills and practices to make working together easier are typical of Stage 3.

Learning to share leadership and getting past the tendency to agree in order to avoid conflict are the challenges at the integration stage.

The integration stage can be quite short, depending on the ease of resolving feelings of dissatisfaction and integrating new skills. If members prolong conflict avoidance, there is a possibility that the team could return to the dissatisfaction stage.

Team Development Stage 4 (TDS4): Production

At this stage, both productivity and morale are high and reinforce one another. There is a sense of pride and excitement in being part of a high performing team. The primary focus is on performance.

Purpose, roles, and goals are clear. Standards are high, and there is a commitment not only to meeting standards, but also to continuous improvement. Team members are confident in their ability to perform and overcome obstacles. They are proud of their work and enjoy working together. Communication is open, and leadership is shared. Mutual respect and trust are the norms. The team is flexible and handles new challenges as it continues to grow.

The compensation task force started to hum, and the completion of the job became a reality in our minds after many meetings and a careful study of alternatives. It finally began to feel as if the effort was worth it, and we were optimistic that the outcomes would be positive for both the company and the consulting partners. We all shared the responsibility for team leadership. We felt this had become a really great team to be on and were proud to be part of it. These feelings of accomplishment, pride, confidence, and a sense of unity are typical of teams who have reached Stage 4.

The challenge in the production stage is sustaining the team's performance through new challenges and continued growth. This stage is likely to continue—with moderate fluctuations in feelings of satisfaction—throughout the life of the team.

Team Development Stage 5 (TDS5): Termination

With ongoing teams, this stage is not reached unless a drastic reorganization occurs. Termination, however, does occur in ad hoc teams or temporary task forces, so team members need to be prepared for its outcomes. Productivity and morale may increase or decrease as the end of the experience draws near. Team members feel sadness or loss—or, on the other hand, a rush to meet deadlines.

After we presented the findings of our compensation task force, we realized that we had some regrets that it was all over. We had shared some tension-filled times and had developed real appreciation for each other, as well as a sense of bonding. This great group of people we had been meeting with for the last several months would probably never be together the same way again. So, while we felt proud of what we had accomplished, we also felt a sense of loss as it was coming to an end. The praise and acknowledgment from the company and the consulting partners helped.

The challenge at the termination stage is to maintain necessary productivity and morale while managing closure, recognition, and celebration. This stage may vary in duration from a small part of the last meeting to a significant portion of the last several meetings, depending on the length and quality of the team experience.

* * *

While the five stages are described as separate and distinct, there is, in fact, considerable overlap among them. Some elements of each stage can be found in every other stage. For example, just because a team is getting started (orientation stage), and needs to focus on developing a clear purpose and building a strong team charter, doesn't mean that it won't need to revisit and refine the charter in Stages 2 or 3. The team's dominant characteristics and needs, however, determine its development stage at any given time. A change in these characteristics and needs signals a change in the team's development level.

Why Is It Important to Understand the Stages of Development and Diagnose Team Needs?

The team stages of development outline a team's needs at any point in its life cycle. Understanding these needs is critically important, because it allows team leaders or members to provide leadership behaviors that will respond to those needs.

Without team leadership training, people who are called to lead a team are usually clueless about what to do. They often operate on instinct. For example, suppose an inexperienced team leader thinks that the only way to lead a team is to use a participative leadership style. From Day 1, she asks everybody for suggestions about how the team should operate. The team members think the leader should answer that question. "After all," they say, "she's the one who called the meeting." They begin to question why they joined this team. The leader, getting little response from her team, gets frustrated and wonders why she agreed to lead the team in the first place. Everyone is confused.

Without understanding the framework of team stages of development, it is only by chance that a leader's behavior matches the team's needs. Combining the Stages of Team Development Model with the Situational Leadership® II Model will help everything begin to make sense.

Team Leadership Styles

As Figure 9.3 illustrates, the leadership styles required to build a high performing organization, just as with self and one-on-one leadership, fall into varying combinations of directive and supportive behavior. Yet the focus is different when applied to teams rather than individuals. The four team leadership styles—**directing**, **coaching**, **supporting**, and **delegating**—vary in the amount of direction provided, the amount of support provided, and the amount of leadership responsibility assumed by team members.

Figure 9.3   Situational Leadership® II Team Leadership Styles

Directive Behavior with Teams

Behaviors that provide direction in teams include *organizing, educating, focusing,* and *structuring.* For example, when you first join the team, you want to know how it will be organized. What do you need to learn to be a good team member? Where will the team focus its efforts? What's the structure? Does anybody report to anybody? Who does what? When? And how?

Supportive Behavior with Teams

Behaviors that provide support in teams include *praising, involving, listening,* and *encouraging.* For example, in developing team harmony and cohesion, people want to be involved in decision making, encouraged to participate, acknowledged and praised for their efforts, valued for their differences, and able to share leadership when appropriate.

The directive and supportive behaviors of the Situational Leadership® II model provide a framework for meeting team needs and can be used by any member of the team.

Matching Leadership Style to Team Development Stage

When we combine the four leadership styles with the stages of team development, as illustrated in Figure 9.4, we have a framework for matching each stage with an appropriate leadership style.

For team leaders and members to determine the appropriate leadership style, first diagnose the team's stage of development in relation to its goal, considering both productivity and morale. Then locate the team's present stage of development on the Stages of Team Development Model and follow a perpendicular line up to the curve on the Situational Leadership® II Model. The point of intersection indicates the appropriate leadership style for the team.

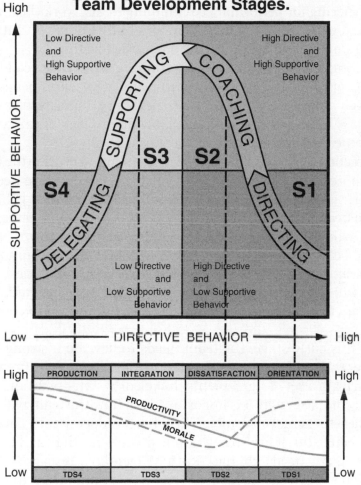

Figure 9.4   Situational Leadership® II:
Matching Leadership Style to Team Development Stages

Intervening with the appropriate leadership style at each stage will help the team progress to or maintain high performance. Matching leadership style to stages of team development, similar to partnering for performance with individuals, works best when the team leader(s) and members all know Situational Leadership® II and are doing the diagnosis together.

At Stage 1, the **orientation stage**, a **directing** leadership style is appropriate. At the beginning of any team, people are relatively eager to be there, and they have high expectations. Morale is high, but productivity is low due to lack of knowledge about the task and each other.

Direction or structure is needed at this stage to provide the information necessary to get the team started. There is some need for support, but much less than the need for task-oriented behavior. People need to be clear about the team's purpose and values and about what kind of participation is expected from them. Norms should be established around communication and accountability. There should be consensus on structure and boundaries: what work will get done and by whom, what the timelines are, what tasks are to be completed, and what skills are needed to complete them.

At this early stage, the team needs to develop a strong team charter that creates a solid foundation for the team's future work. A charter is a set of agreements that clearly states what the team is to accomplish, why it is important, and how the team will work together to achieve results. The charter documents common agreements, but it is also a dynamic document that can be modified as team needs change. Ruth Wageman's research clearly illustrates that a strong team charter is more important to superb team functioning than effective leadership.[7] Figure 9.5 shows a model for developing a charter.

Figure 9.5   The Team Charter Model

At Stage 2, the ***dissatisfaction stage***, a ***coaching*** leadership style is appropriate. The dissatisfaction stage is characterized by a gradual increase in task performance and a decrease in morale. Anger, frustration, confusion, and discouragement can arise due to the discrepancy between initial expectations and reality.

The dissatisfaction stage calls for continued high direction and an increase in support. Team members need encouragement and reassurance as well as skill development and strategies for working together and for task achievement. At this stage, it is important to clarify the big picture and reconfirm the team's purpose, values, and goals. It is also important to give the team more input on decision making. Recognizing team members' accomplishments and giving feedback on progress reassures people, encourages progress, and boosts morale. This is a good time to encourage active listening and reaffirm that the team values differences of opinion. It is also helpful at this stage to have open and honest discussions about issues such as emotional blocks and coalitions, and to resolve any personality conflicts.

At Stage 3, the ***integration stage***, a ***supporting*** leadership style is appropriate. The integration stage enjoys increasing levels of morale and harmony and a continued increase in task competence as team members learn to work together. Goals and strategies are becoming clearer or have been redefined. Negative feelings are being resolved. Confidence, cohesion, and trust are increasing but still fragile. There is a tendency to avoid conflict for fear of slipping back to the dissatisfaction of Stage 2. Team members are more willing and able to assume leadership functions.

Support and collaboration are needed in the integration stage to help team members develop confidence in their ability to work together. The team needs less direction around the task and more support focused on building confidence, cohesion, involvement, and shared leadership. This is a time to encourage people to voice different perspectives and share responsibility for leadership and to examine team functioning. Now, the focus should be on increasing productivity, and developing problem-solving and decision-making skills.

At Stage 4, the ***production stage***, a ***delegating*** leadership style is appropriate. At this stage, the team members have positive feelings about each other and their accomplishments. The quality and amount of work produced is high. Teams at this stage often need new challenges to keep morale and task focus high.

The team generally provides its own direction and support at this point and needs to be validated for that accomplishment. People are sharing leadership responsibilities, and team members are fully participating in achieving the team's goals. Continued recognition and celebration of the team's accomplishments are needed at this time, as well as the creation of new challenges and higher standards. Because the team is functioning at a high level, at this stage it is appropriate to foster decision-making autonomy within established boundaries.

At Stage 5, the **termination stage**, a **supporting** leadership style is appropriate. For teams with a distinct ending point, productivity can continue to increase, or it may go down because of a rush to complete the task. The approaching end of an important experience may also cause morale to increase or to drop from previous high levels.

Accepting and acknowledging the feelings that are present during this stage may be helpful. If a significant downturn in productivity and morale occurs, an increase in support, as well as some direction, is needed to maintain high performance.

For example, Hollywood film crews are classic models of teams that are formed for one purpose and terminated upon completion of the process. Late in the grueling filming of *The Lord of the Rings: The Two Towers*, director Peter Jackson allowed cast member Sean Astin, who played the part of Sam Gamgee, to use the film crew and equipment to make a small film about the process of making the larger film. This much shorter film, *The Long and the Short of It*, was included on the DVD. Not only did it share behind-the-scenes insights, but it also showed director Jackson participating in Astin's mini-film and, in the process, increasing morale on the set.

Stay on the Railroad Tracks

As we talked about with one-on-one leadership, it is important in developing a team to stay on the railroad tracks—to follow the leadership style curve as the team progresses through the stages of development. After developing a team charter, a team leader can't go to a delegating leadership style. He or she will go off the tracks, and the team may crash and burn. Building a high performing team requires a leader who can manage the journey from dependence to interdependence. When a great team leader's job is done, team members will say, "We did it ourselves."

Regression

Changes in leadership, task, or membership are not uncommon and can affect the team's productivity or morale. A significant change in the team often causes the team to move backward through the development stages. Careful diagnosis to determine the team's current development stage will indicate the leadership behaviors needed to deal appropriately with the regression.

The Miracle of Teamwork

When teams function well, *miracles can happen.* A thrilling and inspiring example of a high performing team is the 1980 United States Olympic hockey team.[8] Twenty young men—many of whom had never played together before—came from colleges all over the country and six months later won the Olympic gold medal, defeating the best teams in the world—including the Soviet Union, a team that had been playing together for years. No one expected this to happen. It is considered one of the greatest upsets in sports history and is labeled a miracle. When team members were interviewed, all without exception attributed their success to teamwork. The drive, commitment, cohesiveness, cooperation, trust, team effort, and a passionate belief in a common goal—"Go for the gold"—were the reason for their success.

High performing teams are the result of many factors—a clear team purpose and values, attainable goals, mutual accountability for results, trust, and team cohesion. With the right leadership, the commitment and competence of team members, and a clear team charter, team members can accomplish collectively goals that would be impossible to achieve individually.[9]

It's hard to imagine a leader being effective at the organizational level without first having some experience as a situational team leader. After all, organizational leaders are overseeing a number of teams, departments, and/or divisions. Our next chapter focuses on organizational leadership.

Chapter 10

ORGANIZATIONAL LEADERSHIP

Pat Zigarmi, Ken Blanchard, Drea Zigarmi,
and Judd Hoekstra

Just as team leadership is more complicated than one-on-one leadership, leading an entire organization is more complicated than leading a single team. Why? Because organizational leadership is all about leading change, and managing a change is chaotic and messy.

Today we live in "permanent whitewater." What do we know about whitewater? It's exhilarating and scary! You often have to go sideways or upside down to go forward. The flow is controlled by the environment. There are unseen obstacles. Occasionally it's wise to use an eddy to regroup and reflect, but eddies are often missed because whitewater seems to create its own momentum.

The Importance of Managing a Change

Once there was a time when you could experience change and then return to a period of relative stability. In that era, as things settled down, you could thoughtfully plan and get ready for another change. Kurt Lewin described these phases as unfreezing, changing, and refreezing. The reality today is that there is no refreezing. There's no rest and no getting ready.

In the heat of this chaos, it's hard for people to maintain perspective. The situation reminds us of the story about the little girl who comes home from school one day and asks her mother (today it certainly could be her father), "Why does Daddy work so late every night?" The mother gives a sympathetic smile and replies, "Well, honey, Daddy just doesn't have time to finish all his work during the day." In her infinite wisdom the little girl says, "Then why don't they put him in a slower group?" Alas, there are no slower groups. Constant change is a way of life in organizations today.

Mark Twain once said, "The only person who likes change is a baby with a wet diaper." Like it or not, in the dynamic society surrounding today's organizations, the question of whether change will occur is no longer relevant. Change will occur. That is no longer a probability; it is a certainty.

The issue is, how do managers and leaders cope with the barrage of changes that confront them daily as they attempt to keep their organizations adaptive and viable? They must develop strategies to listen in on the conversations in the organization so that they can surface and resolve people's concerns with change. They have to strategize hard to lead change in a way that leverages everyone's creativity and ultimate commitment to working in an organization that's resilient in the face of change.

Why Is Organizational Change So Complicated?

Consider what happens when someone takes a golf lesson. The instructor changes the golfer's swing in an effort to improve his score. However, golfers' scores typically get worse while they are learning a new swing. It takes time for golfers to master a new swing and for their scores to improve. Now, think about what happens when you ask each member of a team of golfers to change their respective swings at the same time. The cumulative performance drop is larger for the team than it is for any one golfer.

The same performance drop occurs in organizations where large numbers of people are asked to make behavior changes at the same time. When one person on a team is learning a new skill, the rest of the team can often pick up the slack and keep the team on track. However, when everyone is learning new skills, who can pick up the slack?

When a change is introduced in an organization, an initial drop in organizational performance typically occurs before performance rises to a level above the prechange level. Effective change leaders, being aware of this and understanding the process of change, can minimize the drop in performance caused by large numbers of people learning new behaviors at the same time. They can also minimize the amount of time to achieve desired future performance. Furthermore, they can improve an organization's capacity to initiate, implement, and sustain successful changes. That's exactly what we hope you will be able to learn from this chapter.

When Is Change Necessary?

Change is necessary when there is a discrepancy between an actual set of events—something that is happening right now—and a desired set of events—what you would like to happen. To better understand where your organization might be in relation to needed change, consider the following questions:

- Is your organization on track to achieve its vision?
- Are your organization's initiatives delivering the desired outcomes?
- Is it delivering those outcomes on time?
- Is it delivering those outcomes on budget?

- Is your organization maintaining high levels of productivity and morale?
- Are your customers excited about your organization?
- Are your people energized, committed, and passionate?

If you found it difficult to say yes to these questions, your focus on leading change should be more intense.

Most managers report that managing change is not their forte. In a survey of 350 senior executives across 14 industries, 68 percent confirmed that their companies had experienced unanticipated problems in the change process.[1] Furthermore, research indicates that 70 percent of organizational changes fail, and these failures can often be traced to ineffective leadership.

Change Gets Derailed or Fails for Predictable Reasons

Our research and real-world experience have shown that most change efforts get derailed or fail for predictable reasons. Many leaders don't recognize or account for these reasons. As a result, they make the same mistakes again and again. As is often said:

> *Insanity is doing the same things over and over and expecting different results.*

Fortunately, there is hope. By recognizing the reasons change typically gets derailed or fails, leadership can be proactive, thereby increasing the probability of success when initiating, implementing, and sustaining change.

Predictable Reasons Why Change Efforts Typically Fail

1. People leading the change think that announcing the change is the same as implementing it.
2. People's concerns with change are not surfaced or addressed.
3. Those being asked to change are not involved in planning the change.
4. There is no compelling reason to change. The business case is not communicated.
5. A compelling vision that excites people about the future has not been developed and communicated.
6. The change leadership team doesn't include early adopters, resisters, or informal leaders.
7. The change isn't piloted, so the organization doesn't learn what's needed to support the change.
8. Organizational systems and other initiatives aren't aligned with the change.
9. Leaders lose focus or fail to prioritize, causing "death by 1,000 initiatives."
10. People are not enabled or encouraged to build new skills.
11. Those leading the change aren't credible—they undercommunicate, give mixed messages, and do not model the behaviors the change requires.
12. Progress is not measured, and no one recognizes the changes that people have worked hard to make.

continues

13. People are not held accountable for implementing the change.
14. People leading the change fail to respect the power of the culture to kill the change.
15. Possibilities and options are not explored before a specific change is chosen.

When most people see this list, their reaction depends on whether they have usually been the target of change or the change agent. Targets of change frequently feel as though we have been studying their organization for years, because they have seen these reasons why change fails in action, up close and personal. The reality is that while every organization is unique in some ways, they often struggle with change for the same reasons.

When change agents look at this list, they get discouraged, because they realize how complicated implementing change can be and how many different things can go wrong. Where should they start? Which of the fifteen reasons why change fails should they concentrate on?

Over the years it has been our experience that if leaders can understand and overcome the first three reasons why change typically fails, they are on the road to being effective leaders of change.

Focus on Managing the Journey

In working with organizations for more than three decades, we have observed a leadership pattern that sabotages change. Leaders who have been thinking about a change for a while know why the change needs to be implemented. In their minds, the business case and imperative to change are clear. They are so convinced the change has to occur that, in their minds, no discussion is needed. So they put all their energy into announcing the change and very little effort into involving others and managing the journey of change. They forget that:

> *Effective organizational leadership is more about managing the journey of change than announcing the destination.*

In Situational Leadership® II terms, using a directing style 1, these leaders tell everybody what they want to have happen and then disappear, using an inappropriate delegating style 4—expecting the change to be automatically implemented. Unfortunately, that never happens. They have gotten off the railroad track. As a result, the change gets derailed. Why?

Change gets derailed because people know they can outlast the announcement, or at least the person making the announcement. Because they haven't been involved up to this point, they sense that the organization is concerned only with its own self-interests, not with the interests of everyone in the organization. Change that is done to people creates more resistance. The moment there's vocal resistance, the people leading the change break ranks. The minute they do, their lack of alignment signals that there's no need for others to align to the change, because it's going nowhere.

A poor directing style 1, followed by an inappropriate delegating style 4—announcing the change and then abdicating responsibility for the change—means that the change will never be successfully implemented. Instead, take the time to respectfully and thoughtfully listen for and respond to the concerns people have about the change.

Surfacing and Addressing People's Concerns

As we mentioned earlier, Situational Leadership® II applies whether you are leading yourself, another individual, a team, or an organization. In the self and one-to-one context, the leader diagnoses the competence and commitment of a direct report on a specific task. In the team context, a leader diagnoses the team's productivity and morale. In the organizational context, the focus is on diagnosing the predictable and sequential stages of concern that people go through during change.

A U.S. Department of Education project originally conducted by Gene Hall and his colleagues at the University of Texas[2] suggests that people who are faced with change express six predictable and sequential concerns:

1. Information concerns

2. Personal concerns

3. Implementation concerns

4. Impact concerns

5. Collaboration concerns

6. Refinement concerns

People going through a change often ask questions that give leaders clues about which stage of concern they are in. Most of the time, the people managing a change don't hear these questions because there are no forums for people to express them. If people are not asking questions similar to those discussed next, the concerns may have been addressed appropriately, or people may be demonstrating what is considered to be covert or overt resistance to the change. In reality, most people—"resisters" or not—are simply seeking answers to legitimate questions, albeit not always in a constructive manner.

Let's look at each stage of concern and the questions people are asking themselves and their peers.

STAGES OF CONCERN

Figure 10.1   The Stages of Concern Model

Stage 1: Information Concerns

At this stage, people ask questions to get information about the change. For example: What is the change? Why is it needed? What is wrong with the way things are now? How much and how fast does the organization need to change?

People with information concerns need the same information used by those who made the decision to move forward with the change. They don't want to know if the change is good or bad until they understand it. Assuming that the rationale for change is based on solid information, share this information with people, and help them see what you see. Remember, in the absence of clear, factual communication, people tend to create their own information about the change, and rumors become facts.

In a recent SAP[3] implementation where the change leadership team had done a good job explaining the business case, people said:

"There will be fewer errors with a single data entry. It will save money because we will eliminate double entries. There will be fewer manual steps and more functionality/collaboration across work groups. It will be ten times easier to access information. In the long run, it will save time because things will be done in the background. It will eliminate redundancy."

Their information concerns were largely answered by the data the leadership team provided them through multiple vehicles.

Stage 2: Personal Concerns

At this stage, people ask questions about personal concerns. For example: How will the change impact me personally? What's in it for me to change? Will I win or lose? Will I look good? How will I find the time to implement this change? Will I have to learn new skills? Can I do it?

People with personal concerns want to know how the change will play out for them. They wonder if they have the skills and resources to implement the change. As the organization changes, existing personal and organizational commitments are threatened.

These personal concerns have to be addressed in such a way that people feel they have been heard. As Werner Erhard often said, "What you resist, persists." If you don't permit people to deal with their feelings about what's happening, these feelings stay around. The corollary to this principle is that *if you deal with what is bothering you, in the very process of dealing with your feelings, the concerns often go away*. Have you ever said to yourself, "I'm glad I got that off my chest?" If so, you know the relief that comes from sharing your feelings with someone. Just having a chance to talk about your concerns during change clears your mind and stimulates creativity that can be used to help rather than hinder change efforts. This is where listening comes in. Leaders and managers must permit people to express their personal concerns openly, without fear of evaluation, judgment, or retribution.

Personal concerns are the most often ignored
stage of concern during a change process.

In some cases, personal concerns will not be resolved to an individual's satisfaction, but the act of listening to these concerns typically goes a long way toward reducing resistance to the change effort.

If you don't take time to address individual needs and fears, you won't get people beyond this basic level of concern. For that reason, let's look at some of the key personal concerns people often have with regard to change.

People are at different levels of readiness for change. Although almost everyone experiences some resistance to change, some individuals may quickly get excited by an opportunity to implement new ideas; others need some time to warm up to new challenges. This doesn't mean there's any one "right" place to be on the readiness continuum; it just means that people have different outlooks and degrees of flexibility about what they've been asked to do. Awareness that people will be at different levels of readiness for change can be extremely helpful in effectively implementing any change effort. It helps you identify "early adopters" or change advocates who can be part of your change leadership team. This awareness will help you reach out to those who appear to be resisting the change. Their reasons for resisting may represent caution, or they could be clues to problems that have to be resolved if the change is to be successfully implemented.

People initially focus on what they have to give up. People's first reactions to a suggested change often tend to be a personal sense of loss. What do we mean by "losses"? These include, among other things, the loss of control, time, order, resources, coworkers, competency, and prestige. To help people move forward, leaders need to help them deal with this sense of loss. It may seem silly, but people need to be given a chance to mourn their feelings of loss, perhaps just by having time to talk with others about how they feel. Remember, what you resist persists. Getting in touch with what you think you will be losing from the change will help you accept some of the benefits.

Ken Blanchard and John Jones, cofounder of University Associates, worked with several divisions of AT&T in the early 1980s during the breakup of the corporation into seven separate companies.[4] When they announced it, the leaders of this change started out by talking about the benefits. Ken and John realized that nobody could hear these benefits at that time, because people's personal concerns had not been dealt with. To resolve this, they set up "mourning sessions" throughout these divisions where people could talk openly about what they thought they would have to give up with this change. The following were the biggest issues that surfaced:

Loss of status. When you asked people at that time who they worked for, their chests would puff out as they said, "AT&T." It just had a much better ring to it than "Jersey Bell" or "Bell South."

Loss of lifetime employment. A classmate of Ken's, after he graduated from Cornell, got a job with AT&T. When he called home to tell his mother, she cried with joy. "You're set for life," she said. In those days, if you got a job with AT&T, the expectation was that you would work for them for thirty or thirty-five years, have a wonderful retirement party, and then ride off into the sunset. In these days of constant change, people have personal concerns about long-term employment.

Ken and John found that after people had expressed their feelings about these kinds of losses, they were much more willing and able to hear the benefits of divestiture.

People feel alone even if everyone else is going through the same change. When change hits, even if everyone around us is facing the same situation, most of us tend to take it personally: "Why me?" The irony is that for the change to be successful, we need the support of others. In fact, we need to ask for such support. People are apt to feel punished when they have to learn new ways of working. If change is to be successful, people need to recruit the help of those around them. We need each other. This is why support groups work when people are facing changes or times of stress in their lives. They need to feel that their leaders (partners), coworkers, and families are on their side in supporting the changes they need to make. Remember, you can't create a world-class organization by yourself. You need the support of others, and they need your support, too.

People are concerned that they won't have sufficient resources. When people are asked to change, they often think they need additional time, money, facilities, and personnel. But the reality today is that they will have to do more with less. Organizations that have downsized have fewer people around, and those who are around are being asked to accept new responsibilities. They need to work smarter, not harder. Rather than providing these resources directly, leaders must help people discover their own ability to generate them.

People can handle only so much change. Beyond a few changes—or even only one, if the change is significant—people tend to get overwhelmed and become immobilized. That's why it's probably not best to change everything all at once. Choose the key areas that will make the biggest difference.

Whatever you do, make sure people have some success experiences to build on before implementing more change.

In the SAP implementation referenced earlier, what personal concerns were expressed, and how were they addressed? In interviews, people said:

"I saw the databases yesterday and realize I don't have to do anything right now. It's less intimidating now that I've been able to play with it a little. I'm worried about the timing—the 'go live' date is in the middle of everything else. It will definitely take more time. I'm concerned that it will be hard to learn and use. I don't think my team leader can speak for us. She doesn't have a good-enough view of our day-to-day work. I hope there will be one-on-one support, because the training won't create the sense of security I'll need to be able to use the system confidently. If things run smoother, what will we do with our time? We have to answer the question 'What does this mean for me?' now. I can't do this and my real job at the same time. When this project is over, I'll have to go back and fix everything else."

Once people feel that their personal concerns have been heard, they tend to turn their attention to how the change will really shake out. These are called implementation concerns.

Stage 3: Implementation Concerns

At this stage, people ask questions about how the change will be implemented. For example: What do I do first, second, third? How do I manage all the details? What happens if it doesn't work as planned? Where do I go for help? How long will this take? Is what we are experiencing typical? How will the organization's structure and systems change?

People with implementation concerns are focused on the nitty-gritty—the details involved in implementing the change. They want to know if the change has been tested. They know the change won't go exactly as planned, so they want to know "Where do we go for technical assistance and solutions to problems that arise as the change is being implemented?" People with implementation concerns want to know how to make the best use of information and resources. They also want to know how the organization's infrastructure will support the change effort (the performance management system, recognition and rewards, career development).

In the SAP implementation referenced earlier, implementation concerns such as these were voiced:

"I'm concerned that people will hold onto their pet systems. Some other applications may survive, and we'll end up with redundant systems. We don't have the hardware to run the software. I'm concerned that there won't be enough time to clean up the data or verify the new business processes we've designed. I want to touch it now, sooner rather than later. We need more information about what we can expect and when we can give suggestions. I could really use a timeline—what I've seen has been too detailed or too sparse. I need to know when I'll be involved/crunched. Will people really be held accountable for using the new system?"

Stage 4: Impact Concerns

People at this stage ask questions about the change's impact. For example: Is the effort worth it? Is the change making a difference? Are we making progress? Are things getting better? How?

People with impact concerns are interested in the change's relevance and payoff. The focus is on evaluation. This is the stage where people *sell themselves* on the benefits of the change based on the results being achieved. This is also the stage where leaders lose or build credibility for future change initiatives. If the change doesn't positively impact results—or if people don't know how to measure success—it will be more difficult to initiate and implement change in the future. Conversely, this is the stage where you can build change leaders for the future.

Stage 5: Collaboration Concerns

People at this stage ask questions about collaboration during the change. For example: Who else should be involved? How can we work with others to get them involved in what we are doing? How do we spread the word?

People with collaboration concerns are focused on coordination and cooperation with others. They want to get everyone on board because they are convinced the change is making a difference. During this stage, get the early adopters to champion the change and influence those who are still on the fence.

Stage 6: Refinement Concerns

People at this stage ask questions about how the change can be refined. For example: How can we improve upon our original idea? How can we make the change even better?

People with refinement concerns are focused on continuous improvement. During the course of an organizational change, a number of learnings usually occur. As a result, new opportunities for organizational improvement often come to the surface at this stage.

Impact, collaboration, and refinement concerns were barely audible in our SAP example, since it was still being planned. But we heard the following:

"We expect a drop in productivity when we go live. We have to begin to define who owns which work processes and who upstream/downstream needs to change when we go live. SAP isn't just the implementation of new technology; it's business process redesign. We have to build the linkages and do the data conversions now. The experienced SAP users in the company haven't been tapped. I'm concerned we'll ship late when we make the conversion. Exceptions to usual flows are not being anticipated. Old-timers won't be able to take the shortcuts they are used to.

Real-time processing will help us eventually, but at first it will add time. It's important to be thinking about integration across all processes now. I'm sure things will get worse in the first few weeks. What will the next phases focus on?"

* * *

While dealing with people's concerns about change may seem like a lot of hand-holding, each stage of concern can be a major roadblock to the change's success. Since the stages of concern are predictable and sequential, it is important to realize that, at any given time, different people are at different stages of concern. For example, before a change is announced, the leaders of the change often have information that others in the organization don't. In addition, these change leaders typically have figured out how the change will affect them personally and even have gone so far as to formulate an implementation plan before others in the organization are even aware of the proposed change. As a result, the change leaders have often addressed and resolved information, personal, and implementation concerns; now they are ready to address impact concerns by communicating the change's benefits to the organization. The rest of the organization, however, still has not had a chance to voice their concerns. As a result, they will not be ready to hear about the change's benefits until their information, personal, and implementation concerns have been addressed.

Organizational Leadership Styles

If a leader can diagnose people's stage of concern, the leader can respond by communicating the right information at the right time to address and lower or even resolve these concerns. This requires the flexibility to respond differently to the concerns that people have going through change.

Resolving concerns throughout the change process builds trust in the leadership team, puts challenges on the table, gives people an opportunity to influence the change process, and allows people to refocus their energy on the change.

To help people resolve the questions and concerns they have at each stage of the change process, it is most helpful to respond with the right combination of direction and support. By doing so, the questions are answered, and people are prepared to move to the next stage of change. Not addressing the questions will hold people back and delay, if not stop, the process of moving forward. It is here that Situational Leadership® II can be used by leaders and team members alike to deliver the leadership style that is needed at the right time, thus keeping the process moving forward.

The leadership styles required still fall into varying combinations of directive and supportive behavior, and yet the focus is different when applied to organizations rather than to self, individuals, or teams.

Directive Behavior for Organizational Change

Behaviors that provide direction in leading organizations are primarily related to *focusing energy on performance and making the change happen.* These directive behaviors, when applied to change leadership, help define and prioritize the changes required of the organization. This includes explaining the business case for the change. In other words, why are we doing this? People also want to know who will be leading the change and whether they will be consulted or involved. Once again, a clear vision is important here so that people can see where the organization is headed and can determine whether they fit into this picture of the future. They also want to see the implementation plan. They'll want direction about test-driving the change. They'll want to know how resources will be deployed. Leaders providing appropriate direction must see that the organizational structure and systems are aligned to support the desired change. Finally, direction also involves holding everyone accountable for making the change.

Supportive Behavior for Organizational Change

Behaviors that provide support in leading organizations are primarily related to *facilitating the change process and inspiring everyone to work together.* These supportive behaviors, when applied to the organization, help demonstrate that the change leadership team is passionately committed to the change. They also make sure that people's concerns are surfaced and heard. The key here is involvement, involvement, and more involvement. Buy-in and cooperation are increased when change leaders listen to and involve others at each step of the change process. This means sharing information broadly across the organization, asking for input, sponsoring pilots, celebrating small successes, and recognizing people who are changing.

Situational Leadership® II and Change

New work by Patricia Zigarmi, Ken Blanchard, Drea Zigarmi, and Judd Hoekstra on Situational Leadership® II and Change provides guidance for matching leadership style to people's concerns.

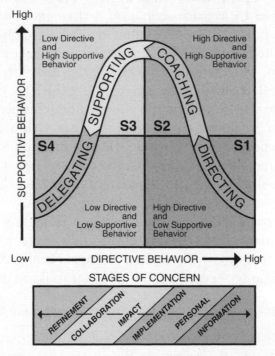

Figure 10.2   The Organizational Change Model

For Information Concerns, Use Leadership Style 1: Directing

When a change is introduced, people lack knowledge about it but tend to have naively high morale. They wonder what it's all about. They have information needs: "What will we be doing differently?" People need direction and focus much more than support or inspiration. To guide the process, leaders should identify desired outcomes and share an image of what successful change would look like. They need to describe what is and what could be. Meeting people's information needs means providing an action plan to reduce the gap between reality and people's idealized concept of the change. It is important to share detailed information that clarifies where the organization is now and where it is going. Effective leaders using the directing style provide credible role models. They use creative methods for leading the change by putting people face-to-face with data about the need to change and allowing people to reach their own conclusions.

For Personal Concerns, Use Leadership Style 2: Coaching

As information is shared and knowledge increases, people realize they need to develop new skills. Anxiety increases. They want to know: "How will the change affect me personally? Will I be successful?" People still need direction and focus, but there is a growing need for support and engagement.

Leaders can help people with personal concerns about the change by providing forums for team members to say what's on their minds. It is important at this stage to provide encouragement and reassurance. Leaders should continue to explain to team members why the change is important and provide consistent messages about the organization's vision, goals, and expectations. They should ask people what it would take for them to see themselves as part of the future. They should create vehicles for early adopters in the organization and users of the change outside the organization to influence peer to peer. They should also provide resources that help resolve personal concerns—clear goals, time, management support, and coaching.

For Implementation Concerns, Use Leadership Style 2: Coaching

After personal concerns have been dealt with, people begin to question whether enough planning has been done. They can often see what hasn't been done quicker than the people leading the change can, because they are closer to day-to-day reality. This is the time to set up small experiments, tests, or pilots to learn what still needs to be done. This is the time to broadly involve others—asking them to flesh out a robust implementation plan with you. This is the time to go forward with resisters to learn why they are resisting (beyond personal concerns). This is the time to increase the frequency of contact between change advocates and early adopters and people who are neutral. People still need both direction/focus and support/engagement to address their implementation concerns.

Leaders can help people through this phase in the change process by working to align systems—performance planning, tracking, feedback, and evaluation systems—with the change. They can offer perspective about how long the change should take and whether performance is on track. Leaders can boost morale by walking the talk, modeling the behaviors they expect of others—openness, transparency, flexibility, responsiveness, and resilience. Leaders can also address discouragement by providing individual training and coaching on how to implement the change, not mass training. By demonstrating that they want to listen and by responding honestly to the questions people raise, leaders build trust. At this stage, it is equally important to look for small wins, recognize progress, and share excitement and optimism about the change.

For Impact Concerns, Use Leadership Style 3: Supporting

As the third stage of concern winds down, people begin to see the payoff in using their new skills. There's a tipping point. There's some momentum—but only if information, personal, and implementation concerns have been surfaced and resolved and only if people have been asked to shape the change they are being asked to make. They begin to feel more confident that they will succeed. They want to know: "How are we doing on our change journey? Can we measure our progress to date?" The need for direction and focus can decline, but people continue to need support, engagement, and inspiration to let them know that progress is being made.

At this stage of the change, leaders and team members need to collect and share information and success stories. By telling stories, they can anchor the change in the company's culture. Working together, leaders and team members can solve problems and remove barriers or obstacles to implementing the change. It is important at this stage for leaders to encourage people to keep up their effort and desire to change.

For Collaboration Concerns, Use Leadership Style 3: Supporting

When people are firmly in the final stages of the change process, they can clearly see that their efforts are paying off, and they want to expand the positive impact on others. They begin to have more ideas that they want to share with others. The question on their minds is "Who else should be involved in our change effort?" They need very little direction and focus but continue to need support and inspiration to encourage them to use the new talents they have developed and to leverage the success they have had.

The focus now should be on encouraging teamwork and interdependence with other teams. Leaders can support the change by cheerleading the improvements in the team's performance and encouraging people to take on even greater challenges.

For Refinement Concerns, Use Leadership Style 3: Supporting, Blending into Style 4: Delegating

The destination is now in sight. People know new ways to behave and how to work in the changed environment. They are ready to ask questions such as "Can we identify new challenges and think of new ways to do things? Can we leverage what we've done so far?" The need for both direction/focus and support/inspiration is declining. This is where integration of everything they have learned during the change journey occurs.

Team members and leaders at this point need to support continuous improvement and innovation by the organization. They should encourage each other to continue to challenge the status quo and to explore new options and possibilities.

* * *

As teams reach the destination of the desired change, there is less and less need for either directive or supportive behaviors from any one team member or leader. Because the destination has been reached, focus and inspiration come from the team members and leader functioning as a collaborative unit. Their only remaining concern—which is now more of a desire and a commitment—is to keep the change alive and thriving.

Involvement and Influence in Planning the Change

As we have been emphasizing, once a leader has diagnosed people's stages of concern, the leader must learn to use the appropriate change strategy and corresponding behaviors to address the specific concerns people have in each stage of organizational change. Doing so significantly increases the probability of implementing successful change, because it expands opportunities for involvement and influence.

People often resent change when they have no involvement in how it should be implemented. So, contrary to popular belief, people don't resist change—they resist being controlled.

When leaders expand people's involvement and influence during a change, there is more buy-in for the change, because people are less likely to feel they are being controlled. When leaders expand opportunities for involvement and influence, they get a chance to hear people's concerns. When they've heard the concerns, they can often resolve them. This builds trust and increases the credibility of the change leadership team.

In this chapter, we have focused on the first three Predictable Reasons Why Change Efforts Typically Fail.

Combining Situational Leadership® II with the concerns people have about change gives leaders the necessary guidance not only to stay on the tracks and manage the journey to successful change, but also to surface and address people's concerns and involve them in planning the change. In the next chapter, we introduce a Change Strategy model that defines eight change leadership strategies. This will be helpful for overcoming the remaining reasons on the list of Reasons Why Change Efforts Typically Fail.

Chapter 11

STRATEGIES FOR MANAGING A CHANGE

Pat Zigarmi and Judd Hoekstra

Leaders often get overwhelmed when they have to implement change. In many ways, they feel caught in a lose-lose proposition. If they try a necessary change, they risk unleashing all kinds of pent-up negative feelings in people. The resisters are seen as troublemakers trying to ruin something good. On the other hand, if leaders don't constantly drive change, their organization will become obsolete, and everyone will lose their jobs. It's been said that if you don't change, you are dying.

Add to that lose-lose perspective a glance at the list of fifteen Predictable Reasons Why Change Efforts Typically Fail, which we discussed in the last chapter, and leaders could become immobilized around change. That's why Pat Zigarmi and Judd Hoekstra developed a Change Stategy Model—to make the seemingly complicated simple (see Figure 11.1).[1]

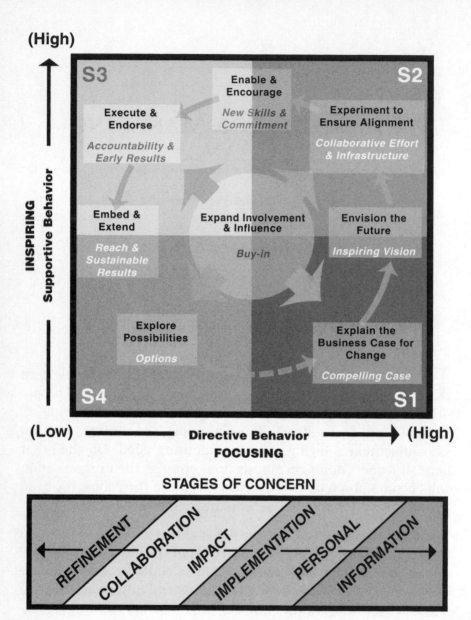

Figure 11.1   The Change Strategy Model

Eight Change Leadership Strategies

In Chapter 10, "Organizational Leadership," we focused on the first three predictable reasons why change efforts typically fail: people leading the change think that announcing the change is the same as implementing it; people's concerns with change are not surfaced or addressed; and those being asked to change are not involved in planning the change.

The Change Strategy Model defines eight change leadership strategies and their respective outcomes. While these strategies are integrated with the six stages of concern, they focus on the remaining twelve reasons why change efforts typically fail. They also describe a process for managing change that differs dramatic-ally from how change is introduced in most organizations.

Strategy 1: Expand Opportunities for Involvement and Influence

Outcome: Buy-In

As the Change Strategy Model shows, the first change leadership strategy, **Expand Opportunities for Involvement and Influence**, must be used consistently throughout the change process. It's at the heart of Blanchard's Change Strategy Model.

The core belief of our approach to leading organizational change is that the best way to initiate, implement, and sustain change is to increase the level of influence and involvement from the people being asked to change, surfacing and resolving concerns along the way. This was a key strategy in the last chapter, when we discussed dealing with the first three reasons why change efforts typically fail. Without this strategy, you cannot achieve the cooperation and buy-in you need from those responsible for making the changes you've proposed.

*Which of the following are you more likely
to commit to: a decision made by others
that is being imposed on you, or a decision
you've had a chance to provide input on?*

What may seem obvious to you isn't obvious to many leaders trying to implement organizational changes. They believe changes will be implemented much faster if they make quick decisions, and it is quicker to make decisions with fewer people providing input into the decision-making process. *While it is true that decisions can be made faster when fewer people are involved, faster decisions do not usually translate into faster and better execution.* The "top-down, minimal involvement" leadership approach ignores the critical difference between compliance and commitment. People may comply with the new directive for a short time until the pressure is off and then return to old behavior.

Providing opportunities for involvement and influence produces long-term, sustainable commitment to a new way of doing business, rather than short-term compliance. Keep Figure 11.2 in mind as you think about how much you want to involve people in the change process: Resistance increases the more people sense that they cannot influence what is happening to them.

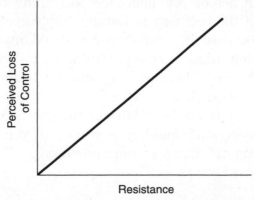

Figure 11.2   Perceived Loss of Control Increases Resistance to Change

If people aren't treated as if they are smart and would reach the same conclusion about the need to change as the change leadership team, they perceive a loss of control. Their world is about to change, but they have not been asked to talk about "what is," explore options, or consider possibilities. Their information concerns have not been addressed. Similarly, if personal concerns are not surfaced and acknowledged, people lose a sense of autonomy. They collude with others, they become anxious, and their resistance increases. Then, when T-shirts with a slogan are given out and everyone is sent to "one size fits all" training, people begin to believe that the organization really is out of control. This puts their sense of control in jeopardy, which again increases resistance. The bottom line is that people have to influence the change they are expected to make, or, as Robert Lee said:

> *"People who are left out of shaping change have a way of reminding us that they are really important."*

Flexibility: Using a Number of Different Change Leadership Strategies to Successfully Lead Change

The seven organizational change leadership strategies on the perimeter of Blanchard's Change Strategy Model proactively address the other twelve Predictable Reasons Why Change Efforts Typically Fail. They also illustrate a sequential process for initiating, implementing, and sustaining change.

To help make the remaining seven change strategies come alive, we offer the following case study involving a problem that has plagued millions of Americans.

Case Study: Non-Support-Paying Parents

As many as 20 million children in America may have noncustodial parents who avoid their child support obligations. According to the Federal Office of Child Support, the total unpaid child support in the U.S. is close to $100 billion; 68 percent of child support cases were in arrears. An overwhelming majority of children—particularly minorities—residing in single-parent homes, where child support is not paid, live in poverty.

In the United States, child support enforcement is a loose confederation of state and local agencies with different guidelines that answer to the federal Office of Child Support Enforcement.

Getting agencies to work together is the greatest challenge. While legislation exists to enforce child support payments, there is too much bureaucracy and not enough manpower to pursue non-support-paying parents across state lines and bring them into custody. As a result, many of these parents have beaten the system.

Up until the 1990s, information on these parents was stored in paper files in clerks' offices in the county where the parent resided. County clerks were responsible for using this information to try to enforce the collection of child support. Often, as a county clerk got close to tracking down a parent not paying court-ordered child support payments, the parent would move on to a different county or even a different state.

With the major challenge of sharing information stored in paper files across county lines, even across state lines, it became nearly impossible to catch the non-support-paying parents. As a result, custodial parents and kids who were due to receive child support ended up losing.

As frustration grew over this situation, the federal government decided to take on the challenge. In the early 1990s, federal legislation mandated that each state implement an electronic tracking system that facilitated the sharing of current information across county and state lines to better enable the tracking of these parents. This may sound like a relatively simple change to make, considering that computers and the Internet are now commonplace in most businesses. However, many county clerks were in their fifties and sixties, lived in rural areas, had never used a computer, and had been trying to track non-support-paying parents with a notepad, pencil, and telephone for decades.

Do you think the county clerks being asked to change had concerns with the proposed change? Of course they did. Many of these county clerks had questions regarding ***information concerns***, such as how having a new computer would improve the situation in their county. In counties that were already doing a good job of collecting child support, people wondered if they needed to participate, or if they could continue to use their paper files as long as they were successful. Counties that had been using a computer system for years to track cases wondered if they needed to use the new computer system, or if they could keep using the current system. People had questions about how long it would take to move the information from their paper files to the computer.

Many of the county clerks had questions and comments around ***personal concerns*** as well. People said things like, "I've never used a computer. Will I be taught how? Can I do it? If I can't learn to use the new computer system, will I still have a job? Besides using the new computer system, how else is my job changing? This sounds like a lot of extra work. I'm not ready for this." These questions are typical at this stage.

In addition, the clerks had questions regarding ***implementation concerns***. They wanted to know when they would be trained on the new computer system. They wanted to know who to contact if they needed help after training. Many wondered if any counties were "going live" before they were, and they wondered if they could talk with people in those counties. They also wondered when the whole state would be up and running on the new system. Finally, they wondered what would happen if the computer system went down or was unavailable for a period of time.

Once the change was in motion, some of the clerks brought forward questions about ***impact concerns***. For example, they wanted to know if they were catching any non-support-paying parents they wouldn't have caught without the new system. They wanted to know how much more money they were collecting compared to when they were doing things the old way. Many were curious to know if their customers (custodial parents) saw a positive change in how they were working with them and the results they were achieving.

In time, the clerks' **collaboration concerns** began to surface. Here are some of their comments:

"I've seen the success of this new system firsthand. Is there anybody who is not yet convinced that this is a good idea?"

"I'm so glad I got to be part of the pilot. I can't wait to go back to my county and share the good news. They are currently pretty skeptical about this new system."

"The system is working pretty well within the counties around us that have 'gone live.' Are there other counties or states we should be working with that we haven't connected with yet?"

Once the new system was up and running, the clerks brought forward their **refinement concerns**. While they acknowledged that the new system was an improvement over how things used to be, they suggested areas that might be improved. For example, a question came up about how they could connect their system to other systems (other county and state child support systems, the Department of Motor Vehicles, the new-hire database, the IRS) so that they could better track people and enforce the collection of child support.

Strategy 2: Explain the Business Case for Change
Outcome: Compelling Case for Change

The second leadership strategy, Explain the Business Case for Change, addresses *information concerns*.

When leaders present and explain a rational reason for the change, the outcome is a compelling case that helps people understand the change being proposed, the rationale for the change, and why the status quo is no longer a viable option. This leadership strategy addresses the following reason why change efforts fail.

Why Change Efforts Typically Fail: Reason #4

4. There is no compelling reason to change. The business case is not communicated.

Expect that many people in the organization will not understand the need for a change; they will feel good about the job they are currently doing. As a result, they will have *information concerns* and likely will ask questions such as: What is the change? Why is it needed? What is wrong with the way things are now? How much and how fast does the organization need to change?

Most likely, those initiating the change were frustrated by something wrong with the status quo or were anxious about an opportunity that would be lost by continuing with business as usual. This spirit of discontent with the status quo needs to be shared and felt by those being asked to change.

Suppose a leader mistakenly attempts to create and communicate a change-specific vision to the organization before demonstrating that the status quo is no longer a viable option. The inertia of the status quo will likely prove too strong, and the very people whose cooperation the leader needs are much less likely to embrace the picture of the future the leader intends to create. As John Maynard Keynes said:

"The difficulty lies not so much in developing new ideas as in escaping old ones."

In the child support example described earlier, it was critical to have custodial parents and county clerks share their stories regarding the frustration and hopelessness they felt in trying to track down and enforce the collection of child support from non-support-paying parents with only pen-and-paper support from government agents. Without county clerks feeling this frustration in some way, shape, or form, it was very unlikely that they would be willing to learn a new computer system and adopt new ways of working just because it was mandated by federal legislators.

As you build the case for change, one of the best ways to get buy-in from employees is to share information broadly and then ask people at all levels in the organization to tell you why they believe the organization needs to change. *Ask people for their reasons why the organization needs to change, even if you already think you know the answers.* By doing so, your case for change will be more compelling in people's eyes, because they came up with it. As a result of their ownership in the case for change, people are much more likely to leave the status quo behind.

Using the example we cited in Chapter 4, "Empowerment Is the Key," The Ken Blanchard Companies needed to make a number of changes as a result of the economic downturn following the terrorist attacks on September 11, 2001. The leaders shared information broadly with the organization regarding projected revenue, current expenses, and break-even figures. This brought people face to face with the reality of the situation and ensured that the organization understood that "business as usual" was no longer a viable option. Then the leaders asked associates what would happen if the status quo were maintained. The associates clearly stated that the company's survival was at stake. As a result of their involvement in building the case for change, associates bought into a number of cost-cutting initiatives, even when the initiatives weren't in their own best interests.

Strategy 3: Envision the Future

Outcome: Inspiring Vision

The third leadership strategy, Envision the Future, addresses both *information* and *personal concerns*. To quote Proverbs 29:18, "Where there is no vision, the people perish."

When leaders envision the future, they create an inspiring vision that motivates people in the organization and that unleashes their power and potential. This leadership strategy addresses the following reason why change efforts fail.

Why Change Efforts Typically Fail: Reason #5

5. A compelling vision that gets people excited about the future has not been developed and/or communicated.

In Chapter 2, "The Power of Vision," we described the importance of a compelling vision for the organization that inspires and excites people and causes them to want to stay. When any organizational change is considered, it is always important to revisit the organization's vision to provide rationale for the change. At times, this may mean modifying the organization's vision or creating a new one, such as what happened when Louis Gerstner took over IBM. A new, compelling picture of the future when the proposed change is implemented must support the organization's vision, including its purpose and values.

The process used to create a vision, whether it is for an entire organization or for a specific change initiative, is the same. This process was described in detail in Chapter 2. As Ken Blanchard and Jesse Stoner point out in *Full Steam Ahead!: Unleash the Power of Vision in Your Company and Your Life*, the process you use to develop a vision is as important as the vision itself.[2] In other words, if people are involved in the process and feel the vision is theirs—as opposed to some words on a poster from an executive retreat—they are more likely to see themselves as part of the future organization. When this happens, people are more likely to show the tenacity needed during the challenging times that inevitably accompany change.

Getting people involved in the visioning process is also a key way to help them resolve the *personal concerns* they experience during a change. The more you can get people involved in the visioning process, the more likely it is they will want to be part of the future organization. They need to be able to see themselves in the picture of the future for it to inspire them.

In our earlier child support example, the change leadership team was responsible for drafting the initial vision. Because there was no existing vision for the state's Child Support Program to compare it to, they needed to create a vision for the entire program, not just for the implementation of an electronic tracking system. Next they took the draft vision to the county clerks across the state and asked them for input. The result was the creation of a shared vision that was compelling for the vast majority of those being asked to change:

> *Our state's Child Support Program helps children thrive by providing financial stability to their families and offering the highest-quality service as a nationally recognized model of excellence for child support enforcement.*

While a small group of leaders could have come up with these words, giving county clerks an opportunity to provide input ensured that the vision was understood and embraced.

Strategy 4: Experiment to Ensure Alignment
Outcome: One Voice and Aligned Infrastructure

The fourth change leadership strategy, Experiment to Ensure Alignment, is for *personal* and *implementation concerns.*

When leaders engage others in planning and experimenting, they encourage collaborative effort and help build the infrastructure that is needed to support the change. The Experiment to Ensure Alignment strategy addresses the following reasons why change efforts fail.

Why Change Efforts Typically Fail: Reasons #6, 7, 8, and 9

6. The change leadership team doesn't include early adopters, resisters, or informal leaders.

7. The change isn't piloted, so the organization doesn't learn what's needed to support the change.

8. Organizational systems and other initiatives aren't aligned with the change.

9. Leaders lose focus and/or fail to prioritize, causing "death by 1,000 initiatives."

Expand the change leadership team. It is not possible to bring about change in an organization with a single leader. As David Nadler says, "The scope of today's changes is too much for one CEO—even a very charismatic one—to pull off alone." Change requires a strong and broad-based change leadership team that is aligned and speaks with one voice to the larger organization. The outcome is a unified message that minimizes ambivalence and confusion, a message that is compelling and inspiring.

In Chapter 9, "Situational Team Leadership," we described the importance of teamwork and how to build a high performing team. How do you build a change leadership team? First, it is important to select both sponsors and day-to-day change leadership team members. A sponsor is an executive who can legitimize the change and who has the formal authority to deploy resources to support the initiation, implementation, and reinforcement of the change. A member of the change leadership team is responsible for the day-to-day leadership of the change (the execution of the change strategies described by the Change Strategy Model). As you identify potential sponsors and members of the change leadership team, consider whether they possess the skills and traits required to lead change. Consider the following questions: Have they led or been part of successful change efforts in the past? Do they have the time and availability required of a change leader? Do they have the respect of their peers? Are they highly skilled? Are they willing to play the role of devil's advocate? Are they effective communicators who are willing to raise the concerns of colleagues who may be less inclined to do so? Do they have the diversity necessary to think outside the box and come up with the best solutions to challenges that arise?

In our child support example, it was critical that the change leadership team include county clerks representing a diverse set of counties across the state: rural and urban counties, a county already using computers to track non-support-paying parents, a county using only pen and paper to track non-support-paying parents, a county with good performance regarding collection of child support, and a county with poor performance regarding collection of child support.

The change leadership team should be a representative sample of the organization—advocates and resisters, formal and informal leaders, and leaders at all levels of the organization.

It's important to embrace the resisters to change. We once worked with a company where a manager appeared to be very resistant to the changes being proposed by the executive team. This manager had lots of credibility within his department and could sway people to support or block the change. Once the executive proposing the changes allowed this manager to be involved in many of the decisions regarding the change and to take an active leadership role, this manager ended up being one of the strongest supporters and leaders of the change. It's been said that

---

Those who plan the battle rarely battle the plan.

It's important to include a variety of perspectives and roles that represent the entire organization on the change leadership team. This way, various perspectives can be surfaced and worked through before final decisions are made. Although it may feel uncomfortable at first, it is very helpful to include at least one or two people who might be considered "resistant" and who can articulate the concerns of those who share that perspective.

When you include a representative sample of the organization, people throughout the organization feel that their point of view and concerns are being heard. A diverse team also means that there are more opportunities for advocates to be in contact with people who are neutral, before they become resistant. When resisters have a forum to surface and address their concerns, they often become the most effective problem solvers and spokespeople for the change.

Build a high performing change leadership team. Once the change leadership team is expanded to increase opportunities for involvement and influence, consider how important it is for this to be a high performing team. It is extremely damaging to an organization when its leaders are not on the same page and are communicating inconsistent messages to the organization during times of change.

We worked with an organization where the top executive was trying to get buy-in from his executive team for a series of changes. Some of his team did not agree with what was proposed. Although there were meetings to discuss the changes, one executive did not voice his concerns. By being silent, he implied that he supported the change leadership team's recommendations and that he would communicate a consistent message to his people. Instead, the team member chose to publicly criticize the top executive and the changes that were being proposed to members of his department. He tried to subvert the change outside the change leadership team.

When people see a lack of alignment at the top, they know they don't have to align. In addition, they know that without alignment, the change will stall or derail and that they can outlast it. In this example, as a result of his actions, the subversive executive was fired. The team members agreed to this action during the team chartering session. It sent a strong message about alignment to the whole organization. It is important to note that the executive was fired as much for not voicing his concerns to his team as for disparaging the top executive and the proposed changes.

While it may not always lead to someone being fired, communication of inconsistent messages during a change effort results in people freezing and waiting for the leaders to sort out the inconsistencies. Negative spin from one member of a change leadership team will kill a change effort. Again, with a broad, diverse team, there are more people to communicate, but the challenge is to get them to communicate one message and to get them to listen when they communicate as much as talk. Remember: Sustainable organizational change happens through conversation and collaboration, not by unilateral action by a few.

Involve others in planning and pilots. We've all seen or been part of changes that have not gone so well. In most of these cases, the implementation plan was not developed by people anywhere near the front line. As a result, the plan did not account for some real-world realities and was shrugged off as flawed, unrealistic, and lacking the details required for action—or, worse yet, flat-out wrong.

As with the earlier change strategies we described, when you involve people and give them a chance to influence, you get not only their buy-in, but also a better outcome. Also, your planning process needs to account for the fact that you won't have it all figured out ahead of time. Run some experiments or pilots with early adopters in an effort to work out the kinks and learn more about the best way to implement the change with the larger organization. Ensure that your change implementation plan is dynamic. By getting others involved in the planning process, you can resolve a number of *personal and implementation* concerns. Test drives, pilots, or experiments can also teach you what else needs to change in terms of policies, procedures, systems, and structures so that the probability of successful implementation across the larger organization improves. The positive outcomes of engaging others at this stage of the change process are collaborative effort and the right infrastructure.

Many change plans underestimate the momentum generated by short-term wins. Short-term wins are improvements that can be implemented within a short time frame—typically three months—with minimal resources, at minimal cost, and at minimal risk. Short-term wins have several benefits. First, they proactively address impact concerns (such as "Is the change working?"). Second, they provide good news early in the change effort, when good news is hard to come by. Third, they reinforce behavior changes made by early adopters. Fourth, they help sway those who are "on the fence" regarding action.

In the child support case study pilot described earlier, it was critical to select counties that had the greatest probability of seeing significant short-term results from implementing the new electronic tracking system. This would help grease the skids and build momentum for post-pilot implementations with other counties where the impact was more in question.

Avoid death by 1,000 initiatives. With limited resources, it is critical to make choices about what change initiatives will allow your organization to achieve its vision most effectively and efficiently. Individual change initiatives need to be scheduled and implemented in light of other activities and initiatives competing for people's time, energy, and mind share.

During times of change, it is critical to provide your people with direction regarding priorities. Like a sponge, after a certain amount of change, people cannot absorb any more, no matter how resilient and adaptive they are.

Decide what not to do. While it is important to provide direction on what to do, it is just as important to provide direction on what *not* to do. Ask the following questions when deciding what to do and what not to do: What project or initiative will have the greatest impact on your vision? What provides the greatest value for resources expended (money, people, time)? Can the people responsible for working on the project handle it in light of all the things they are tasked with doing? Are there enough qualified people who can dedicate time to work on the project? Are there any synergies between this project and other critical projects?

Once you have prioritized and sequenced a list of possible change projects, recognize that, because we live in a dynamic environment, priorities can shift and resources can become more abundant or scarce. This may shift the type and number of projects an organization undertakes at any point in time.

Decide what, how, and when to measure and assess progress. The adage is true: *What gets measured gets done*. Because it is difficult to predict human behavior with absolute certainty—especially in the face of major change—assess the progress being made on a number of fronts in an effort to identify potential risks to the change's success. These areas include sponsor commitment, employee commitment and behavior change, achievement of project milestones, and interim business results.

The plan crafted at this step of the change process needs to describe what will be measured, how it will be measured, and the frequency of measurement. To increase the probability of successful change, consider using the Organizational Change Readiness Assessment (see page 313) to determine what's working well and what requires additional work.

Communication, communication, communication. Much has been written about the importance of communication during times of change. Why is it so important? A significant amount of resistance encountered during organizational change is caused by a lack of information, especially the *what* and *why* types of information. In the absence of honest, passionate, and empathetic communication, people create their own information about the change, and rumors begin to serve as facts.

For example, we worked with an organization going through a tremendous amount of change. As we started our work, we quickly realized that little or no rationale was being provided for key decisions that affected a large number of people. Without supporting rationale, the facts appeared harsh to team members:

- The development project I am working on was stopped.
- My budget was cut.

Based on these facts alone, many people assumed that the company's future was bleak. As a result, tremendous effort was required to overcome the rumor mill that led to drops in productivity and morale and that caused some people to begin looking for other jobs.

Let's consider these same facts, only this time with supporting rationale. Can you see how providing this rationale could have prevented the rumors and resistance that occurred?

- The project I am working on was stopped because we found that customer safety was at risk. Customer safety is our highest-priority value, so we made a decision in line with our values.

- My budget was cut because the organization is reallocating these funds toward another drug development project based on a recent licensing agreement we signed.

Some of the strongest resistance to change occurs when reality differs from expectations. Therefore, understanding the current expectations of those affected by the change is critical if leaders are to manage and shape or transform those expectations effectively.

Recognize that covert resistance kills change. Effective leaders not only tolerate the open expression of concerns, they actually reward their people for sharing their concerns in an open, honest, and constructive manner. It is critical that leaders provide opportunities for two-way communication, because concerns cannot be surfaced and resolved without give-and-take dialog.

It is also important to recognize that communicating your message once is not enough for most people to act on it. People in organizations are so bombarded with information that one of the best ways to sort out what requires action versus what does not is to listen for the messages that are communicated repeatedly over time. These can be distinguished from the flavor-of-the-month messages that come and go. Communicate your key messages at least seven times in seven different ways. Better yet, at least ten times in ten different ways.

Strategy 5: Enable and Encourage

Outcome: New Skills and Commitment

The fifth change leadership strategy, Enable and Encourage, is for *implementation* and *impact concerns.*

When leaders enable and encourage people throughout the organization to embrace the change, associates can develop new skills and make a deeper commitment to the organization. This leadership strategy addresses the following reason why change efforts fail.

Why Change Efforts Typically Fail: Reason #10

10. People are not enabled and/or encouraged to build new skills.

Our experience has shown that most organizations jump into this change strategy much too soon. In many cases, executives announce the change and try to get people into training as soon as possible. Unfortunately, people's *information* and *personal concerns* have not been addressed, so the results of the training are less than optimal. Also, training often is delivered before all the kinks are worked out, contingencies are planned for, help desks are created, or systems are aligned. Finally, early training usually fails because it's "one size fits all." After the learnings from pilots and experiments are culled and the right infrastructure is in place, training for the change should be done in as individualized a way as possible. Ideally, a training strategy for each individual should be delivered at just the right time.

Notice how many other change strategies precede the Enable and Encourage change strategy in our model. Our model is front-loaded for a reason—namely, because most organizations don't do a good job on the early work that needs to be done to set up a successful change. The rallying cry we hear often in our work with organizations going through change is, "We're raising the bar!" This rallying cry is not bad in and of itself. However, nothing kills motivation faster than telling people to raise their performance but failing to provide them with new skills, tools, and resources required to leap over the recently raised bar. As a result, people's reaction to leadership's statement that "We're raising the bar!" is often along the lines of "What does that mean? I'm not doing a good job now?"

After you determine the roles, responsibilities, and competencies required for lasting change, skill gaps need to be closed. Leaders need to use directing leadership style 1 (with high direction and low support) or more likely coaching leadership style 2 (with high direction and high support) to build people's competence and

commitment. Leaders need to use mistakes as opportunities for further learning, and they need to praise progress.

In the child support case study we described earlier, a group of
county clerks involved in the pilots were chosen to train other
county clerks on the new electronic tracking system and new
work processes. This brought county clerk trainees face to face
with others in similar positions who had gone down the path
before them. Because the trainers were speaking from a position
of experience, they were credible and could set realistic expectations for what other county clerks could expect when their
county "went live."

In addition, the county clerks facilitating the training used the
sessions as opportunities to gather additional input and ensure
that the implementation plan was as strong as it could be.

Strategy 6: Execute and Endorse
Outcome: Accountability for Results

The sixth change leadership strategy, Execute and Endorse, is for
impact and *collaboration concerns*. James Champy articulates this
strategy well:

> *A leader needs to attract followers ... but if*
> *the mobilization process is to succeed,*
> *those followers must become leaders too,*
> *finding their own sense of purpose in*
> *the shared challenge and spreading*
> *the call and vision of the change.*

When leaders execute and endorse the change, they create
conditions for accountability and early results. This leadership
strategy addresses the following reasons why change efforts fail.

Why Change Efforts Typically Fail: Reasons #11, 12, and 13

11. Those leading the change aren't credible—they undercommunicate, give mixed messages, and do not model the behaviors the change requires.

12. Progress is not measured, and/or no one recognizes the changes that people have worked hard to make.

13. People are not held accountable for implementing the change.

Much has been written about the importance of execution. We do not argue with the emphasis being placed on execution. That being said, execution is much easier if you lead the change using the strategies we've described up to this point. If you don't, you will fight an uphill battle.

Walking the talk. Although it is critical for the change leadership team to communicate with one voice, it is even more important that the change leaders walk their talk and model the behaviors they expect of others.

It is estimated that a leader's actions are at least three times as important as what he or she says. Leaders need to display as much or more commitment to the change as the people they lead. People will assess what the leader does and doesn't do to assess the commitment to the change. The minute that associates or colleagues sense that their leader is not committed or is acting inconsistently with the desired behaviors of the change, they will no longer commit themselves to the effort.

Measure, praise progress, and redirect when necessary. As stated earlier, what gets measured gets done. Keep in mind that people's thoughts and actions are leading indicators of business and financial performance. Leading indicators allow you to drive by "looking through the windshield" rather than relying solely on lagging indicators such as financial performance, which is akin to driving while looking in the rearview mirror.

Once measurement occurs, praise the progress that is being made. Don't wait for perfect performance. If you do, you'll be waiting a long time. This concept has been key to our teachings for decades:

The key to developing people and creating great organizations is to catch people doing things right and to accentuate the positive.

Because you've planned for short-term wins, you should be able to find and share success stories as a means of influencing people who remain on the fence.

Follow through on your promise to recognize and reward the behavior you expect, and follow through on your promise to impose consequences for anyone attempting to derail the change program. This is the stage where you get rid of the people who are still resisting.

In our child support case study, the state government called monthly meetings for county clerks across the state who had similar "go live" dates. During these meetings, each county was asked to share a success story as well as any challenges they were having. The idea of holding each county accountable for sharing a success story in front of their peers created some healthy competition to make the new tracking system work. It allowed early-adopting counties to sway those that were on the fence. Discussing the challenges also provided opportunities for learning that could be fed back into the design of the tracking system, the planning process, and the training of county clerks.

In another example, a change leadership team we worked with instituted the use of a "performance dashboard" to continually measure progress against a set of key performance indicators. The change leadership team met twice a month to discuss the plan's progress, as seen by green, yellow, and red indicators on the performance dashboard. If a key performance indicator was green, this was praised and celebrated. If a key performance indicator was yellow or red, the team would discuss how best to respond to get that indicator back on track. This process held people accountable for performance and also ensured that people got the direction and support they needed to get back on track.

Strategy 7: Embed and Extend
Outcome: Sustainable Results

The seventh change leadership strategy, Embed and Extend, is for *collaboration* and *refinement concerns*. Here's a good rule of thumb:

> *Organizations should spend ten times more energy reinforcing the change they just made than looking for the next great change to try.*

When leaders embed and extend the desired change, they can reach and sustain the desired results. This leadership strategy addresses the fourteenth reason why change efforts fail.

Why Change Efforts Typically Fail: Reason #14

14. People leading the change fail to respect the power of the culture to kill the change.

Culture can be defined as the predominating attitudes, beliefs, and behavior patterns that characterize an organization's functioning. While a high performing change leadership team can generate enthusiasm and short-term success during times of change, it is critical that the change be embedded in the organization's culture if it is to be sustainable over the long haul.

If a change is introduced that is not aligned with the current culture, you must alter the existing culture to support the new initiative or accept that the change may not be sustainable in the long term. The best way to alter the culture is to go back to the organization's vision and examine its values. Identify which values support the new culture and which don't. Choose the most critical values. Then, define the behaviors that are consistent with the values and create rewards and accountability for behaving consistently with the values. It is energizing for an organization to do this in the context of implementing change.

In many cases, a change is implemented within one business unit before other business units are engaged. The change process defined by the Change Strategy Model needs to be repeated for the new units that have not yet gone through the process.

Citing our child support case study once again, it was critical to ensure that all obstacles to using the new tracking system were removed. While there were some common obstacles to overcome for most counties, many obstacles differed by county. As a result, embedding the change on a local level required attention at the local level. Because ongoing support was provided, obstacles were removed, and the counties themselves sold each other on the benefits of implementing the new tracking system. Doing so allowed the initiative to be extended across an entire state and eventually the entire country.

Strategy 8: Explore Possibilities

Outcome: Options

The eighth change leadership strategy, Explore Possibilities, is for *refinement concerns*. By involving others in exploring possibilities, you immediately lower information concerns as a new change is announced, because people are "in the loop" about deciding what needs to change. This leadership strategy addresses the following reason why change efforts fail.

Why Change Efforts Typically Fail: Reason #15

15. Possibilities and options are not explored before a specific change is chosen.

Ideally, those who are closest to the problems and opportunities in an organization are the ones who come up with the options to be considered by the change leadership team. To ensure face validity and inclusion of the best options, the options identified should be reviewed by a representative sample of those being asked to change.

In our child support case study, noncustodial parents and county clerks across the country expressed frustration with the fact that non-support-paying parents were getting harder to track and more elusive than ever. As a result, the federal government took this input, explored the root causes of the problem, and identified a number of possible responses. A number of change projects were chosen as part of an integrated strategy to enforce the collection of child support payments. These projects included but were not limited to withholding income from the noncustodial parent's employer and interception of income tax refunds (state and federal), unemployment compensation benefits, and lottery winnings. The projects also included credit bureau reporting, driver's and professional license suspension, financial institution data match (locating of bank assets), cross-matching new-hire reporting, hunting and fishing license suspension, passport denial, liens, federal loan data matching, and computer automation of child support operations, including interfaces with numerous other state agency systems.

Some of these options were potentially more feasible and would have more impact than others. By simply having options, people felt they had choices and could influence what changed.

Since 1995, annual child support collections in the state where the enforcement tracking system was implemented have increased from $177 million to more than $460 million. Increased collections means that more children are receiving the child support they deserve, and fewer families will have to resort to public assistance to survive.[3]

It is our hope that instructing leaders how to address each stage of concern during organizational change has taken much of the mystique out of the process and shown you how you can lead at a higher level. Responding to others' concerns and paying attention to how you increase involvement and influence at each step in the change process is the best way we know to build future change receptivity, capability, and leadership.

In Chapter 1, "Is Your Organization High Performing?," we argued that if being a high performing organization is the destination, leadership is the engine. While that is true, it's important to have the ***right kind of leadership***. This will be the focus of the last section of our book.

Visit **www.LeadingAtAHigherLevel.com** to access the free virtual conference titled *Treat Your People Right*. Use the password "People" for your FREE access.

HAVE THE RIGHT KIND OF LEADERSHIP

Chapter 12

SERVANT LEADERSHIP

Ken Blanchard, Scott Blanchard,
and Drea Zigarmi

When people lead at a higher level, they make the world a better place, because their goals are focused on the greater good. Making the world a better place requires a special kind of leader: a servant leader.

Robert Greenleaf first coined the term "servant leadership" in 1970 and published widely on the concept for the next 20 years.[1] Yet it is an old concept. Two thousand years ago, servant leadership was central to the philosophy of Jesus, who exemplified the fully committed and effective servant leader.[2] Mahatma Gandhi, Dr. Martin Luther King, Jr., and Nelson Mandela are more recent examples of leaders who have exemplified this philosophy.

What Is Servant Leadership?

When people hear the phrase servant leadership, they are often confused. They immediately conjure up thoughts of the inmates running the prison, or of trying to please everyone. Others think servant leadership is only for church leaders. The problem is that they don't understand leadership. They think you can't lead and serve at the same time. Yet you can if you understand—as we have emphasized a number of times—that leadership has two parts: vision and implementation. In the visionary role, leaders define the direction. It's their responsibility to communicate what the organization stands for and wants to accomplish.

Max DuPree, legendary former chairman of Herman Miller and author of *Leadership Is an Art*, compared this role to that of a third-grade teacher who keeps repeating the basics. "When it comes to vision and values, you have to say it over and over and over again until people get it right, right, right!"

As you now know, the responsibility for this visionary role falls to the hierarchical leadership. Kids look to their parents, players look to their coaches, and people look to their organizational leaders for direction. *The visionary role is the leadership aspect of servant leadership.*

Once people are clear on where they are going, the leader's role shifts to a service mindset for the task of implementation— the second aspect of leadership. How do you make the dream happen? *Implementation is where the servant aspect of servant leadership comes into play.* In a traditional organization, managers are thought of as responsible, and their people are taught to be responsive to their boss. "Boss watching" becomes a popular sport, and people get promoted on their upward-influencing skills. That activity doesn't do much for accomplishing a clear vision. All people try to do is protect themselves rather than move the organization in the desired direction.

Servant leaders, on the other hand, feel their role is to help people achieve their goals. They constantly try to find out what their people need to perform well and live according to the vision. Rather than wanting people to please their bosses, servant leaders want to make a difference in the lives of their people and, in the process, impact the organization. With its emphasis on bringing out the magnificence in people, Situational Leadership® II is a servant leadership model.

Applying Servant Leadership

To help you realize that servant leadership can occur in any organization, consider the following example from the Department of Motor Vehicles (DMV). The DMV has such a multitude of people to take care of—basically, everybody with a driver's license—that it's no surprise they sometimes treat you like a number instead of a person. In most states, after you have passed your initial tests, you can avoid the DMV for years if you fill out the proper form and mail it in.

Ken Blanchard had avoided his local DMV like the plague. But several years ago, he lost his driver's license about three weeks before he was scheduled to leave on a trip to Europe. He knew he had to go to the DMV and get a new license to back up his passport on his trip. So he said to his executive assistant, "Dana, would you put three hours on my calendar next week sometime so I can go to the DMV?" In Ken's experience, that's about how long it usually took to get anything done there. He'd wait for a long time, and then they'd tell him he was in the wrong line, he'd filled out the wrong form, or he'd done something that meant he had to start all over.

As a result, Ken headed over to the DMV with low expectations. (Remember, he hadn't been there in years.) He knew immediately something had changed when he walked in the front door, because a woman charged him and said, "Welcome to the Department of Motor Vehicles! Do you speak English or Spanish?"

"English," Ken replied.

She said, "Right over there." The guy behind the counter smiled and said, "Welcome to the Department of Motor Vehicles! How may I help you?" It took Ken nine minutes to renew his license, including getting his picture taken. He said to the woman who took his picture, "What are you all smoking here? I mean, this isn't the Department of Motor Vehicles that I used to know and love."

She replied, "Haven't you met the new director?"

"No," he said.

So she pointed to a desk behind all the counters, right out in the open. Clearly the director had no privacy. His office was in the middle of everything. Ken went over, introduced himself, and said, "What's your job as the director of the Department of Motor Vehicles?"

What the man said is the best definition of management we've ever heard:

> *"My job is to reorganize the department*
> *on a moment-to-moment basis,*
> *depending on citizen (customer) need."*

The director obviously had a compelling vision for this department. The point of their business was to serve the citizens and their needs, and to serve them well.

What did this director do? He cross-trained everybody in every job. Everyone could handle the front desk; everyone could take the pictures. You name it—everyone could do it! Even the people in the back, who normally weren't out in front, could do every job. Why? Because if suddenly there was a flood of citizens, why have people in the back doing bookkeeping, accounting, or secretarial work when there were customers who needed help? So he'd bring them out when they were needed.

The DMV director also insisted that nobody go to lunch between 11:30 and 2:00. Why? Because that's when the customers showed up. Ken told this story at a seminar one time, and a woman came up to him at the break and said, "Where is your Department of Motor Vehicles? I can't believe what you've been telling us." She continued, "I recently waited in line for about forty-five minutes at our DMV, and I was just about to get to the front of the line when the woman announced, 'It's break time.' We had to stand around for fifteen minutes while they all went for coffee and stretched their legs."

That didn't happen at this "new" Department of Motor Vehicles, where the director had created a motivating environment. Those team members were really committed. Even employees Ken recognized from past visits who had joined in on the "fun" of abusing the customers were now excited about serving.

Often you see people at one point and they are so excited about their work. Then you see them three months later and they're discouraged. In 90 percent of these cases, the only thing that has changed is that they've gotten a new boss. Someone who jerks them around, who doesn't listen to them, who doesn't involve them in decision making, and who treats them as if they really are *subordinates*. The reverse is also true. People can be unhappy in a job situation when suddenly a new leader comes in and their eyes brighten, their energy increases, and they are really ready to perform well and make a difference.

When leaders make a positive difference, people act like they own the place, and they bring their brains to work. Their managers encourage their newfound initiative. Another example from the "new" DMV punctuates this point.

Great Leaders Encourage Their People to Bring Their Brains to Work

Just about the time Ken had his inspiring experience with the DMV, Dana, his executive assistant, decided to buy a big motor scooter and bop around southern California. When she got this beauty, somebody told her, "You have to get a license." She had never thought about needing a license for a motor scooter. So, she went to the DMV to do the right thing. The woman behind the counter went into the computer and found Dana's name and driving record. It turns out that Dana had a perfect driving record. She never had a traffic violation.

"Dana," the woman said, "I noticed that in three months you have to retake your written driving test. Why don't you take both tests today?"

Caught off guard, Dana said, "Tests? I didn't know I was supposed to take a test." And she started to panic.

The woman reached across the counter, patted Dana's hand, and said, "Oh, Dana, don't worry. With your driving record, I'm sure you can pass these tests. And besides, if you don't, you can always come back."

Dana took the tests. She went back to the woman, who graded the tests. Dana fell one correct answer short of passing each test, so officially she failed both. But, in a kind way, the woman said, "Oh, Dana. You are so close to passing. Let me try something. Let me re-ask you one question on each test to see if you can get it right so I can pass you." Not only was this a wonderful offer, but the fact was, each question had only two answers. So the woman said, "Dana, you chose B. What do you think would be the right answer?"

When Dana said, "A!" this helpful woman said, "You're right! You pass!"

Ken once told this story at a seminar, and a bureaucrat came racing up to the platform during the break. He started yelling, "Why are you telling this story? That woman broke the law! Your assistant failed both of those tests!"

So Ken went back to see his DMV director friend. He told him about this bureaucrat, and the director said, "Let me tell you one other thing. When it comes to decision making, I want my people to use their brains more than rules, regulations, or laws. My person decided that it was silly to make someone like your assistant Dana, with her perfect driving record, come back to retake a test on which she missed only one question. I guarantee you, if she had missed four or five questions, my person wouldn't have given her the same deal. And to show you how important I think this is, *I would back that person's decision with my job.*"

Would any of you like to work for this kind of leader? You'd better believe it. Why? Because he is a servant leader. In Rick Warren's best-selling book *The Purpose Driven Life*, the first sentence is "It's not about you."[3] Just like our DMV director, servant leaders realize that leadership is not about them. It's about what and who they are serving. What's the vision, and who's the customer? The vision answers Hayes and Stevens' question, "What's the point?" As the authors of *The Heart of Business* insist, "profit can be a by-product of the pursuit of a higher purpose and even part of the planned process in pursuit of that higher purpose, but it should never be the purpose and motive itself."[4] If profit is your reason for being an organization, it will eventually drive your people and customers to be self-serving, too. As we argued in Chapter 3, "Serving Customers at a Higher Level," everyone has a customer. Who is a manager's customer? The people who report to that manager. Once the vision and direction are set, managers work for their people.

What Impacts Performance the Most?

To find out what kind of leadership has the greatest impact on performance, Scott Blanchard and Drea Zigarmi worked with Vicky Essary to study the interaction between organizational success, employee success, customer loyalty, and leadership.[5] In their year-long study, which included an exhaustive literature review of hundreds of studies from 1980 to 2005, they examined two kinds of leadership: **strategic leadership** and **operational leadership**.

Strategic leadership is the "what" that ensures everyone is going in the same direction. It's where the answer to the question "What's the point of your business?" is found. Strategic leadership includes activities such as establishing a clear vision, maintaining a culture that aligns a set of values with that vision, and declaring must-do initiatives or strategic imperatives that the organization needs to accomplish. Vision and values are enduring, whereas strategic imperatives are short-term priorities that could last a month or two, or a year or two. An example of a strategic initiative is David Novak, chairman and CEO of Yum! Brands, declaring a customer-mania focus for all the company's restaurants around the world. Strategic leadership is all about the vision and direction aspect of leadership, or the *leadership* part of servant leadership.

Operational leadership is everything else. It provides the "how" for the organization. It includes the policies, procedures, systems, and leader behaviors that cascade from senior management to the frontline employees. These management practices create the environment that employees and customers interact with and respond to on a daily basis. Operational leadership is all about the implementation aspect of leadership, or the *servant* part of servant leadership.

Blanchard and Zigarmi discovered that employee success included things like employee satisfaction (I am happy), employee loyalty (I am going to stay on my job), employee productivity (how I am performing), perceptions of one's relationship with his or her manager and the teamwork in the environment, as well as more tangible measures, like absenteeism, tardiness, and vandalism. They identified all these factors as *employee passion*.

When it came to customers, their reactions to the environment of the organization fell into three bodies of research: satisfaction (I am happy with how this organization serves me), loyalty (I will continue to do business with this organization), and advocacy (I am willing to speak positively about my experience with this company). The net result of these three factors they labeled *customer devotion*.

Blanchard and Zigarmi combined all the hard (profitability, growth over time, and economic stability) and soft (trust in the company and a sense of its integrity) measures of organizational success into a concept they called *organizational vitality*. In many ways, organizational vitality depicts that triple-bottom line— being the provider of choice, employer of choice, and investment of choice—that we discussed in Chapter 1, "Is Your Organization High Performing?"

If leadership is the engine that drives a high performing organization, Blanchard and Zigarmi were interested in how the two aspects of leadership—strategic leadership and operational leadership—interact with and impact employee passion, customer devotion, and organizational vitality. As indicated in Figure 12.1, there is a leadership-profit chain of events.

Figure 12.1   The Leadership-Profit Chain

Interestingly, Blanchard and Zigarmi found that while strategic leadership is a critical building block for setting the tone and direction, it has only an indirect impact on organizational vitality. The real key to organizational vitality is operational leadership. If this aspect of leadership is done effectively, employee passion and customer devotion will result from the positive experiences and overall satisfaction people have with the organization.

It is also interesting to note that positive employee passion creates positive customer devotion. At the same time, when customers are excited about and devoted to the company, it has a positive effect on the work environment and the employees' passion. People love to work for a company where customers are raving fans. It makes them gung ho, and together the customers and employees directly impact organizational vitality.[6]

The big-picture conclusion from the research of Blanchard and Zigarmi is that the *leadership* part of servant leadership (strategic leadership) is important—because vision and direction get things going—but the real action is with the *servant* aspect of servant leadership (operational leadership). If the vision and direction are compelling and motivating, and leaders do a good job of implementing them in the eyes of the employees and customers, organizational vitality and success are assured.

To do a good job, effective servant leaders must be environmentalists whose jobs are to create and maintain cultures that turn on employees so that they can turn on customers. These leaders do that by looking down the traditional hierarchy and saying, "What can I do for you?" rather than having their people look up the hierarchy and say, "What can we do for you?" That's why Yum! Brands calls its corporate headquarters "The Support Center" and has changed all manager titles to "coach."

When managers focus only on organizational indicators of vitality—such as profit—they have their eyes on the scoreboard, not the ball. Profit, a key aspect of organizational vitality, is a by-product of serving the customer, which can be achieved only by serving the employee. *So profit really is the applause you get from taking care of your customers and creating a motivating environment for your people.*

If the servant aspect of servant leadership has a greater impact on organizational vitality, how do leaders develop their serving qualities?

Being a Servant Leader Is a Question of the Heart

Most of our work in the past has focused on leadership behavior and how to improve leadership style and methods. We have attempted to change leaders from the outside. In recent years, though, we have found that effective leadership is an inside job. It is a question of the heart. It's all about leadership character and intention. Why are you leading? Is it to serve or to be served? Answering this question in a truthful way is so important. You can't fake being a servant leader. We believe that if leaders don't get the heart right, they simply won't ever become servant leaders.

The most persistent barrier to being a servant leader is a heart motivated by self-interest that looks at the world as a "give a little, take a lot" proposition. Leaders with hearts motivated by self-interest put their own agenda, safety, status, and gratification ahead of those affected by their thoughts and actions.

In a sense, we all entered this world with a self-focus. Is there anything more self-centered than a baby? A baby doesn't come home from the hospital asking, "How can I help around the house?" As any parent can attest, all children are naturally selfish; they have to be taught how to share.

You finally become an adult when you realize that life is about what you give rather than what you get.

The shift from self-serving leadership to leadership that serves others is motivated by a change in heart.

Driven Versus Called Leaders

When we talk about servant leadership and ask people whether they are a servant leader or a self-serving leader, no one admits to being a self-serving leader. Yet we observe self-serving leadership all the time. What is the difference?

In his book *Ordering Your Private World*, Gordon McDonald discusses an interesting distinction that can help us understand the difference between servant leaders and self-serving leaders.[7] McDonald contends that there are two kinds of people: "driven" people and "called" people. Driven people think they own everything. They own their relationships, they own their possessions, and they own their positions. Driven people are self-serving. Most of their time is spent protecting what they own. They run bureaucracies and believe the sheep are there for the benefit of the shepherd. They want to make sure that all the money, recognition, and power move up the hierarchy and away from the frontline people and the customers. They're great at creating "duck ponds."

Called people are very different. They believe everything is on loan—their relationships, possessions, and position. Do you know your relationships are on loan? One of the tough things about 9/11 was that some loans got called in early. If you knew you might not see someone important in your life tomorrow, how would you treat that person today? Margie Blanchard has a wise saying: "Keep your I-love-yous up to date."

Called people understand that possessions are only temporary, too. In tough economic times, a lot of people get uptight about losing their toys. They think "he who dies with the most toys wins." The reality is, "he who dies with the most toys dies." It's great to have nice things when things are going well, but you might have to give up some of them in hard times. Possessions are on loan.

Called leaders also understand that their positions are on loan from all the stakeholders in the organization, particularly the people who report to them. Since called leaders don't own anything, they figure their role in life is to shepherd everybody and everything that comes their way.

Self-serving leaders give themselves away in two ways. The first is how they receive feedback. Have you ever tried to give feedback to someone up the hierarchy, and that person killed the messenger? If that has ever occurred, you were dealing with a self-serving leader. They hate feedback. Why? Because if you give them any negative feedback, they think you don't want them to lead anymore. And that's their worst nightmare, because they *are* their position. The second giveaway for self-serving leaders is their unwillingness to develop other leaders around them. They fear the potential competition for their leadership position.

Called leaders have servant hearts, and they love feedback. They know the only reason they are leading is to serve, and if anybody has any suggestions on how they can serve better, they want to hear them. They look at feedback as a gift. When they receive feedback, their first response is, "Thank you. That's really helpful. Can you tell me more? Is there anybody else I should talk to?"

Called leaders also are willing to develop others. They think leadership is not the province of just the formal leaders. To them, leadership should emerge everywhere. Since they believe their role in life is to serve, not to be served, they want to bring out the best in others. If a good leader rises, servant leaders are willing to partner with that person, and even step aside and take a different role if necessary. They thrive on developing others and the belief that individuals with expertise will come forward as needed throughout the organization.

Robert Greenleaf said it well: "The true test of a servant leader is this: Do those around the servant leader become wiser, freer, more autonomous, healthier, and better able themselves to become servant leaders?"[8]

The Plight of the Ego

What keeps people from becoming servant leaders? The human ego. We believe that ego can stand for edging good out and putting yourself in the center. That's when we start to get a distorted image of our own importance and see ourselves as the center of the universe. The greater good is a foreign thought.

There are two ways our ego gets in the way. One is *false pride*, when you start thinking more of yourself than you should. That's when you start pushing and shoving for credit and thinking leadership is about you rather than those who are led. You spend much of your time promoting yourself. Your ego also gets in your way through *self-doubt* or *fear*—thinking less of yourself than you should. You are consumed with your own shortcomings and are hard on yourself. You spend a great deal of time protecting yourself. With both false pride and self-doubt, you have a hard time believing you are okay. To borrow the title from an old song, you are "looking for love in all the wrong places." Now you think that, as Robert S. McGee warns, "your self-worth is a function of your performance plus others' opinions."[9] Since your performance varies from day to day and people are often fickle, with that belief your self-worth is up for grabs every day.

It's easy to understand that self-doubt comes from lack of self-esteem, because people afflicted with it on a daily basis act as if they are worth less than others. It is less obvious with people who have false pride, because they behave as if they are worth more than others. People with false pride, who act as if they are the only ones who count, are really trying to make up for their lack of self-esteem. They overcompensate for their "not okay" feelings by trying to control everything and everybody around them. In the process, they make themselves unlovable to those around them.

It's interesting to see how false pride and self-doubt play out in managers. When managers are addicted to either ego affliction, it erodes their effectiveness. Managers dominated by false pride are often called "controllers." Even when they don't know what they are doing, they have a high need for power and control. Even when it's clear to everyone that they are wrong, they keep on insisting they are right. These folks aren't much for supporting their people, either. If everyone is upbeat and confident, con-trollers throw out the wet blanket. They support their bosses over their people because they want to climb the hierarchy and be part of the bosses' crowd.

At the other end of the spectrum are the fear-driven managers who are often characterized as "do-nothing bosses." They are described as "never around, always avoiding conflict, and not very helpful." They often leave people alone even when those peo-ple are insecure and don't know what they are doing. Do-nothing bosses don't seem to believe in themselves or trust in their own judgment. They value others' thoughts more than their own—especially the thoughts of those they report to. As a result, they rarely speak up and support their own people. Under pressure, they seem to defer to whoever has the most power.

If any of this sounds a bit too close for comfort, don't be alarmed. Most of us have traces of both false pride and self-doubt, because the issue is really ego. We are stuck, all alone, focusing only on ourselves. The good news is that there is an antidote for both.

Ego Antidotes

The antidote for false pride is humility. True leadership—the essence of what people long for and want desperately to follow—implies a certain humility that is appropriate and elicits the best response from people.

Jim Collins supports this truth in *Good to Great*.[10] He found two characteristics that describe great leaders: *will* and *humility*. Will is the determination to follow through on a vision/mission/goal. Humility is the capacity to realize that leadership is not about the leader; it's about the people and what they need.

According to Collins, when things are going well for typical self-serving leaders, they look in the mirror, beat their chests, and tell themselves how good they are. When things go wrong, they look out the window and blame everyone else. On the other hand, when things go well for great leaders, they look out the window and give everybody else the credit. When things go wrong, these servant leaders look in the mirror and ask questions like "What could I have done differently that would have allowed these people to be as great as they could be?" That requires real humility.

One of the keys, therefore, to becoming a servant leader is humility. We have found two compelling definitions of humility. The first one appeared in a book by Ken Blanchard and Norman Vincent Peale, *The Power of Ethical Management*:[11]

> ***People with humility don't think less of themselves; they just think about themselves less.***

So, people who are humble have solid self-esteem.

The second definition of humility comes from Fred Smith, author of *You and Your Network*:[12]

> ***People with humility don't deny their power; they just recognize that it passes through them, not from them.***

Too many people think that who they are is their position and the power it gives them. Yet that's not true. Where does your power come from? It's not from your position; it's from the people whose lives you touch. Most people would like to make the world a better place. But how many actually have a plan for how they will do that? Very few. And yet we all can make the world a better place through the moment-to-moment decisions we make as we interact with the people we come into contact with at work, at home, and in the community.

Suppose as you leave your house one morning, someone yells at you. You have a choice: You can yell back, or you can hug the person and wish her a good day. Someone cuts you off on your way to work. You have a choice: Will you chase him down and give him an obscene gesture, or will you send a prayer toward his car? We have choices all the time as we interact with other human beings. Humility tames your judgmental nature and motivates you to reach out to support and encourage others. That's where your power comes from.

What's the antidote for fear? It's love. Do you have kids? Do you love your kids? Does this love for your kids completely depend on their success? If they're successful, you love them; if they're not, you won't? Few people would agree with this. You love your kids unconditionally, right? What if you accepted that unconditional love for yourself? You know God doesn't make junk. He unconditionally loves each one of us. Did you know that you can't control enough, sell enough, make enough money, or have a high-enough position to get any more love? You have all the love you need. All you have to do is open yourself to it.

What Servant Leaders Do

The Secret: What Great Leaders Know—And Do[13]—a book Ken Blanchard wrote with Mark Miller, vice president of training and development for Chick-fil-A—illustrates that great leaders *serve*. This book is built around the acronym SERVE. In fact, Chick-fil-A organizes its management training program around the five fundamental ways in which every great leader serves. And since

Chick-fil-A has less than 5 percent turnover among its restaurant managers in more than 1,100 restaurants, this program has a pretty good track record.

S stands for See the Future. This has to do with the visionary role of leaders that we discussed in detail in Chapter 2, "The Power of Vision." Leadership is about taking people from one place to another. We can't say enough about the importance of having a compelling vision. Once a clear vision is established, goals and strategies can be developed within the context of the vision.

Consider these questions as you think about Seeing the Future:

- What is your team's purpose?
- Where do you want your team to be in five years?
- How many members of your team could tell you what the team is trying to become or achieve?
- What values do you want to drive the behavior of your team?
- How can you communicate your vision of the future to your team?

E stands for Engage and Develop People. That's what Section III, "Treat Your People Right," was all about. We took you on a transformational journey from self leadership to one-on-one leadership, to team leadership, to organizational leadership. As a leader, once the vision and direction are set, you have to turn the hierarchical pyramid upside down and focus on engaging and developing your people so that they can live according to the vision. You also must take care of your customers in a way that creates customer maniacs and raving fans.

Consider these questions as you think about Engaging and Developing People:

- How much time do you invest looking for talented people to join your organization?

- What are the key characteristics you look for in the people you select?

- To what extent have you successfully engaged each member of your team?

- What are ten specific things you could do to engage individuals more effectively in the work of your team and the organization?

- What have you done to suggest to your people that when it comes to implementation activities, you work for them?

- How are you encouraging the development of your people?

R stands for Reinvent Continuously. Reinventing Continuously has three aspects. First, great leaders reinvent continuously on a personal level. They are always interested in ways to enhance their own knowledge and skills. The very best leaders are learners. Great leaders find their own approach to learning—some read, some listen to tapes, some spend time with mentors. They do whatever it takes to keep learning. We believe if you stop learning, you stop leading. We feel that everyone in every organization, every year, should have at least one learning goal. What do you hope will be on your resume next year that's not on it this year? For example, maybe you might want to learn Spanish this year, since more and more of your customers are Spanish-speaking. You might want to learn some new computer program that will make your life simpler and help you retrieve the information you need to make effective decisions. Whatever it is, focus on learning something new every year.

Consider these questions as you think about reinventing yourself continuously:

- Who are your mentors?
- What are you reading or listening to on tape?

The second part of Reinvent Continuously applies to systems and processes. Great leaders are always seeking answers to questions like these:

- How can we do the work better?
- How can we do it with fewer errors?
- How can we do it faster?
- How can we do it for less?
- What systems or processes can we change to enhance performance?

Leaders must also work to instill the desire for improvement into the people doing the day-to-day work. The leader may champion this cause, but the people make it happen—or not.

The third part of Reinvent Continuously is the idea of structural invention. Many people assume that an organizational structure is permanent. In many cases, the organizational structure no longer serves the business—the people are serving the structure. Great leaders don't change the structure just for something to do. They understand that their organizational structure should be fluid and flexible. That belief is key to creating the energizing structures and systems that are characteristic of high performing organizations. Other, less proficient leaders tend to let the structure drive their decisions rather than adapting the structure to meet the business's ever-changing demands.

Don Shula, the famous NFL coach and coauthor with Ken Blanchard of *Everyone's a Coach*, was a great believer in this. He said great teams are "audible-ready." Suppose a football quarterback calls "halfback right." When he gets to the line of scrimmage, he sees that the defense is all to the right. He doesn't turn to the halfback and say, "Hold on; I think they're going to kill you." He decides to call a new play. Why? Because the structure and what they've set up is no longer appropriate. Shula always felt it was important to realize that you don't call an audible for nothing. It's good to have a plan; it's good to have your structure in place. But always be watchful and determine whether it's serving you, your customers, and your people well. If it's not, change it.

V stands for Value Results and Relationships. Great leaders—those who lead at a higher level—value both results and relationships. Both are critical for long-term survival. Not either/or, but both/and. For too long, many leaders have felt that they needed to choose. Most corporate leaders have said it's all about results. In reality, there are two tests of a leader. First, does he get results? Second, does he have followers? By the way, if you don't have followers, it's very hard to get long-term results.

The way to maximize your results as a leader is to have high expectations for both results and relationships. If leaders can take care of their customers and create a motivating environment for their people, profits and financial strength are the applause they get for a job well done. You see, success is both results and relationships. It's a proven formula.

Consider these questions as you think about Valuing Results and Relationships:

- How much emphasis do you place on getting results?
- How many of your people would say that you have made a significant investment in their lives?
- What are the ways in which you have expressed appreciation for work well done in the last thirty days?

E stands for Embody the Values. All genuine leadership is built on trust. There are many ways to build trust. One way is to live consistently with the values you profess. If I say customers are important, my actions had better support that statement. If I choose to live as if customers are not important, people will have reason to question my trustworthiness. In the final analysis, if I am deemed untrustworthy by my people, I will not be trusted—or followed as a leader. Embody the Values is all about walking your talk. The leader, above all, has to be a walking example of the vision. Leaders who say "Do as I say, not as I do" are ineffective in the long run.

Consider these questions as you think about Embodying the Values:

- How can you better integrate your organizational values into how your team operates?

- What are some ways you can communicate your core values to your team over the next thirty days?

- How can you alter your daily activities to create greater personal alignment with these values?

- How can you recognize and reward people who embody these values?

The SERVE acronym builds a wonderful picture of how servant leaders operate. But it's a tough act to follow. Continually doing a good job in each of these areas is a significant task, yet it's worth it. Servant leadership is about getting people to a higher level by leading people at a higher level.

Servant Leadership: A Mandate or a Choice

We believe that servant leadership has never been more applicable to the world of leadership than it is today. Not only are people looking for deeper purpose and meaning as they meet the challenges of today's changing world, they are also looking for principles that actually work. Servant leadership works.

As Blanchard and Zigarmi found in their research, when the "what"—the *leadership* aspect of servant leadership—gets things started in the right direction and the "how"—the *servant* part of servant leadership—excites employees and customers, organizational vitality and success are almost guaranteed. If that's true, why wouldn't everyone—even self-serving leaders, who are focused only on making money or their own power, recognition, and status—want to be servant leaders? Doesn't servant leadership benefit their motives, too? The answer is yes, but not for long. Self-serving motivations can't be hidden for long. Your heart will be exposed. As Blanchard and Zigarmi found, there is a direct correlation between bad senior leadership and organizational failure. What happened at Enron, WorldCom, and other companies speaks volumes.

Servant leadership is not just another management technique. It is a way of life for those with servant hearts. In organizations run by servant leaders, servant leadership will become a mandate, not a choice, and the by-products will be better leadership, better service, a higher performing organization, and more success and significance.

Servant leadership provides better leadership. Organizations led by servant leaders are less likely to experience poor leadership. In studying bad leadership, Barbara Gellerman found seven different patterns, falling along a continuum ranging from ineffective to unethical leadership. Ineffective leadership just does not get the job done because of incompetence, rigidity, and lack of self-control or callousness. Unethical leadership, in contrast, is about right and wrong. "Unethical leadership can be effective leadership, just as ineffective leadership can be ethical," Gellerman states. "But unethical leadership cannot make even the most basic claim to decency and good conduct, and so the leadership process is derailed."[14]

Organizations led by servant leaders ward off unethical leadership. When the vision and values are clearly defined, ethical and moral dilemmas are less likely to emerge. Drea Zigarmi, coauthor of *The Leader Within*,[15] contends that a moral dilemma exists when there are no guidelines for decision making, forcing an individual to rely on his or her own values and beliefs. An ethical dilemma arises when the organization has clearly established guidelines for behavior and the individual must consciously decide to go along with or violate those guidelines.

Organizations work more effectively if clear vision and values are established up front, as they are under servant leadership. When unethical leadership occurs, it is often the result of the moral confusion created by the organization's lack of clearly established guidelines that a compelling vision provides.

Servant leadership provides a cure for ineffectiveness as well. Suppose someone who is unqualified accepts a leadership position. What will it take for this person to become effective and get the job done? The key is humility. True servant leadership embraces a humble sincerity that brings out the best in leaders and those they serve. Because servant leaders have solid self-esteem, they are willing to admit when they have a weakness or need assistance. Put in positions over their heads, they can reach out to their people for help.

We had a beautiful example of this in our own company. Because of a leadership crisis, we needed Debbie Blanchard, one of the owners, to take over our sales department. The only sales experience she had was working at Nordstrom in the summer while in college. When she had her first meeting with all her salespeople, her humility showed through. She told them that she needed their help if she were to be effective. She flew around the country, met with her team, found out what their needs were, and figured out how she could help them. Responding to her humility, the salespeople reached out to make sure she had the knowledge she needed to be effective. With Debbie at the helm, the sales department has produced the highest sales in the history of the company, far exceeding its annual goals.

Servant leadership provides better service. Organizations led by servant leaders are more likely to take better care of their customers. As we've pointed out, if you don't take care of your customers today, somebody is waiting, ready and willing to do it. Again, the only thing your competition can't steal from you is the relationship your people have with your customers. Under servant leadership these relationships can really grow, because the people closest to the customer are given the power to soar like eagles rather than quack like ducks. As we pointed out in Chapter 3, the great customer service experiences created by Southwest Airlines and Ritz Carlton were a direct result of servant leadership. Leaders like Herb Kelleher and Horst Shultze set up their organizations to empower everyone—including the frontline people—to make decisions, use their brains, and be servant leaders who could carry out the vision of high-quality customer service.

Servant leadership helps create a high performing organization. When we discussed HPO SCORES in Chapter 1, we said that if becoming a high performing organization is the destination, leadership is the engine. And the kind of leadership we want is servant leadership. The one HPO SCORES element that best characterizes a servant leader is *Shared Power and High Involvement*. They go hand in hand with leaders who realize it's not about them.

Is being a servant leader just about being nice for the sake of niceness? No—it works. Practicing shared power and high involvement strongly impacts financial results through productivity, retention, and employee satisfaction. Using U.S. Department of Labor data and surveys of over 1,500 firms from various industries, Huselid and Becker found that such participative practices significantly improved employee retention, increased productivity, and improved financial performance. In fact, they were able to quantify the financial impact of participative practices with enough confidence to say that each standard deviation in the use of participative practices increased a company's market value between $35,000 and $78,000 per employee.[16]

The servant leaders in high performing organizations understand that day-to-day decision making should occur closest to the action and on the front lines by those directly involved with the customer. Being involved in decisions that affect their lives reduces people's stress and creates a healthier, happier workforce. Involvement in decision making increases their ownership and commitment as well as effectiveness.

For example, Chaparral Steel does not use quality inspectors. The people in their plants are responsible for the products they produce and the quality of those products. Given the power and responsibility for decision making, they act as they are expected to: as owners.

Servant leaders in high performing organizations involve their people at all levels and from multiple areas of the business in complex and strategic decision making. Research demonstrates that decisions and action plans are more effective when people whose commitment is required are part of the planning.[17] Effectiveness increases in quality, quantity, and implementation. These kinds of decisions are often made in a team environment where everyone involved is in the room at the same time, able to benefit from and react to each other's thinking and to arrive at "collective wisdom." W.L. Gore, a company whose watchwords are "commitment, empowerment, and innovation," recognizes the importance of personal contact. Gore even goes so far as to limit the size of its facilities. They will build a new plant rather than expand one where associates would lose contact with each other.

High performing organizations do not depend on a few peak performers to guide and direct, but have broadly developed leadership capacities. This allows for self-management, ownership, and the power to act quickly as the situation requires. Pushing decision making to those closest to the action is an empowering practice. Servant leaders in high performing organizations create environments where people are free to choose to empower themselves.

The benefit of shifting power from top management leaders to the people closest to the action is illustrated by the journey of Summit Pointe, a large state and locally funded behavioral health organization. Eunice Parisi-Carew, one of the HPO SCORES researchers, had the opportunity to collaborate with Erv Brinker, the CEO—a wonderful example of a servant leader. When Erv took his position, he determined that it was critical to share the power concentrated at the top and allow those involved on the front lines to make decisions that impacted their lives and the service they provided. His first step was to hire Dev Ogle, a talented senior consultant, to act as his guide. Dev began by training his senior leaders, using an approach that emphasized the importance of sharing leadership and power. Brinker's expectation was that the senior leaders would act as models as he moved the organization from a hierarchical to a team-based culture. The journey was successful. Summit Pointe is now an organization that supports team performance. For example, each team sets its own performance standards, monitors its progress, and receives pay incentives based on its accomplishments. They use a "pay-for-performance" approach to compensation. Now that they are in control, teams are actually setting higher goals for themselves than had previously been set for them. A collection of both hard and soft data revealed the exceptional results of servant leadership:

- Administrative overhead has been reduced significantly while the number of customers served has increased: It went from 230 staff serving 2,000 customers per year to 100 staff serving 8,000 customers, with a $1.5 million cost savings.

- New services such as prevention have been added, with increased revenue of $5 million.

- Communication across departments has increased dramatically.

- Employee morale has increased, and the isolation that is common in this stressful field has decreased dramatically.

- Whereas the industry average for turnover is 29 percent, Summit Point has averaged 9 percent.

Servant leaders think differently than self-serving leaders. It is not possible to share power without believing that people can and will manage power and decision making responsibly if given the proper training, information, and opportunity. It is also not possible to create a high-involvement culture without including everyone. Servant leaders in high performing organizations not only appreciate but capitalize on cultural diversity; style diversity; social diversity; and diversity in race, religion, sexual orientation, and age. They realize that effective decision making, problem solving, and innovation come from utilizing different perspectives.

Servant leadership brings more success and significance. In his classic book *Halftime*, Bob Buford reveals that most people, later in life, want to move from success to significance—from getting to giving.[18] Organizations led by servant leaders are more likely to create environments where people at all levels can experience both success and significance.

Too many leaders today focus only on success and think it depends only on how much wealth they have accumulated, the amount of recognition they have received, and the power and status they possess. There is nothing inherently wrong with any of those things, as long as you don't identify those things as who you are. As an alternative, we'd like you to focus on the opposite of each of those as you move from success to significance. What's the opposite of accumulating wealth? It's generosity of time, talent, treasure, and touch (reaching out to support others). What's the opposite of recognition? It's service. What's the opposite of power and status? It's loving relationships.

We've found over the years that when you focus only on success, you will never reach significance. That's the problem with self-serving leaders—they never get out of their own way. On the other hand, if you focus on significance—generosity, service, and loving relationships—you'll be amazed at how much success will come your way. Take Mother Teresa. She couldn't have cared less about accumulating wealth, recognition, and status. Her whole life was focused on significance. And yet what happened? Success came her way. Her ministry received tremendous financial backing, she was recognized all over the world, and she was given the highest status wherever she went. She was the ultimate servant leader. If you focus on significance first, your emphasis will be on people. Through that emphasis, success *and* results will follow.

An amazing story of significance occurred during the 100-yard dash at the Special Olympics several years ago in Spokane, Washington. Nine contestants waited eagerly for the starting gun to fire. When it did, they raced toward the finish line as fast as they could, given their physical disabilities. About a third of the way down the track, one of the boys fell. He tried to get up and fell again. In frustration, he lay on the track, sobbing. While six of the other racers continued to push toward the finish line and possible victory, two of the youngsters, hearing the sobs of their opponent, stopped, turned around, headed back toward their fallen competitor, and helped him up. The three boys held hands, walked down the track, and crossed the finish line together, well after the others had finished the race. The crowd was surprised. When they realized what had happened, they rose in unison and gave these youngsters a longer and louder ovation than they'd given the winner of the race.

Life is all about the choices we make as we interact with each other. We can choose to be self-serving or serving. Most of the youngsters in the race chose to focus on their own success—victory—but two tossed aside their dreams in favor of serving someone else. The crowd responded with enthusiasm, because we all yearn to live at a higher level, and these young people modeled what that means. They made a different choice—they were true servant leaders.

We hope you make these kinds of choices. As leaders, life constantly presents us with opportunities to choose to love and serve one another. Someone said to Margie Blanchard recently, "You've lived with Ken for almost 45 years. What do you think leadership is all about?" She said, "Leadership is not about love—it *is* love. It is loving your mission, it's loving your customers, it's loving your people, and it's loving yourself enough to get out of the way so other people can be magnificent." That's what leading at a higher level is all about.

Chapter 13

DETERMINING YOUR LEADERSHIP POINT OF VIEW

Ken Blanchard, Margie Blanchard,
and Pat Zigarmi

All right, you've heard from us. Throughout this book, we have essentially shared with you our leadership point of view—our thoughts about leading and motivating people. Our leadership point of view is based on a belief that to create a great organization, leaders have to make sure everyone's aiming at the right target and vision. They need to make sure everyone is treating both their customers and their people right. As leaders, they need to focus on serving, not being served.

Now it's your turn.

The goal of this chapter is to help you develop your own leadership point of view. Not only will this help you clarify your thoughts on leadership, it will also prepare you to teach your leadership point of view to others.

Why is developing a clear leadership point of view important? Ken Blanchard was sold on this idea after reading Noel Tichy's book, *The Leadership Engine*, and talking with Noel while they were doing consulting work with Yum! Brands. Noel's extensive research has shown that effective leaders have a clear, teachable leadership point of view and are willing to share it with and teach it to others, particularly the people they work with.[1]

This realization so impacted Ken that he and his wife, Margie, created a course called "Communicating Your Leadership Point of View" as part of the Master of Science in Executive Leadership (MSEL) program jointly offered by The Ken Blanchard Companies and the College of Business at the University of San Diego. As we have said, effective leadership is a journey beginning with self leadership, moving to one-on-one leadership, then team leadership, and ending with organizational leadership. This course is the final focus of the self leadership portion of the degree program. The course culminates in all of the students making presentations to the class that describe their leadership points of view. The students deliver their leadership points of view as though they are talking to those who report to them in their organizational leadership positions.

If you can teach people your leadership point of view, they will not only have the benefit of understanding where you're coming from, but they'll also be clear on what you expect from them and what they can expect from you. They may also begin to solidify their own thinking about leadership so that they can teach others, too. Tichy feels strongly that learning, teaching, and leading are intricately intertwined and, therefore, should be considered inherent parts of everyone's job description. Why everyone's? Because as we emphasized in the previous chapter, "Servant Leadership," we are all leaders in some part of our lives.

Elements of a Leadership Point of View

In determining your leadership point of view, you should be able to answer seven questions:

1. Who are the influencers (leaders) in your life who have had a positive (or, in some cases, negative) impact on your life, such as parents, teachers, coaches, or bosses? What did you learn from these people about leadership?

2. Think of your life purpose. Why are you here, and what do you want to accomplish?

3. What are your core values that will guide your behavior as you attempt to live your life "on purpose"?

4. Given what you've learned from past leaders, your life purpose, and your core values, what are your beliefs about leading and motivating people?

5. What can your people expect from you?

6. What do you expect from your people?

7. How will you set an example for your people?

Your Leadership Role Models

When we ask people who most impacted their lives, seldom do they mention bosses or other organizational leaders. More often they talk about their parents, grandparents, friends, coaches, or teachers. When Ken Blanchard is asked this question, he is quick to mention his mother and father:

"My mom was the ultimate positive thinker. She told everyone that I laughed before I cried, I smiled before I frowned, and I danced before I walked. With those kinds of messages, how could I have ended up anything but a positive thinker? My dad was a career naval officer who retired as an admiral. He was a powerful leadership role model for me. He didn't think leadership was choosing between people or results. He thought leadership was a 'both/and' relationship—both people and results were important to him. He taught me that position power and 'my way or the highway' are not the way to lead. I'll never forget when I was elected president of the seventh grade and came home all excited. Dad said, 'It's great, Ken, that you're president of your class. But now that you have a position, don't use it. Great leaders are followed not because they have position power, but because they're respected and trusted as individuals.' He always supported and involved his people, yet he demanded high performance.

"My mom instilled in me a strong belief in God. That helped me keep things in perspective. Mom said, 'Ken, don't act like you're better than anybody else. But don't let anyone act like they are better than you, either. We are all children of God.' The one-two punch I received from my mom and dad gave me the belief that in life, I was here to serve, not to be served."

Who influenced *your* life and gave you a sense of what leadership is all about?

Your Life Purpose

Why are you here? What business are you in? As we suggested in Chapter 2, "The Power of Vision," if an organization doesn't have a clear purpose and sense of what business it's in, we think there's something wrong. Yet few people have a clear sense of their life's purpose. How can you make good decisions about how you should use your time if you don't know what business you're in?

The following is a simple process that will help you create a good first draft of your life purpose.[2] First, list some personal characteristics you feel good about. Use nouns, such as

computer expertise	enthusiasm
physical strength	wit
sense of humor	sales ability
mechanical genius	happiness
people skills	charm
problem-solving skills	good looks
teaching skills	artistic ability
example	creativity
energy	patience

For example, Ken chose *sense of humor*, *people skills*, *example*, and *teaching skills*.

Next, list ways you successfully interact with people. These will be verbs, such as

teach	inspire
produce	manage
educate	motivate
encourage	plan
stimulate	act
lead	sell
love	coach
help	write

Ken picked *educate*, *help*, *inspire*, and *motivate*.

Finally, visualize what your perfect world would be. What would people do or say? Write a description of this perfect world.

> To Ken, a perfect world is where everyone is aware of the presence of God in their lives and all people are servant leaders, reflecting God's light and shining that light on others.

Now combine two of your nouns, two of your verbs, and your definition of your perfect world, and you'll have a good start on a definition of your life purpose.

Ken's life purpose is to be "a loving teacher and an example of simple truths that helps and motivates myself and others to awaken to the presence of God in our lives."

One of our MSEL students said his life purpose was "*to use my humor and people skills to help and inspire others to be successful in achieving their goals.*" He went on to say, "I would like our workplace to become a company where people want to come to work and a place where people can grow to feel better about who they are and what they are accomplishing."

Your Core Values

Values are beliefs you feel strongly about because you choose them over other alternatives. It has been said that

---

*The most important thing in life
is to decide what's most important.*

When you were a kid, your parents and other adults tended to dictate your values, but at some point in life we all choose what is important to us. Your boss might value results more than people. You might be the opposite. People don't all value the same things. Some people value wealth and power, while others are more concerned with safety or survival. Success is a value; integrity and relationships are values as well. The following is a sample list of personal values:

truth	influence	fairness
efficiency	integrity	order
initiative	peace	spirituality
environmentalism	loyalty	adventure
power	clarity	cooperation
control	security	humor
courage	love	collaboration
competition	persistence	resources
excitement	sincerity	trust
creativity	fun	excellence
happiness	relationships	teamwork
honor	wisdom	quality
innovation	flexibility	hard work
obedience	perspective	responsiveness
financial	commitment	fulfillment
growth	recognition	purposefulness
community	learning	self-control
support	honesty	cleverness
service	originality	success
profitability	candor	stewardship
freedom	prosperity	support
friendship	respect	

In trying to determine what your values are, you might start with a long list. You probably like a lot of the values just listed, plus others you might think of. But fewer are better, particularly if you want your values to guide your behavior. In *Managing by Values*, Ken Blanchard and Michael O'Connor contend that more than three or four values is too many and can become immobilizing.[3] So, see if you can pick out what you think are your most important values. If you're having trouble narrowing down your top values, you might combine a couple. For example, Ken combined two words to create "spiritual peace" as his number one value, followed by *integrity*, *love*, and *success*.

Your number one value is often your core value—something you want to be present no matter what you're doing. So, if your number one value is integrity, living with integrity is not an option.

In talking about a core value, the implication is that your values should be rank-ordered. Why? Because values are sometimes in conflict, as we discussed in Chapter 2, "The Power of Vision." For example, if you value financial growth but integrity is your core value, any activities that could lead to financial gain must be checked against your integrity value.

How do you know when you're living according to a particular value? You have to define that value as specifically as possible. Let's take something that you might not think is easy to define, like love. According to Ken, "I value love. I know I am living by this value anytime I feel loving toward myself and others, anytime I have compassion, anytime I feel love in my heart, anytime I feel the love of others, anytime my heart fills up with love, and anytime I look for the love of others."

Your Beliefs About Leading and Motivating People

Your beliefs are where you will find the essence of your leadership point of view. These should flow naturally from the people who have influenced you and from your purpose and values.

For example, let's look at some of the beliefs about leading and motivating people that Ken shares with others. You'll

283

recognize that his beliefs represent some of the key themes in this book:

"I believe people who produce good results feel good about themselves. Therefore, my leadership role as your manager is to help you win—to accomplish your goals. I want you to get an A. To make that a reality, I have learned that there are three aspects to managing people's performance: *performance planning*, *performance coaching*, and *performance review*.

"*Performance planning* gets things going in the right direction, because during that process you learn what you'll be held accountable for—your goals—and what good behavior looks like—your performance standards. In essence, performance planning is like giving you the final exam at the beginning of class.

"During *performance coaching* I focus, on a day-to-day coaching basis, on teaching you 'the right answers'—how to accomplish your goals and get an A. To do that, I have to manage by wandering around—either personally or through a good information system, so that I can observe your performance. If things are going in the right direction, I should cheer you on with an 'attaboy' or 'attagirl.' If progress is not being made, I should redirect your efforts and get you back on course. In other words, you should know when you are getting 'wrong answers' so that we can discuss what would make a 'good answer.'

"In most organizations, managers spend more time on the annual *performance review* than they do on planning and coaching. I feel that is a mistake. If I do a good job of performance planning and performance coaching with you, the annual performance review will, in essence, be just that—a review. You will hear nothing new from me that you have not already heard during my day-to-day coaching. This is the time you should be receiving your A. If you don't, I have to take major responsibility for this less-than-expected performance.

"In some cases—when you don't receive an A and I have made every effort to help make you an A student—we both might decide that you are in the wrong position for your talents. Then our discussion naturally will move toward career planning. Everything I do as a manager with you should be geared toward helping you produce good results and, in the process, feel good about yourself."

What People Can Expect from You

Letting people know what they can expect from you underscores the idea that leadership is a partnership process. It gives people a picture of how things will look under your leadership.

For example, one of the students in the MSEL program at the University of San Diego described what his people could expect from him:

"Knowing that I like building things will help you understand what you can expect from me. In fact, I look at many different things in the context of building. I like building houses. I like building my family. I like building businesses, and I like building and developing people. I'm happy to roll up my sleeves to help build most anything. It's what I enjoy most. So you can expect that I will give you plenty of my time, and I will listen to you when you see the need.

"I love to teach and coach, so you can expect that I will teach and coach you. You'll be empowered to manage your business the way you see fit, and we'll debrief frequently so that we are always on the same page. You'll be allowed to make mistakes. In fact, I encourage you to run fast and not be afraid of mistakes. When you make them, we'll talk about them, and we'll seek better alternatives. I have high standards, so you should know I will hold high expectations for you, but I think you'll like the support.

I believe one continues to learn each day of one's life, and I enjoy doing it. In short, I am here to serve you."

What You Expect from Your People

Because leading is a partnership process, it is perfectly reasonable—in fact, it's imperative—that you let people know what you expect from them. This gives people a picture of what their behavior will look like under your leadership.

Here is another example from one of the students in the MSEL program at USD:

> "My expectations of you can be combined into a saying known as the Golden Rule: *Do unto others as you would have them do unto you.* What do I mean by that? I expect you all to act ethically in everything you do. There are many opportunities to take shortcuts and do things that will result in short-term gains. Plenty of business examples in recent years have shown how disastrous this can be. I expect you to stand tall on this issue and to not allow anyone to think that you tolerate fraud or anything unethical. You manage hundreds of employees. While each of them may not know you that well, they need to know your feelings on this topic by way of your word and example."

How You Will Set an Example

Your leadership point of view should let others know how you will set an example for the values and behaviors you are encouraging. As most parents know, people learn from your behavior, not from your words. Leaders must walk their talk.

For example, the MSEL student just mentioned made clear how he would set an example for his people:

> "All of you know that I released our company's top sales-person about nine months ago for questionable activities. He thought that he was untouchable due to his status as a top-producing account executive. No one, including

myself, is above the ethical standards that are expected of a person working at our company."

Developing Your Own Leadership Point of View

Now it's your turn to pull together all seven elements and create your own leadership point of view. To serve as a guide, we'll share a couple of examples from our MSEL students. The first example is from Stephanie Rosol, who works in human resources for Harrah's Entertainment, Inc. We picked hers because she presents the seven elements of her leadership point of view in an engaging and motivating way.

My Background

I grew up in a single-parent household, a product of an early 1970s California divorce by the age of three. I am the oldest of my siblings and cousins. As a result, I was naturally the first to do things. I wasn't used to waiting around for someone else to do them for me.

From my mom, I learned perseverance and optimism. She believed your life is what you make of it and you don't need a lot to be happy. The one thing you do need is choice. This is huge for me. I believe we have a choice in how we perceive and react to the world around us. We have a choice in everything, and in that, we are powerful.

The other piece that influenced me early on was the lack of structure. Nothing was overtly prescribed. While basic rules applied, the theory of "life is yours to figure out" prevailed. On one hand, I didn't have a lot of clear role models for how I wanted to be, but on the other hand, the only limitations were self-imposed. While no one was telling me what I should be, no one was telling me what I couldn't be, either.

Early experiences in life led me to believe the world isn't always safe for those who are vulnerable. Because of that, I had a strong need to control my environment, and I was in a hurry to be a grown-up. From an early age, I've worked to take care of myself. While I wasn't the most reliable papergirl or fast-food worker in town (I had difficulty with timeliness—sometimes I still do), from the age of thirteen, I worked to be able to do the things others took for granted. I believed if it were to be, it was up to me.

I started out pretty focused on achievement and accomplishment. Once I started acquiring the safety, security, and love I sought in the world, my perspective began to shift. My basic needs for survival are now satisfied, and I am now more focused on meaning and purpose. My leadership role models were my teachers and counselors. With their support, I've been able to move to a place where I seek to serve others.

My Purpose and Values

I believe my responsibility in a leadership position is to serve those I work with. My goal is for my interactions to encourage people to grow and become healthier, wiser, freer, more autonomous, and more likely to serve others inside and outside the workplace.

I want to give you every opportunity to identify, stretch toward, and reach your potential. By doing this, you grow, I grow, and the people we serve all benefit. *My life mission is to work with people to build their confidence and recognize their capabilities.* I believe we all do the best we can, based on our awareness. I pledge to give you the opportunity to increase your awareness on a daily basis.

Wouldn't it be great if only we could act with the confidence others have in us? Why is it that the validation we seek most often comes from outside of us? For example, when we are uncertain about how we will do on a big project, on a test, or with delivering a presentation, our supporters tell us things like "You'll do great" or "I don't know what you're worried about. You always do well." Why is it so easy for others to express confidence in us while we undermine ourselves with worry and doubt? My theory is that we are conditioned to focus on our weaknesses. We undervalue what comes naturally to us. We end up *performing not to fail* instead of doing what we love.

How many of you have heard this story? After a man's untimely death, his family went through his personal items and found a tattered piece of paper the deceased had held onto since third grade. The paper listed the qualities his classmates valued about him (runs fast, makes funny jokes, has good handwriting, etc.). The man had held onto it all that time. The point is that for many of us, our desire for validation and appreciation never goes away. It doesn't come along often enough.

My Beliefs About Leading and Motivating People

I want to increase your focus on your strengths and encourage you to internalize your appreciation of your best qualities. I believe we are born good and that we all have the capacity to be great. But our success doesn't come from identifying and/or "fixing" our weaknesses. It comes from leveraging our strengths. We grow the most where we know the most. Excellent performers are not well-rounded; in fact, they are sharp. The tragedy in life is not that we do not have enough strengths; it is that we fail to use the ones we have.

One of my favorite quotes comes from Marianne Williamson, although Nelson Mandela is often credited with it, because it was part of his inauguration speech. Mandela is an amazing leader who used adversity to look inward. He used his experiences to better serve the world. Here is the quote:

> *Our deepest fear is not that we are inadequate. Our deepest fear is that we are powerful beyond measure. It is our light, not our darkness, that most frightens us. We ask ourselves, "Who am I to be brilliant, gorgeous, talented, and fabulous?" Actually, who are you not to be? Your playing small doesn't serve the world. There's nothing enlightened about shrinking so that other people won't feel insecure around you. We were born to make manifest the glory that is within us. It is not just in some of us, it is in everyone, and as we let our own light shine, we unconsciously give other people permission to do the same. As we are liberated from our own fear, our presence automatically liberates others.*

I want to support you in eliminating those doubts and fears, to see weaknesses as simply underdeveloped strengths.

What You Can Expect from Me

You can expect that I will be honest and understanding, but that I will have high expectations for you and for myself. I pledge to provide you with development. My feedback for you will be to educate, facilitate, and support rather than dictate, suffocate, and control. I want to have fun with you and laugh with you. I will work toward an ease of communication that will help us both achieve our goals. We will get there by building trust. Please know that I have only the best of intentions for you, our relationship, and the work we do together.

What I Expect from You

I expect that you will take responsibility for your role and the contribution you can make. In our regular meetings, I will ask you to help me by letting me know the answers to the following questions:

What am I doing that helps you succeed?

What am I not doing that you need to succeed?

What am I doing that you would like to do?

How can we make sure you have the opportunity to do what you do best in your role?

How I Will Set an Example for You?

I promise to continue to learn and grow to better serve you. I will strive to model behaviors required for a healthy balance between work and home. I promise to be open to your "feedforward" (ideas and things you think I could benefit from developing or concentrating on) and feedback (thoughts on something that wasn't everything it could be).

I thank you for your attention, your audience, and your valuable time. As I mentioned, my intent in communicating my leadership point of view is to enhance our relationship, build that ease of communication, selfishly get you in my corner, and let you know I'm in yours.

What questions can I answer for you?

Our second example of a leadership point of view is from Eddie Hiner, an MSEL student who is an officer in the Navy SEALs. We include this for a couple of reasons. Although Eddie doesn't follow the seven elements perfectly, he talks from his heart and makes it clear to his people where he comes from, what he believes, and how his beliefs will impact them. So, don't get hung up on following our formula to a T. Your leadership point of view is about who you are and how you intend to be with your people. We also included Eddie's leadership point of view because it illustrates how a military officer can be a servant leader in the context of a hierarchical organization. We believe that servant leadership should be the foundation for all leadership, no matter where you find yourself leading.

How I Learned My Leadership Point of View

By the time I was eleven, both my parents had moved away, leaving my brother and me with our grandmother. We lived in a remote town in the Blue Ridge Mountains of Virginia, where my grandmother had lived her entire life. My grandfather had passed away about seven years earlier, so it was only my grandmother, my brother, and I. She was retired and living on Social Security. Needless to say, we were not wealthy.

My brother and I grew up without parental guidance. We made our own decisions in life, learning by trial and error. My brother was my first mentor—and by far the most influential. Even though he was only thirteen at the time, he had vision and was wise beyond his years. He knew that life had a lot to offer us. He constantly encouraged me to strive to be better and not let my situation determine my future. He taught me what I later learned in the SEAL teams as "offensive mind-set." Offensive mind-set is to be the cause of the effect, not the effect that was caused. Essentially, it means to control your destiny rather than letting your environment control it.

My brother was two years older than I, so he taught me the hard lessons he had learned. We were a *team*. These two concepts are extremely important in my current profession.

My senior year I met my next mentor when I received a baseball scholarship. Coach Guzzo taught me discipline, teamwork, honor, and how to be a winner. He didn't care how good a player you were; if you weren't a team player, you didn't play. During one game he benched one of our best players because he ignored the signal to sacrifice bunt and decided, on his own, to swing at the pitch. His hit scored the winning run, but Coach Guzzo benched him for not being willing to sacrifice himself for the team.

Shortly after leaving school, I decided I wanted to be a Navy SEAL. From the moment I found out about the SEAL teams, I knew that was where I needed to be. I have learned nearly my entire leadership point of view from living it in the teams. The training is centered on core values and team values. Part of the selection requires you to adopt the team's values. Your character is stressed more than your skills or physical ability. I don't know of any other organization in the world that is as good at training character as this one.

My Leadership Point of View

I approach my job as a responsibility and a privilege; I work for you. I compare myself to a stagecoach driver. By driving the stagecoach, I am responsible for leading the team of horses, but without the team, I'm a pedestrian. Without me, you would still be pulling the stagecoach, and you would still be a team. The bottom line is, without you, I don't have a job. Without me, you still have a job. Therefore, I am here because of you, not the other way around.

I realize that everyone makes mistakes. If you make a mistake or use poor judgment because of lack of experience, own up to it and move on. I can deal with that. If it's a character issue, that's a different story. When making a decision, I find it useful to ask myself a few questions. Does it look right? Sound right? Feel right? If I answer no to any one of these, I know it probably isn't the right thing to do. I also consider whether the decision supports the mission and whether I would be willing to walk into the commanding officer's office and tell him about my decision. If I am not willing to do that, I reconsider my decision.

Remember that we are all here for the same reason: to accomplish the mission. This means that sometimes I'll have to make decisions that not all of you agree with. I don't expect you to. If we are all thinking alike, none of us is thinking at all. It is crucial that each one of you think for himself. But sometimes I will make decisions that may not be popular. That is my job and my responsibility. Remember, you fight for a democracy; you don't work for one—and neither do I. We all take orders. Just keep in mind that I am always trying to do the best for the team and that I will shield you from the top. Most of the time, I will leave the decisions up to you. I trust your judgment, because you are the experts. You have the authority to use that judgment. I'm here to guide you; I'm not a dictator. On the rare occasion when I do need to give a direct order, I expect it to be followed both in practice and in spirit. Remember that there is a reason for it.

The past ten years with the teams has had the greatest influence on my leadership perspective. The adversity I have encountered in the teams has helped stimulate a powerful bond between me and the men I work with. The sense of brotherhood that comes from that bond has really influenced the way I approach leadership.

Every leader I have worked for has given me the same advice: Take care of your men. That's why the concept of servant leadership is not a new idea to me. This concept is deeply rooted in the SEAL teams.

> As a platoon commander, I am not only responsible for my team's performance at work; I am also accountable for helping you deal with your personal lives. Being a team is not a part-time job. The whole man goes into combat, not just the one at work.
>
> When you finally make it into the teams, you realize why the character traits we value are crucial to our success. It's simple: We either live by them, or we might die by not doing so.

During the writing of this book, Eddie was in Iraq. No matter how dangerous the assignment, wouldn't you like to have him as your leader?

In this book, we've done our best to give you the leadership point of view that we have been developing over the last 25 years. So, as you develop your own leadership point of view, don't be hard on yourself. This might be your first time thinking about your beliefs about leading and motivating people. Feel free to incorporate any of the ideas you have learned in these pages.

The world needs more leaders who are leading at a higher level. As we said in the introduction, our dream is that someday everyone will know someone who is leading at a higher level. We dream of the day when self-serving leaders are history, and leaders serving others are the rule, not the exception.

You can be a leader who makes a positive difference on our planet. So, go out and do it! We're counting on you.

COMPANION ONLINE RESOURCE

Visit **www.LeadingAtAHigherLevel.com** to access the free virtual conference titled *The Right Kind of Leadership*. Use the password "Leadership" for your FREE access.

ENDNOTES

Introduction

1 Matt Hayes and Jeff Stevens, *The Heart of Business* (Bloomington, IN: Author House, 2005).

2 Robert Greenleaf, *Servant Leadership: A Journey into the Nature of Legitimate Power and Greatness*, 25th Anniversary Edition (New Jersey: Paulist Press, 2002).

Chapter 1

1 John Elkington uses the phrase "triple bottom line accounting" in his 1998 book *Cannibals with Forks*. Elkington's use of the phrase includes environmental and social responsibility measures in accounting reports. Our use of the phrase "triple bottom line" has a different focus: success with customers, employees, and investors.

2 For more information on the HPO SCORES model and the research conducted, see "High-Performing Organizations: Scores" by Don Carew, Fay Kandarian, Eunice Parisi-Carew, and Jesse Stoner. Ken Blanchard Companies, 2001.

3 The HPO SCORES Profile is a psychometrically sound organizational assessment, with strong validity and reliability, that provides feedback on the extent to which the practices in your organization are similar to those in high performing organizations. Developed by Don Carew, Fay Kandarian, Eunice Parisi-Carew, and Jesse Stoner, The HPO SCORES Profile is published by The Ken Blanchard Companies.

4 Supplement to the HPO SCORES quiz.

Chapter 2

1 Jesse Stoner, "Visionary Leadership, Management, and High Performing Work Units" (doctoral dissertation, University of Massachusetts, 1988).

2 Ford Motor Company documents indicate that company officials had data that Firestone tires installed on Explorer sport-utility vehicles had little or no margin for safety in top-speed driving at the tire pressures that Ford recommended. The papers were part of a collection of documents that Congressional investigators released before the third round of Congressional hearings investigating Ford's and Bridgestone/Firestone Inc.'s handling of tire failures.

3 Jim Collins and Jerry Porras, *Built to Last: Successful Habits of Visionary Companies* (New York: HarperCollins, 1994).

4 Research studies described in *Leaders: The Strategies for Taking Charge* by Warren Bennis, 1985, and *The Leadership Challenge* by Kouzes and Posner, among others.

5 *New York Times*, August 2, 1995.

6 Jesse Stoner and Drea Zigarmi, "From Vision to Reality" (Escondido, CA: The Ken Blanchard Companies, 1993). The elements of a compelling vision were also described by Jesse Stoner in "Realizing Your Vision" (Provo, UT: *Executive Excellence*, 1990).

7 Charles Garfield and Hal Bennett, *Peak Performance: Mental Training Techniques of the World's Greatest Athletes* (New York: Warner Books, 1989).

8 Ken Blanchard and Michael O'Connor, *Managing by Values* (San Francisco: Berrett-Koehler, 1997).

9 Ken Blanchard and Jesse Stoner, *Full Steam Ahead!: Unleash the Power of Vision in Your Company and Your Life* (San Francisco: Berrett-Koehler, 2003).

Chapter 3

1 Rick Sidorowicz, "Back to the Beginning—Core Values," *The CEO Refresher*, Ontario, Canada: Refresher Publications, Inc., 2002.

2 Ken Blanchard and Sheldon Bowles, *Raving Fans: A Revolutionary Approach to Customer Service* (New York: William Morrow, 1993).

3 Ken Blanchard, Jim Ballard, and Fred Finch, *Customer Mania!* (New York: Simon & Schuster/Free Press, 2004).

4 Thomas Peters and Nancy Austin, *A Passion for Excellence* (New York: Random House, 1997).

5 Ken Blanchard and Don Shula, *Everyone's a Coach* (Grand Rapids, MI: Zondervan, 1995).

6 Ken Blanchard and Sheldon Bowles, *Gung Ho: Turn On the People in Any Organization* (New York: William Morrow, 1998).

Chapter 4

1 The Sarbanes-Oxley Act of 2002 is a U.S. federal law also known as the Public Company Accounting Reform and Investor Protection Act of 2002 (and commonly called SOX or SarbOx).

2 Edward Lawler, *Creating High Performance Organizations: Practices and Results of Employee Involvement and Total Quality Management* (San Francisco: Jossey-Bass, 1995).

3 In a more recent and rigorous research study, S. R. Silver investigated the relationship between organizational empowerment and "hard" measures of team performance for 50 teams of applied research engineers. The study found that organizational empowerment had a positive impact on the quality, timeliness, and financial outcomes of the team's performance.

S. R. Silver, "Perceptions of Empowerment in Engineering Workgroups: The Linkage to Transformational Leadership and Performance," unpublished doctoral dissertation, 1999, Washington, D.C., George Washington University.

In a highly rigorous study, S. E. Siebert, S. R. Silver, and W. A. Randolph analyzed data collected from 375 employees in 50 work teams in one division of a Fortune 100 manufacturer of high-technology office and printing equipment. They determined that a climate of empowerment was positively related to manager ratings of work unit performance and job satisfaction.

S. E. Siebert, S. R. Silver, and W. A. Randolph, "Taking Empowerment to the Next Level: A Multiple-Level Model of Empowerment, Performance, and Satisfaction," *Academy of Management Journal 47* (2004).

4   T. W. Malone, "Is Empowerment Just a Fad? Control, Decision Making, and IT," *Sloan Management Review*, Winter (1997): 23–35.

5   Inaugural address of John Fitzgerald Kennedy, January 20, 1961.

6   Ken Blanchard, John Carlos, and Alan Randolph, *Empowerment Takes More Than a Minute* (San Francisco: Berrett-Koehler, 1996).

7   As described in the HPO SCORES model in Chapter 1, "Is Your Organization High Performing?"

8   Jim Harris, "Five Principles to Revitalize Employee Loyalty and Commitment," *R&D Innovator* 5, No. 8 (August 1996).

9   Thomas H. Davenport and Laurence Prusak, *Working Knowledge* (Boston: Harvard Business School Press, 2000).

10 Jim Harris, "Five Principles to Revitalize Employee Loyalty and Commitment," *R&D Innovator* 5, No. 8 (August 1996).

11 Ken Blanchard, Alan Randolph, and Peter Grazier, *Go Team: Take Your Team to the Next Level* (San Francisco: Berrett-Koehler, 2005).

12 Ken Blanchard, Jim Ballard, and Fred Finch, *Customer Mania!: It's Never Too Late to Build a Customer-Focused Company* (New York: Simon & Schuster/Free Press, 2004).

13 Barney Bunnell and Marcelina Gilliam, two of the shift leaders, presented this story with Don Carew at the 2000 Blanchard Client Conference. They got a standing ovation.

Chapter 5

1 The original Hersey-Blanchard model gained prominence in 1969 in the authors' classic text, *Management of Organizational Behavior*, now in its eighth edition. After finding that some critical aspects of the model were not being validated in practice by thousands of users and it didn't fit the research on team development, Ken and the founding associates of The Ken Blanchard Companies— Margie Blanchard, Don Carew, Eunice Parisi-Carew, Fred Finch, Drea Zigarmi, and Patricia Zigarmi—created Situational Leadership® II. *Leadership and the One Minute Manager,* coauthored with Drea Zigarmi and Patricia Zigarmi, marked a new generation of Situational Leadership® II for managers everywhere.

2 Derived from The Leadership Behavior Analysis II (LBAII), an instrument designed to measure both your own and others' perceptions of leader flexibility, as well as the leader's effectiveness in choosing an appropriate leadership style.

Drea Zigarmi, Carl Edeburn, and Ken Blanchard, *Getting to Know the LBAII: Research, Validity, and Reliability of the Self and Other Forms*, 4th Edition (Escondido, California: The Ken Blanchard Companies, 1997).

3   The application of the original Situational Leadership® II model was advanced when Don Carew and Eunice Parisi-Carew developed the team leadership program; Susan Fowler and Laurie Hawkins championed Situational Self Leadership; and Drea Zigarmi, Pat Zigarmi, and Judd Hoekstra focused energy on organizational leadership.

Chapter 6

1   See the HPO SCORES model in Chapter 1, "Is Your Organization High Performing?"

2   Ken Blanchard, Jim Ballard, and Fred Finch, *Customer Mania!: It's Never Too Late to Build a Customer Focused Company* (New York: Simon & Schuster/Free Press, 2004).

3   Jim Belasco and Ralph Stayer, *Flight of the Buffalo: Soaring to Excellence, Learning to Let Employees Lead* (New York: Warner Books, 1994).

4   Robert Slater, *The New GE: How Jack Welch Revived an American Institution* (New York: McGraw-Hill, 1993).

5   Based on the Situational Self Leadership program, which was developed to teach Situational Leadership® II skills to direct reports and other associates.

6   Ken Blanchard, Susan Fowler, and Laurence Hawkins, *Self Leadership and The One Minute Manager* (New York: William Morrow, 2004).

Chapter 7

1 Jim Belasco and Ralph Stayer, *Flight of the Buffalo: Soaring to Excellence, Learning to Let Employees Lead* (New York: Warner Books, 1994).

2 "Management by Wandering Around" was developed by executives at Hewlett-Packard in the 1970s. It was popularized in a book written by Tom Peters and Robert Waterman in the early 1980s, *In Search of Excellence*. Their research revealed that managers of the most successful companies in America stayed close to the customers and the people doing the work; they were involved in rather than isolated from the business's daily routines.

3 Doing an Internet search for "handling performance problems" will provide excellent insight into the content of the literature and training programs.

4 Marjorie Blanchard and Garry Demarest, *One on One Conversations* (Escondido: The Ken Blanchard Companies, 2000).

Chapter 8

1 Ken Blanchard and Spencer Johnson, *The One Minute Manager* (New York: William Morrow, 1982 and 2003).

2 An introduction to the research on goal setting can be found in E. A. Locke and G. P. Latham, *Goal Setting: A Motivational Tool That Works* (New Jersey: Prentice Hall, 1984). Two excellent quick summaries can be found in Gary P. Latham, "The Motivational Benefits of Goal Setting" (New York: *Academy of Management Executive*, 2004, Vol. 18, No. 4, pp. 126–129). Also see Stephan Kerr and Landauer Steffen, "Using Stretch Goals to Promote Organizational Effectiveness and Personal Growth" (New York: *Academy of Management Executive*, 2004, Vol. 18, No. 4, pp. 134–138).

3   Scott Meyers, *Every Employee a Manager* (New York: McGraw-Hill, 1970).

4   Gerard Seijts and Gary Latham, "Learning Versus Performance Goals: When Should Each Be Used?" (New York: *Academy of Management Executive*, 2004, Vol. 18, No. 4, pp. 124–131).

5   David McClelland, J.W. Atkinson, R.A. Clark, and E.L. Lowell, *The Achievement Motive* (Princeton: Van Nostrand, 1953).

6   Based on data from the U.S. Census Bureau and National Center for Health Statistics as cited in "U.S. Divorce Statistics" (Toronto: *Divorce Magazine*, 2002).

7   Ken Blanchard, Jim Ballard, Thad Lacinak, and Chuck Tompkins, *Whale Done!: The Power of Positive Relationships* (New York: The Free Press, 2002).

8   Ken Blanchard and Robert Lorber, *Putting the One Minute Manager to Work* (New York: William Morrow, 1984).

9   Ken Blanchard and Margret McBride, *The One Minute Apology: The Way to Make Things Better* (New York: William Morrow, 2003).

Chapter 9

1   Ken Blanchard, Sheldon Bowles, Don Carew, and Eunice Parisi-Carew, *High Five!: The Magic of Working Together* (New York: William Morrow, 2001).

2   J.V. Johnson, W. Stewart, and E.M. Hall, "Long Term Psychological Work Environment and Cardiovascular Mortality," *American Journal of Public Health* (March 1996).

3   C. Southers, E. Parisi-Carew, and D. Carew, *Virtual Teams Handbook* (Escondido, CA: The Ken Blanchard Companies, 2002).

4   J. Despain and J.B. Converse, *And Dignity for All* (New Jersey: Financial Times/Prentice-Hall, 2003).

5   B. Tuckman, "Developmental Sequence in Small Groups," *Psychological Bulletin*, 1964; R.B. Lacoursiere, *The Life Cycle of Groups: Group Development Stage Theory* (New York: Human Science Press, 1980); J. Stoner and D. Carew, "Stages of Group Development and Indicators of Excellence" (unpublished manuscript, 1991); S.A. Whelan and J.M. Hochberger, "Validation Studies of Group Development Questionnaire" (Thousand Oaks, CA: Small Group Research, 1996).

6   Adapted from R.B. Lacoursiere, *Ibid.*

7   R. Wageman, "Critical Success Factors for Creating Superb Self-Managing Teams," *Organizational Dynamics*, Summer 1997).

8   ABC Video Enterprises, *Do You Believe in Miracles?*, 1981. Also, Disney's *Miracle* is a 2004 film that tells the story of Herb Brooks and the 1980 U.S. Olympic hockey team.

9   Ken Blanchard, Don Carew, and Eunice Parisi-Carew, *The One Minute Manager Builds High Performing Teams* (New York: William Morrow, 1990).

Chapter 10

1   International Consortium for Executive Development Research.

2   Gene E. Hall and Susan Loucks, "Teacher Concerns as a Basis for Facilitating and Personalizing Staff Development," Lieberman and Miller, eds. *Staff Development: New Demands, New Realities, New Perspectives* (New York: Teachers College Press, 1978).

3   SAP is the acronym for Systems, Applications, Products. It is a mainframe system that provides users with a soft real-time business application.

4   In an interesting development, in 2005 SBC Communications purchased AT&T, thus reuniting the venerable
phone company with three of its offspring (SBC was
composed of Southwestern Bell, Pacific Telesis, and
Ameritech). The merged company is named AT&T Inc.

Chapter 11

1   For some of the pioneering work on change leadership,
see Warren Bennis, *Managing the Dream: Reflections on
Leadership and Change* (New York, NY: Persus Book Group,
2000), John Kotter, *Leading Change* (Boston, MA:
Harvard Business School Press, 1996), and Daryl R.
Conner, *Managing at the Speed of Change* (New York, NY:
Random House, 1993).

2   Ken Blanchard and Jesse Stoner, *Full Steam Ahead!:
Unleash the Power of Vision in Your Company and Your Life*
(San Francisco: Berrett-Koehler, 2003).

3   Indiana Department of Child Services website:
http://www.in.gov/dcs.

Chapter 12

1   A collection of Greenleaf's most mature writings on the
subject can be found in *The Power of Servant Leadership*
(San Francisco: Berrett-Koehler, 1998). The Greenleaf
Center for Servant Leadership (www.greenleaf.org) is a
source of all his writings.

2   Ken Blanchard and Phil Hodges, *Lead Like Jesus: Lessons
from the Greatest Leadership Role Model of All Time*
(Nashville, TN: Thomas Nelson, 2005).

3   Rick Warren, *The Purpose Driven Life: What on Earth Am
I Here For?* (Grand Rapids, MI: Zondervan, 2002).

4   Matt Hayes and Jeff Stevens, *The Heart of Business* (Bloomington, IN: Author House, 2005).

5   Scott Blanchard, Drea Zigarmi, and Vicky Essary, "Leadership-Profit Chain," *Perspectives* (Escondido, CA: The Ken Blanchard Companies, 2006).

6   Ken Blanchard and Sheldon Bowles, *Gung Ho!: Turn On the People in Any Organization* (New York: William Morrow, 1998).

7   Gordon MacDonald, *Ordering Your Private World* (Nashville: Nelson Books, 2003).

8   Robert Greenleaf, *The International Journal of Servant Leadership*, Vol. 1, No. 1 (Spokane, WA: 2006).

9   Robert S. McGee, *The Search for Significance* (Nashville, TN: W. Publishing Group, 2003).

10 Jim Collins, *Good to Great: Why Some Companies Make the Leap—And Others Don't* (New York: Harper Collins, 2001).

11 Ken Blanchard and Norman Vincent Peale, *The Power of Ethical Management* (New York: William Morrow, 1988).

12 Fred Smith, *You and Your Network* (Mechanicsburg, PA: Executive Books, 1998).

13 Ken Blanchard and Mark Miller, *The Secret: What Great Leaders Know—And Do* (San Francisco: Berrett-Koehler, 2004).

14 Barbara Gellerman, "How Bad Leadership Happens," *Leader to Leader*, No. 35 (Winter 2005).

15 Drea Zigarmi, et al., *The Leader Within: Learning Enough About Yourself to Lead Others* (Upper Saddle River, NJ: Prentice-Hall, 2004).

16 M.A. Huselid, "The Impact of Human Resource Management Practices on Turnover, Productivity, and Corporate Financial Performance," *Academy of Management Journal*, 38 (1995).

17 E. Trist, "The Evolution of Socio-technical Systems," Ontario Quality of Working Life Centre, 1981.

18 Bob Buford, *Halftime* (Grand Rapids, MI: Zondervan, 1997).

Chapter 13

1 Noel Tichy, *The Leadership Engine: How Winning Companies Build Leaders at Every Level* (New York: HarperCollins, 1997).

2 Susan Fowler developed this process for the Situational Self Leadership program offered by The Ken Blanchard Companies. For more information, see www.kenblanchard.com.

3 Ken Blanchard and Michael O'Connor, *Managing by Values* (San Francisco: Berrett-Koehler, 1997).

ORGANIZATIONAL CHANGE READINESS ASSESSMENT

Directions: Think about a current change effort in your organization where you have an opportunity to influence the change process. Respond to each of the following statements by placing a score from the scale in the following box next to each question. Then, complete the scoring by following the scoring instructions at the end.

1	**Strongly Disagree**	**3**	**Neutral**	**5**	**Strongly**
2	**Disagree**	**4**	**Agree**		**Agree**

❑   1. The people leading this change explored a number of options before initiating this change.

❑   2. This is the best option.

❑   3. This change is necessary for the organization.

❑   4. There is a compelling reason associated with this change.

❑   5. The organization's top managers are strong supporters of this change.

❑   6. I have confidence in the people leading this change.

❑   7. Communication regarding the change is consistent, regardless of who is communicating.

❑   8. I have a clear picture of how the organization will be different after the change has been implemented.

❑   9. I see myself in the "picture of the future."

❑ 10. I am excited about the future of this organization.

continued

☐ 11. I understand the priority of this change in relation to other initiatives within the organization.

☐ 12. The organization will experiment with and/or pilot the change before rolling it out to everyone.

☐ 13. Mistakes will be treated as opportunities to learn rather than punished as failures.

☐ 14. I will be provided with the resources I need to implement the change (such as time, tools, coaching, and feedback).

☐ 15. I will get the training I need to build the new skills needed for this change.

☐ 16. I know where to go for help/support if I have questions, concerns, or challenges related to the change.

☐ 17. The people leading this change "walk their talk."

☐ 18. I will be held accountable for contributing to the success of this change.

☐ 19. I will be recognized and/or rewarded for contributing to the success of this change.

☐ 20. The organization is constantly looking for ways to refine the change to improve performance.

☐ 21. I am confident in the ability of the organization to sustain this change.

☐ 22. I believe a critical mass of people will champion versus resist this change.

☐ 23. The people leading this change believe it's important to involve others in planning for this change.

☐ 24. I have had an opportunity to express my concerns with the proposed change.

☐ 25. I have the opportunity to influence decisions related to this change.

Bonus: My recommendations for the people leading the change/me are:

a. Start:

b. Stop:

c. Continue:

Scoring Instructions

1. Calculate the total score for questions 1–25.
2. Interpret your total score. Depending on how creative you think your recommendations are, award bonus points:

110–125 At this time, the change is set up effectively. The most common reasons why change efforts fail or get derailed have been addressed, increasing the probability of a successful implementation.

86–109 At this time, the change is set up effectively in some ways, but it requires further work in other areas to improve the probability of a successful implementation.

85 or less At this time, the change is not set up to succeed. A significant amount of work needs to be done across a number of areas to improve the probability of a successful implementation.

3. Circle each question that has a score of 3 or less. These areas represent the most likely "derailers" of the change.

ACKNOWLEDGMENTS AND PRAISINGS

From Ken Blanchard

This is one of the biggest and most significant writing projects in which I have ever been involved. As I indicated in my Introduction, this book pulls together the thinking from The Ken Blanchard Companies over the past 25 years. This certainly wasn't a solo flight. Many people contributed to bringing to reality the dream of *Leading at a Higher Level*.

Let me start with my coauthors. The idea for creating an organization where *we could work with people we love and care about and make a difference in organizations* was born in the early 1970s by eight of us who were faculty members or doctoral students at the University of Massachusetts in Amherst. This group, including **Margie** and me, **Don Carew**, **Eunice Parisi-Carew**, **Fred Finch**, **Laurie Hawkins**, **Drea Zigarmi**, and **Pat Zigarmi**, is what we call the Founding Associates of The Ken Blanchard Companies.

In the early 1980s, this group changed the original Situational Leadership® theory to Situational Leadership® II, which is the cornerstone of the Blanchard leadership programs. These Founding Associates are the people I went to when I first thought of writing this book. Without their encouragement and important contributions, this book would have remained a dream.

After the Founding Associates got underway on the book, we invited a number of other consulting partners and associates to join us in writing it, because of the major part they have played in the development of our work. Big hugs and appreciation to **Scott Blanchard**, **Susan Fowler**, **Judd Hoekstra**, **Fay Kandarian**,

Alan Randolph, and **Jesse Stoner**, who have made important contributions to this book.

One other writer was instrumental in this book becoming a reality. Without **Martha Lawrence**, the senior editor on my team, we would still be talking about this book. She made it happen. She nurtured every section, every chapter, and every word. Martha hates attention and recognition, but she has no choice. Everyone who has worked on this book loves her and recognizes the important role she has played. Martha and I could never do what we do without the support of the other members of our team: **Dottie Hamilt**, **Anna Espino**, and **Nancy Jordan**. They all light up my life.

Two other Blanchard people have been key to the creation of this book. First, **Richard Andrews**, who is a miracle worker when it comes to writing win-win contracts. Not only does he believe "among friends, clear accounts," but he is always making sure that our intellectual property is protected. I'd also like to thank **Kevin Small**, a new member of our team and a marketing genius who has been a constant director and cheerleader for the distribution of this book.

As an editor, **Tim Moore** is every author's dream—brilliant, insightful, and always encouraging. A huge thank-you to Tim and his top-notch publishing team at Pearson/Prentice Hall: **Russ Hall**, **Susie Abraham**, **Amy Neidlinger**, **Lori Lyons**, and **Gloria Schurick**.

I have had the pleasure of coauthoring books with a number of other authors. Several deserve special mention:

Paul Hersey, my partner in developing the original Situational Leadership® model that led to Situational Leadership® II, the foundational concept for our company.

Spencer Johnson, my coauthor on *The One Minute Manager*, the book that catapulted my career and our company to a new level.

Sheldon Bowles, my coauthor on *Raving Fans* and *Gung Ho!*, two bestsellers that have taken our company in new directions.

Jim Ballard, a key writing partner who worked with me on *Managing by Values* (coauthored with Michael O'Connor), *Everyone's a Coach* (coauthored with Don Shula), and *The Heart of a Leader*. We also wrote two books together: *Whale Done!* (coauthored with Thad Lacinak and Chuck Thompkins) and *Customer Mania!* (coauthored with Fred Finch). Jim has made me a better writer and has been a constant spiritual encouragement.

Bob Lorber, my coauthor on *Putting the One Minute Manager To Work*, the follow-up book that started The One Minute Manager Library.

Margret McBride, my coauthor on *The One Minute Apology* and the literary agent who introduced me to mainstream publishing.

Norman Vincent Peale, my coauthor on *The Power of Ethical Management* and a wonderful inspiration for my spiritual growth.

Phil Hodges, my coauthor on *Leadership by the Book* (with Bill Hybels), *The Servant Leader*, and *Lead Like Jesus*, books that began my writing about Jesus as one of the greatest leadership role models of all time and led to our founding of The Center for FaithWalk Leadership.

My work with Paul, Spencer, Sheldon, Jim, Bob, Margret, Norman, and Phil is cited throughout this book. They all have had a major impact on my thinking and my life.

ABOUT THE AUTHORS

Ken Blanchard

Few people have impacted the day-to-day management of people and companies more than Dr. Ken Blanchard. A prominent, gregarious, sought-after author, speaker, and business consultant, Dr. Blanchard is universally characterized by his friends, colleagues, and clients as one of the most insightful, powerful, and compassionate individuals in business today.

From his phenomenal best-selling book *The One Minute Manager®*, coauthored with Spencer Johnson (which has sold more than 13 million copies and has remained on best-seller lists for 20 years) to the library of books he has coauthored with Sheldon Bowles (including the blockbuster best-sellers *Raving Fans* and *Gung Ho!*), Ken's impact as a writer is far-reaching. In July 2005, he was inducted into the Amazon Hall of Fame as one of the top 25 best-selling authors of all time.

Dr. Blanchard is chief spiritual officer of The Ken Blanchard Companies, an international management training and consulting firm that he and his wife, Dr. Marjorie Blanchard, founded in 1979 in San Diego. He is also a visiting lecturer at his alma mater, Cornell University, where he is a trustee emeritus of the Board of Trustees. Along with his wife, he teaches a course in leadership for the Master of Science in Executive Leadership program at the University of San Diego. He is also cofounder of Lead Like Jesus, a nonprofit organization dedicated to inspiring and equipping people to walk their faith in the marketplace.

Dr. Blanchard has received many awards and honors for his contributions in the fields of management, leadership, and speaking. The National Speakers Association awarded him its highest honor, the Council of Peers Award of Excellence, and he received the Golden Gavel Award from Toastmasters International. He was inducted into the HRD Hall of Fame by *Training* magazine and Lakewood Conferences. He was awarded the Thought Leadership Award for continued support of work-related learning and performance by ISA—The Association of Learning Providers. The College of Business at Grand Canyon University in Phoenix, Arizona bears his name.

Marjorie Blanchard

Dr. Marjorie Blanchard has earned a reputation worldwide as a compelling motivational speaker, an accomplished management consultant and trainer, a best-selling author, and an entrepreneur. She was the corecipient with her husband, Dr. Kenneth Blanchard, of the Entrepreneur of the Year award from Cornell University.

Coauthor of *The One Minute Manager Gets Fit* and *Working Well: Managing for Health and High Performance*, Dr. Blanchard is well-versed in a variety of topics and often speaks on leadership, balance, managing change, and life planning. As cofounder of The Ken Blanchard Companies, she works diligently with Ken, developing the company into one of the world's premier management consulting and training companies.

Dr. Blanchard now heads the firm's Office of the Future, a think tank charged with shaping the future of both the training industry and the company.

Dr. Blanchard received her bachelor's and master's degrees from Cornell University and her doctorate from the University of

Massachusetts. Along with Ken, she teaches a course in leadership for the Master of Science in Executive Leadership program at the University of San Diego.

Scott Blanchard

Scott Blanchard is a stimulating author, motivational speaker, accomplished corporate trainer, and passionate champion of coaching in the workplace. Scott founded Coaching.com, a Web-enabled corporate coaching and personal development service. Under his leadership, his organization is revolutionizing corporate coaching by offering the most advanced, accessible, and research-driven services in the industry. His personal philosophy is based on a fundamental shift occurring in the discipline of leadership: Great leaders do not succeed by doing what they are good at; instead, they succeed by getting things done with and through others.

Scott is senior vice president of The Ken Blanchard Companies. As a Blanchard family member and part owner, he represents the "next generation" charged with leading the business into the future. In addition, Scott is the principal architect of Blanchard's strategic alliance with Ninth House® Network.

Scott is the coauthor of *Leverage Your Best, Ditch the Rest*, a book on corporate coaching. As a senior consulting partner for more than six years, Scott led major training interventions at numerous Fortune 500 companies. Scott is well-versed in Blanchard's training programs, including Situational Leadership® II and Raving Fans®. He is also a certified facilitator and trainer for the Myers-Briggs Type Indicator®, a well-known temperament assessment tool.

Scott was educated at Cornell University and received his master's degree in organizational development from American University in Washington, D.C.

Donald K. Carew

Dr. Don Carew is a founding associate of The Ken Blanchard Companies and a professor emeritus at the University of Massachusetts Amherst. He is an accomplished and respected management consultant, trainer, educator, and author. Don's primary academic and consulting interests have been in collaboration and teamwork in organizations, leadership, and building high performing teams and organizations. While a full-time faculty member at the University of Massachusetts from 1969 to 1994, he was chair of the Organization Development Graduate Program. As a consultant, Don has worked with dozens of organizations in the United States, Mexico, Canada, and Europe in a wide range of industries, including manufacturing, health care, hospitality, retail, human services, education, and government, as well as with The Ken Blanchard Companies themselves.

Don's interest in teamwork and high-involvement organizations goes back to his teenage years, when he worked in two different manufacturing plants. He soon realized that the democratic values of participation, collaboration, and high involvement were not at work in those plants. This realization planted the seeds of his career-long interests and study. These interests became clearer as he continued in college and graduate school and developed connections with the NTL Institute. It was through T groups (human relations training groups) that he first experienced the tremendous power of teams to enhance the lives of individuals and organizations and to be a spawning ground for creativity and innovation. Don's lifelong commitment to the principle that *people have a right to be involved in decisions that affect their lives* was further strengthened by a post-doctoral internship with NTL in Bethel, Maine.

Don's association with the Blanchard family goes back to 1966, when he and Ken Blanchard were young faculty members at Ohio University. They started a friendship that has continued for 40 years. Don moved to the University of Massachusetts in 1969, and Ken joined the faculty in 1970. It was Don Carew's and Eunice Parisi-Carew's research on group development that led the Founding Associates of The Ken Blanchard Companies to change the Situational Leadership® II model so that it could be used with groups and teams as well as with individuals.

In addition to teaching at the University of Massachusetts, Don has been a faculty member at Trenton State University, Princeton University, and the University of San Diego. He is coauthor of two best-selling books: *The One Minute Manager Builds High Performing Teams* with Ken Blanchard and Eunice Parisi-Carew, and *High Five* with Ken, Eunice, and Sheldon Bowles. He is also a coauthor of the article "High Performing Organizations: Scores."

Don holds a bachelor's degree in business from Ohio University, a master's degree in human relations from Ohio University, and a doctorate in counseling psychology from the University of Florida. He is an associate of the NTL Institute and a licensed psychologist in Massachusetts.

Eunice Parisi-Carew

Dr. Eunice Parisi-Carew is an accomplished management consultant and trainer and a sought-after motivational speaker.

With a broad base of experience in many facets of management and organizational development, she has designed, directed, and implemented training and consulting projects for a number of top North American corporations, including Merrill Lynch, AT&T, Hyatt Hotels, Transco Energy Company, and the Department of Health, Education, and Welfare.

Team building, leadership, organizational change, and life management are among the many topics she addresses in seminars, speeches, and articles. She is also cocreator of the High Performing Teams product line offered by The Ken Blanchard Companies.

She has directed a graduate program in group dynamics and leadership at the University of Hartford and was a part-time faculty member at American University. She is also a member of the Board of Directors of the NTL Institute. She has also served as Vice President of Professional Services at The Ken Blanchard Companies.

She received her doctorate of education in behavioral sciences from the University of Massachusetts and is also a licensed psychologist in the state of Massachusetts.

Currently, she is a senior researcher with the Office of the Future at The Ken Blanchard Companies. Her role is to study trends that occur five to ten years out and their implications for leaders, organizations, and business practices.

Fred Finch

Dr. Fred Finch is the author of *Managing for Organizational Effectiveness: An Experiential Approach*. A founding associate of The Ken Blanchard Companies, he has been a consultant and leadership educator at Harvard University, Merrill Lynch, IBM, Shell International, and many other high-profile organizations. He received his doctorate from the Graduate School of Business at the University of Washington. He served as a professor of management and organizational behavior for 14 years in the Graduate School of Management at the University of Massachusetts Amherst.

Fred is coauthor with Ken Blanchard and Jim Ballard of *Customer Mania! It's Never Too Late to Build a Customer-Focused Company*, which grew out of the study of Yum! Brands, the world's largest quick-service restaurant corporation, with 850,000 employees in more than 100 countries. He is also coauthor with Pat Stewart of Situational Frontline Leadership, a popular training program for frontline leaders.

Susan Fowler

Susan Fowler is coauthor with Ken Blanchard and Laurence Hawkins of *Self Leadership and the One Minute Manager*, published in 2005.

Susan has established a solid and respected track record as a keynote speaker and an innovative product designer and developer in the field of leadership training. She received the

Lifetime Achievement Award for creative training designs from the North American Society for Games and Simulations. As a senior consulting partner with The Ken Blanchard Companies, Susan has consulted with such clients as Pfizer, Harley Davidson, MasterCard, AMF Bowling, Dow Chemical, KPMG, Black & Decker, SC Johnson, TJX Retailers, The National Basketball Association, and dozens of others. Prior to that, she gained extensive, worldwide public seminar presentation experience with CareerTrack.

Susan's goal is to be a catalyst for personal change and a teacher of the skills necessary to sustain self-motivation. Susan brings a unique perspective to her programs because of her extensive professional experience in the field of advertising, her broadcast work in television and radio, and her undergraduate degree in marketing from the University of Colorado. As one of the world's foremost experts on personal empowerment, she has delivered training seminars, workshops, and keynote speeches to more than 50,000 people in over 20 countries and in all 50 states. Audiences applaud her high energy, sense of humor, insight, and pragmatic solutions to workplace issues.

With Ken Blanchard and Laurence Hawkins she created—and is the lead developer of—Situational Self Leadership®, a best-of-class self leadership and personal empowerment program. Her publications include *Overcoming Procrastination*, *Mentoring*, *The Team Leader's Idea-a-Day Guide* (coauthored with Drea Zigarmi), and *Empowerment* (coauthored with Ken Blanchard). Susan is an adjunct professor for the University of San Diego's Master of Science in Executive Leadership program.

Laurence Hawkins

Dr. Laurence Hawkins is one of the founding associates of The Ken Blanchard Companies, as well as an internationally renowned management consultant and motivational speaker. With Ken Blanchard and Susan Fowler, he coauthored the Situational Self Leadership program, which focuses on empowerment and taking initiative when you're not in charge. He is also the coauthor with Ken and Susan of *Self Leadership and the One Minute Manager*, published in 2005.

Laurie has concentrated much of his work on aerospace, particularly Lockheed Martin and McDonnell Douglas, and pharmaceutical giants such as Pfizer, Merck, and GlaxoSmithKline. Laurie has focused his career on applying the Blanchard standards of Situational Leadership® II, Situational Team Leadership, and Situational Self Leadership in the international arena, focusing on Europe, South America, and Saudi Arabia. More recently, he has been teaching the tools, concepts, and philosophy of self leadership to clients in China and Korea—countries where obedience is rapidly shifting to a culture of taking the initiative and entrepreneurship.

Laurie received his bachelor's degree in American history and literature from Williams College and his master's and doctorate degrees in leadership and organizational behavior from the University of Massachusetts Amherst.

Judd Hoekstra

Judd Hoekstra is one of Blanchard's experts in organizational change and is coauthor of its Managing a Change consulting methodology and training program. Judd's approach to change is based on a shared commitment to Don Carew's principle that *people have a right to be involved in decisions that affect their lives* and the concept that *those who plan the battle rarely battle the plan.*

Although he is a relative newcomer to The Ken Blanchard Companies, Judd's impact on the company and his clients has been immediate and far-reaching. His positive attitude, his ability to work well with all people, and his passion for "doing the right things right" help those he works with make great things happen.

Prior to joining Blanchard in 2001, Judd served as a strategy execution consultant with Fourth Floor Consulting. Before that, he was a change management consultant with Accenture. He was primarily responsible for helping client executives lead their organizations through large-scale changes. Judd's experience crosses a number of industries; his clients have included The Dow Chemical Company, Allstate Insurance Company, Anheuser-Busch, and Commonwealth Edison.

He received his bachelor's in business management and marketing from Cornell University and graduated from the Advanced Business Management Program at Kellogg Graduate School of Management. Judd and his wife, Sherry, live in the Chicago area and are the proud parents of Julia and Cole.

Fay Kandarian

Dr. Fay Kandarian has worked as both an internal and independent organizational change consultant over the past 20 years. She has been a consulting partner with The Ken Blanchard Companies since 1998.

Her extensive line, staff, and executive experiences provide constant reference points that inform her consulting. Her areas of expertise include whole-systems change, executive coaching, strategic planning, intervention design, leadership and team development, communications skills, and process consultation.

While doing doctoral research at Columbia University's Department of Organization and Leadership, Fay studied and developed proficiency in using large-group interventions as a new paradigm for organization development and large-scale change.

She researched Polarity Management (B. Johnson, 1996) as a training intervention to help teach systems thinking skills and later introduced Polarity Management's "both/and" thinking to The Ken Blanchard Companies.

Working with fellow HPO team members Jesse Stoner, Eunice Parisi-Carew, and Don Carew, she helped create the HPO SCORES model and coauthored the article "High Performing Organizations: Scores." Using the HPO SCORES conceptual framework, she further investigated how leaders learn to guide their organizations to high performance.

She holds a bachelor's from George Washington University, a master's in business from the University of New Haven, and a master's and doctorate in education from Columbia University.

Alan Randolph

Dr. Alan Randolph is an internationally respected and highly accomplished management educator, researcher, and consultant. His work focuses on empowerment, leadership, teamwork, and project management issues for both domestic and international organizations in the public and private sectors. He has worked in a variety of countries, including most recently Peru, Brazil, China, Germany, France, and Poland.

Dr. Randolph is a professor of management and international business at the Merrick School of Business at the University of Baltimore. He also is a senior consulting partner with The Ken Blanchard Companies. He has developed a variety of leadership and empowerment educational products. He has also published numerous articles in practitioner and academic journals such as *Harvard Business Review*, *Sloan Management Review*, *The Academy of Management Executive*, *Organizational Dynamics*, and *The Academy of Management Journal*.

Dr. Randolph has also written and coauthored a number of books, including *Go Team!: Take Your Team to the Next Level*, *Checkered Flag Projects: 10 Rules for Creating and Managing Projects That Win!*, *Empowerment Takes More Than a Minute*, and *The 3 Keys to Empowerment: Release the Power Within People for Astonishing Results*. Many of his books have become best-sellers and have been translated into many languages around the world.

Jesse Stoner

Dr. Jesse Stoner is widely known as one of the foremost experts on vision and leadership. A highly regarded management consultant and author, Jesse has worked closely with leaders for more than 20 years to help them create organizations in which their people can thrive and make a significant contribution. Her work in vision development has helped individuals, leaders, and companies create compelling visions, identify the strategies to capture them, and ensure that they are lived on a day-by-day basis.

Jesse coauthored with Ken Blanchard the best-seller *Full Steam Ahead!: Unleash the Power of Vision in Your Work and Your Life*. She is also coauthor of *Creating Your Organization's Future*, a program that helps leadership teams develop a shared vision for their department or organization.

Jesse was a member of the original research team investigating the characteristics of high performing organizations. She helped create the HPO SCORES model and coauthored the article "High Performing Organizations: Scores" and the assessment, The HPO SCORES Profile.

Additionally, she has contributed to the development of the Building High Performing Teams programs. She coauthored *Team Development Stage Analysis (TDSA)* and "The Team Member's Role in Building High Performing Teams."

Jesse earned advanced degrees in psychology and a doctorate in organization development from the University of Massachusetts.

Drea Zigarmi

Formerly president of Zigarmi Associates, Inc., Dr. Drea Zigarmi is the director of research and development for The Ken Blanchard Companies. His work has been critical to the company's success with its clients. Almost every product that has been developed at The Ken Blanchard Companies over the past 20 years has Drea's mark on it. He coauthored with Ken Blanchard the well-known Leader Behavior Analysis instrument and the Development Task Analysis form used in all Situational Leadership seminars.

He has coauthored three books: *The Leader Within: Learning Enough About Yourself to Lead Others*, *The Team Leaders' Idea-a-Day Guide*, and *Leadership and the One Minute Manager*.

He received his bachelor's in science from Norwich University. He earned a master's in philosophy and a doctorate in administration and organizational behavior from the University of Massachusetts Amherst.

Patricia Zigarmi

Dr. Patricia Zigarmi is a founding associate of The Ken Blanchard Companies, where she currently serves as vice president for business development. She has contributed to the company's growth as vice president of sales and marketing and as vice president of consulting services. She is a speaker, consultant, product designer, business developer, account strategist, trainer, and team builder for many of Blanchard's clients and is a mentor to many colleagues at Blanchard.

Pat is coauthor of *Leadership and the One Minute Manager*. She also designed Blanchard's premier product line, Situational Leadership® II. With her leadership, ongoing initiatives for Situational Leadership® II training and coaching have been negotiated with many global companies and most of the Fortune 500 companies. She is also the author of Blanchard's Managing a Change program and a number of performance management products on Giving Feedback and Monitoring & Reviewing Performance.

Respected for her ability to listen and build trust, she has been a coach to the executives and managers of many companies.

She received her bachelor's in sociology from Northwestern University and her doctorate in leadership and organizational behavior from the University of Massachusetts Amherst. Her first mentor was Warren Bennis, whom she shadowed in his role as a change agent as president of the University of Cincinnati. Her doctoral dissertation is a study of Warren's leadership of four change initiatives. Pat met Ken Blanchard on her first day of graduate school, and they have worked together and inspired each other ever since.

In addition to her contributions to The Ken Blanchard Companies, Pat teaches Managing a Change for the Master's in Executive Excellence program at the University of San Diego. She is also a member of the San Diego Women's Foundation. Pat lives in San Diego and is the mother of two daughters, Lisa and Alexa.

Services Available

For more than 27 years, The Ken Blanchard Companies® has been in the business of helping leaders and organizations lead at a higher level. An award-winning provider of corporate training, the company is a global leader in workplace learning, productivity, performance, and leadership effectiveness that is best known for its Situational Leadership® II program—the most widely taught leadership model in the world. Because of its ability to help people excel as self-leaders and as leaders of others, SLII® is embraced by Fortune 500 companies as well as organizations of all sizes.

The mission of the company is to unleash the potential and power in people and organizations for the greater good. Based on the beliefs that people are the key to accomplishing strategic objectives and driving business results, Blanchard® programs develop excellence in leadership, teams, customer loyalty, change management, and performance improvement. The company's continual research points to best practices for workplace improvement, while its world-class trainers and coaches drive organizational and behavioral change at all levels and help people make the shift from learning to doing. Some examples of our client engagements include:

- Becoming the best-in-class by developing and retaining key talent
- Fostering a culture of principled and ethical leadership
- Ensuring change management that keeps companies competitive
- Creating vision that captures the energy and commitment of employees
- Helping companies develop leadership bench strength

The company has delivered training and performance improvement best practices in more than 50 countries. For many of these clients, Blanchard has helped to align learning and development needs with business strategies for long-term organizational impact. Blanchard consulting partners are also available for training initiatives, consulting engagements, and keynote addresses around the world.

Global Headquarters
The Ken Blanchard Companies
125 State Place
Escondido, CA 92029
www.kenblanchard.com
+1.800.728.6000 from the U.S.
+1.760.489.5005 from anywhere

INDEX

empowerment. *See also* self
   leadership
  defined, 68-69, 103-104
  example of, 71-72
  in high performing teams, 172
  keys to
    boundaries, 78-79, 81
    self-direction, 82-85
    sharing information,
      74-78
  language of hierarchical
    culture versus, 72-74
  performance and, 69-70
  resistance to, 70-71
  servant leadership and,
    273-274
Enable and Encourage change
    strategy, 237-239
energizing systems and
    structures
  customer service and, 61-62
  importance of, 13
enthusiastic beginner (develop-
    ment level), 89-91
Envision the Future change
    strategy, 228-230
ethics, unethical leadership, 270
Everyone's a Coach (Blanchard
    and Shula), 3, 52
examples, setting, 286-287
Execute and Endorse change
    strategy, 239-242

Expand Opportunities for
    Involvement and
    Influence change
    strategy, 221-223
expectations
  accountability and, 147
  what people can expect from
    you, 285-286
  what you expect from your
    people, 286
Experiment to Ensure Alignment
    change strategy,
    230-237
Explain the Business Case for
    Change strategy,
    226-228
Explore Possibilities change
    strategy, 243-245
external customers, internal
    customers versus, 44-45

F

failure of change, reasons for,
    198-200, 221, 227-230,
    238-244
failure of teams, reasons for,
    169-170
false pride, 261-262
  antidote to, 263-264
fear. *See* self-doubt
feedback, 149-150
  servant leaders and, 260